7th Seminar on Industrial Control Systems: Analysis, Modeling and Computing (ICS 2018)

ITM Web of Conferences Volume 18 (2018)

Moscow, Russia
27-28 February 2018

Editors:

E. Nikulchev **G. Bubnov**

ISBN: 978-1-5108-6103-9

Printed from e-media with permission by:

Curran Associates, Inc.
57 Morehouse Lane
Red Hook, NY 12571

Some format issues inherent in the e-media version may also appear in this print version.

Printed by Curran Associates, Inc. (2018)

For additional information, please contact EDP Sciences – Web of Conferences at the address below.

EDP Sciences – Web of Conferences
17, Avenue du Hoggar
Parc d'Activité de Courtabœuf
BP 112
F-91944 Les Ulis Cedex A
France

Phone: +33 (0) 1 69 18 75 75
Fax: +33 (0) 1 69 28 84 91

contact-edps@webofconferences.org

Additional copies of this publication are available from:

Curran Associates, Inc.
57 Morehouse Lane
Red Hook, NY 12571 USA
Phone: 845-758-0400
Fax: 845-758-2633
Email: curran@proceedings.com
Web: www.proceedings.com

TABLE OF CONTENTS

Statement of Peer review

In submitting conference proceedings to *Web of Conferences*, the editors of the proceedings certify to the Publisher that

1. They adhere to its **Policy on Publishing Integrity** in order to safeguard good scientific practice in publishing.
2. All articles have been subjected to peer review administered by the proceedings editors.
3. Reviews have been conducted by expert referees, who have been requested to provide unbiased and constructive comments aimed, whenever possible, at improving the work.
4. Proceedings editors have taken all reasonable steps to ensure the quality of the materials they publish and their decision to accept or reject a paper for publication has been based only on the merits of the work and the relevance to the journal.

Title, date and place of the conference

7th Seminar on Industrial Control Systems: Analysis, Modeling and Computing (ICS2018)
Moscow, Russia
27-28 February 2018

Proceedings editor(s):

Evgeny Nikulchev, professor, Moscow Technological University, Russia

Date and editor's signature

28/03/2018

Multipoint Numerical Criterion for Manifolds to Guarantee Attractor Properties in the Problem of Synergetic Control Design

Askhat Diveev[1], *Elizaveta* Shmalko[1,*], and *Elena* Sofronova[1]

[1] Federal Research Center Computer Science and Control of the Russian Academy of Sciences, 119333 Moscow, Russia

Abstract. The paper presents the results of our research on the application of symbolic regression methods for the numerical solution of the problem of synthesis of synergetic control. Synergetic control is characterized by the presence of manifolds in the state space that must have the properties of an attractor, in particular terminal manifolds, as well as the existence of regions of state space through which system solutions do not pass, for example, phase constraints, that must have the properties of repellers. In the present paper we formulate a numerical criterion for ensuring the property of an attractor for a terminal manifold of arbitrary dimension, taking into account the dynamic behavior of the system in a neighborhood of a given manifold. The results of computational experiments on the effective application of the proposed criterion are presented. It is shown that the proposed approach makes it possible to automate the synthesis of synergistic control using the methods of symbolic regression.

1 Introduction

Herman Haken [1] defines synergetic as the field of science which study self-organization in physical systems and also other related phenomena in wider class of systems.

Synergetic control as an approach to solve the problems of control synthesis was proposed in the works of A.A. Kolesnikov. [2-4]. The main idea of the approach is following. When control is synthesized that is control function that depends on the vector of coordinates of state space of control object is found, we are able to receive such system of differential equations describing dynamics of the control object together with the control system which does not contain a free vector of control in the right parts of the equations because we replace the control by the synthesized function. So all solutions of the received system of the differential equations have the properties set by the developer. Properties that must be satisfied by solutions of the differential equations describing the received closed control system are determined by the presence of manifolds in the state space, in particular terminal manifolds must possess properties of an attractor, and phase constraints must point to regions of the state space through which solutions of the system do not pass or possess the properties of repellers.

Unfortunately, the most qualitative examples of control synthesis on the basis of the synergetic theory consider objects of a low order, in particular not above the second order where properties of solutions of systems of the differential equations are obviously displayed on the plane. Practically all synergetic approaches [2], despite general conclusions, are limited to consideration of examples of second-order systems. Such low order of systems as the condition of application of the synergetic theory cannot satisfy experts in the field of control because modern control objects, such as robots or groups of robots, are described by the systems of the differential equations of much higher order. The main mathematical apparatus for synergetic control is a method of analytical construction of aggregated controllers [3-6]. This method uses the solution of a system of algebraic equations, and if the dimension of control and terminal manifold do not match, a subjective approach is required to choose the solution. The method works only for the systems of a low order too.

In this of work we consider application of modern numerical methods of symbolic regression [7-9] for the solution of tasks of control on the basis of the synergetic theory. We formulate numerical criteria to check properties of an attractor for manifolds in the state space. The presented numerical criteria take into account not only hit of the solution into the neighbourhood of the manifold but also the very behaviour of the solutions in the neighbourhood of this manifold. The proposed criterion turns out to be especially important for one-dimensional manifolds, for which it is necessary not only to get into the neighbourhood of a manifold, but also to provide a definite form of solution changing in time in the neighbourhood of the manifold.

We provide the results of numerical experiments which show efficiency of the proposed numerical criterion to check attractor properties.

* Corresponding author: e.shmalko@gmail.com

2 Method of Analytical Construction of Aggregated Controllers

Consider the method of analytical construction of aggregated controllers.

Given a model of control object

$$\dot{\mathbf{x}} = \mathbf{f}(\mathbf{x},\mathbf{u}) . \quad (1)$$

We want to receive such control that a terminal manifold became an attractor

$$\psi_i(\mathbf{x}) = 0 ,\ i = 1,\ldots,r . \quad (2)$$

Let

$$\boldsymbol{\psi}(\mathbf{x}) = [\psi_1(\mathbf{x}) \ \ldots \ \psi_r(\mathbf{x})]^T . \quad (3)$$

Notice

$$(Tp+1)\boldsymbol{\psi}(\mathbf{x}) = 0 , \quad (4)$$

where T is a positive constant, p is a differentiation operator.

Differentiate

$$T\frac{d}{dt}\boldsymbol{\psi}(\mathbf{x}) + \boldsymbol{\psi}(\mathbf{x}) = 0 , \quad (5)$$

$$T\frac{\partial \boldsymbol{\psi}(\mathbf{x})}{d\mathbf{x}}\mathbf{f}(\mathbf{x},\mathbf{u}) + \boldsymbol{\psi}(\mathbf{x}) = 0 . \quad (6)$$

We have obtained a system of r algebraic equations with m unknown components of control vector. We need to solve these equations concerning the vector of control. If $r = m$, then the system (6) has the only one solution. If $r < m$, the system (6) has many solutions, and if $r > m$, the system has no solution.

3 Problem Statement of Numerical Control Synthesis

Consider the formulation of the problem of control synthesis, taking into account the possibility of solving it numerically.

Given a model of control object

$$\dot{\mathbf{x}} = \mathbf{f}(\mathbf{x},\mathbf{u}) , \quad (7)$$

where $\mathbf{x} \in \mathbf{R}^n$, $\mathbf{u} \in \mathrm{U} \subseteq \mathbf{R}^m$, U - is a compact set, $\mathbf{x}$ is a vector of state space, $\mathbf{x} = [x_1 \ \ldots \ x_n]^T$, $\mathbf{u}$ is a vector of control, $\mathbf{u} = [u_1 \ \ldots \ u_m]^T$, $\mathbf{f}(\mathbf{x},\mathbf{u}) : \mathbf{R}^n \times \mathbf{R}^m \to \mathbf{R}^n$, $\mathbf{f}(\mathbf{x},\mathbf{u}) = [f_1(\mathbf{x},\mathbf{u}) \ \ldots \ f_n(\mathbf{x},\mathbf{u})]^T$, $m \le n$.

Given a region of initial conditions

$$\mathrm{X}_0 \subseteq \mathbf{R}^n . \quad (8)$$

Given a terminal manifold

$$g_i(\mathbf{x}) = 0 ,\ i = 1,\ldots,r ,\ r \le n . \quad (9)$$

Given a quality criterion

$$J = \int_0^{t_f} f(\mathbf{x},\mathbf{u})dt \to \min , \quad (10)$$

where t_f is a given time of the control process.

It is necessary to find control in the form of function of coordinates of state space

$$\mathbf{u} = \mathbf{h}(\mathbf{x}) , \quad (11)$$

where $\mathbf{h}(\mathbf{x}) : \mathbf{R}^n \to \mathbf{R}^m$.

Function $\mathbf{h}(\mathbf{x})$ satisfies the following conditions: the system of differential equations

$$\dot{\mathbf{x}} = \mathbf{f}(\mathbf{x},\mathbf{h}(\mathbf{x})) ,$$

for any initial condition from the region (8)

$$\forall \mathbf{x}(0) \in \mathrm{X}_0 \subseteq \mathbf{R}^n ,$$

has a solution

$$\mathbf{x} = \mathbf{v}(\mathbf{x}(0),t) ,$$

such that it attains in a given time t_f the terminal manifold (9)

$$g_i(\mathbf{v}(\mathbf{x}(0),t_f)) = 0 ,\ i = 1,\ldots,r ,$$

and does not violate constraints of control

$$\mathbf{h}(\mathbf{v}(\mathbf{x}(0),t)) \in \mathrm{U} ,\ 0 \le t \le t_f ,$$

and provides minimum to the quality criterion (10)

$$\int_0^{t_f} f(\mathbf{v}(\mathbf{x}(0),t),\mathbf{h}(\mathbf{v}(\mathbf{x}(0),t)))dt = \min_{\mathbf{u}(\cdot)\in \mathbf{U}^*} \int_0^{t_f} f(\mathbf{x},\mathbf{u})dt ,$$

where U^* is a set of admissible controls that satisfy the control constraints and ensure the achievement of the terminal manifold (9) for the same initial conditions of the object $\mathbf{x}(0) \in \mathrm{X}_0$.

For synthesis of control we use methods of symbolic regression [7-9] which allow to find the coded mathematical expression of the required synthesizing function by means of an evolutionary algorithm.

On the basis of the synergetic theory the terminal manifold as a result of synthesis of control must possess the property of an attractor. If the terminal manifold has dimension zero, $n - r = 0$, i.e. it is a point in state space, then in numerical synthesis, the fulfilment of terminal conditions in the form

$$\|\mathbf{g}(\mathbf{x})\| \le \varepsilon , \quad (12)$$

where $\mathbf{g}(\mathbf{x}) = [g_1(\mathbf{x}) \ \ldots \ g_n(\mathbf{x})]^T$, ε is a set positive small value, ensures the obtaining of properties of an attractor for the terminal manifold. Here in (12) $r=n$ because the manifold is a point and it has zero dimension.

If dimension of terminal manifold is bigger than zero, $n-r>0$, than the condition (12) is not enough for obtaining properties of attractor. It is necessary to describe behaviour of the control object after achievement of terminal manifold.

For example, the system of equations (9) at $r<n$ has many solutions. Let $\mathbf{x}^*$ is one of these solutions, $g_i(\mathbf{x}^*)=0$, $i=1,\ldots,r$. Then condition

$$||\mathbf{x}-\mathbf{x}^*||\le\varepsilon, \tag{13}$$

is equivalent to the condition (12) and, in the synthesis, the point $\mathbf{x}^*$ can be found, which belongs to terminal manifold (9). In this case we at synthesis will provide stability of system concerning a point $\mathbf{x}^*$ of state space on terminal manifold, but not the movement of the control object on a set of points of terminal manifold.

4 Multipoint Criterion to Provide Attractor Properties

A multipoint criterion is appropriate to apply in the numerical synthesis of synergetic control for terminal manifolds whose dimension is greater than zero.

A multipoint criterion is in establishing additional requirements which consider peculiarities of the motion of an object after hitting to the neighborhood of a terminal manifold. According to the additional requirements, it is needed to reach a certain number of points on the terminal manifold, remaining in the neighbourhood of this manifold.

To determine the requirements to achieve a set of points on a terminal manifold, we introduce an integer function

$$\varphi(K^*,t)=K^*-\min\{K^*,k(t)\}, \tag{14}$$

where K^* is a given number of different points on the terminal manifold that must be achieved, $k(t)$ is the number of different points on the terminal manifold attained by the moment t

$$k(t)\leftarrow\begin{cases}1, \text{ if } t\le t_f,\ k(t)=0,\ ||\mathbf{g}(\mathbf{x}(t))||\le\varepsilon,\\ \qquad X_f=\{\mathbf{x}^1=\mathbf{x}(t)\}\\ k(t)+1, \text{ if } t\le t_f,\ ||\mathbf{g}(\mathbf{x}(t))||\le\varepsilon, \text{and}\\ \qquad \forall\mathbf{x}^j\in X_f,\ ||\mathbf{x}(t)-\mathbf{x}^j||>\varepsilon,\\ \qquad j=1,\ldots,k(t),\\ \qquad X_f\leftarrow X_f\cup\{\mathbf{x}^{k(t)+1}=\mathbf{x}(t)\}\\ 0, \text{ if } t\le t_f,\ ||\mathbf{g}(\mathbf{x}(t))||>\varepsilon\end{cases}. \tag{15}$$

The function $\varphi(K^*,t_f)$ is either zero, if the solution succeeds in reaching K^* different points on the terminal manifold by time t_f, or is equal to the difference between the given K^* and the reached by time t_f number of points $k(t_f)$ on the terminal manifold.

5 Examples of Numerical Synthesis of Synergetic Control

Consider a task of synthesis of control for nonlinear control object of the second order

$$\dot{x}_1=x_2+u_1,$$

$$\dot{x}_2=-x_2-x_1-x_1^3+u_2,$$

where

$$-1\le u_i\le 1,\ i=1,2.$$

In the first example we consider the following terminal manifold

$$x_2=-x_1,\ x_1^-\le x_1\le x_1^+.$$

It is necessary to rich the given terminal manifold from the region of initial conditions

$$X_0=\{[x_1(0)\ x_2(0)]^T:-1.1\le x_i(0)\le 1, i=1,2\}.$$

As criteria of optimality of synthesis we consider the following functional

$$J_1=\alpha\varphi(K^*,t_f)+\int_0^{t_f}\Delta_f(x_2(t),x_1(t))dt,$$

$$J_2=\alpha\varphi(K^*,t_f)+\Delta_f(x_2(t_f),x_1(t_f)),$$

where $\Delta_f(x_2(t),x_1(t))$ is a distance to terminal manifold

$$\Delta_f(x_2(t),x_1(t))=\begin{cases}\min\{\Delta^-(t),\Delta^+(t)\},\\ \quad \text{if } (\beta^-(t)<0)\vee(\beta^+(t)<0)\\ 2S(t)/l_f \text{ -- otherwise}\end{cases},$$

$$\Delta^-(t)=\sqrt{(x_1(t)-x_1^-)^2+(x_2(t)-x_2^-)^2},$$

$$\Delta^+(t)=\sqrt{(x_1(t)-x_1^+)^2+(x_2(t)-x_2^+)^2},$$

$$\beta^-(t)=\sum_{i=1}^{2}(x_i^+-x_i^-)(x_i(t)-x_i^-),$$

$$\beta^+(t)=\sum_{i=1}^{2}(x_i^--x_i^+)(x_i(t)-x_i^+),$$

$$l_f=\sqrt{(x_1^+-x_1^-)^2+(x_2^+-x_2^-)^2},$$

$$S(t)=\sqrt{p(t)(p(t)-\Delta^-(t))(p(t)-\Delta^+(t))(p(t)-l_f)},$$

$$p(t)=\frac{\Delta^-(t)+\Delta^+(t)+l_f}{2},\ x_2^-=-x_1^-,\ x_2^+=-x_1^+,$$

α is a weight coefficient.

Synthesis was carried out by method of binary variational genetic programming [6, 9]. In a computing experiment the following values of constants has been used: $x_1^- = -0.5$, $x_1^+ = 0.5$, $\varepsilon = 0.005$, $\alpha = 0.1$, $K^* = 8$, $t_f = 8$.

The following control has been synthesized

$$u_i = \begin{cases} 1, \text{ if } \tilde{u}_i > 1 \\ -1, \text{ if } \tilde{u}_i < -1 \\ \tilde{u}_i - \text{otherwise} \end{cases}, \quad i = 1,2,$$

where

$$\tilde{u}_1 = \sin((q_2+1)(\cos(q_1)+x_1)+q_3q_2\sin(q_1)) +$$
$$+\operatorname{sgn}(q_2x_1\cos(q_2)+(q_2+1)x_2\sin(q_4)),$$
$$\tilde{u}_2 = -(q_1+1)(q_4+2)\arctan(x_2/q_2) +$$
$$(2q_4+1)\vartheta(-q_1-1+\arctan(q_3/x_1)),$$

$q_1 = 0.5439$, $q_2 = 2.7022$, $q_3 = 0.2197$, $q_4 = 3.69531$
,

$\vartheta(a)$ is a Heaviside function

$$\vartheta(a) = \begin{cases} 1, \text{ if } a \geq 0 \\ 0 - if \end{cases},$$

Fig.1 shows the received solutions for four initial values. The red line notes the terminal manifold.

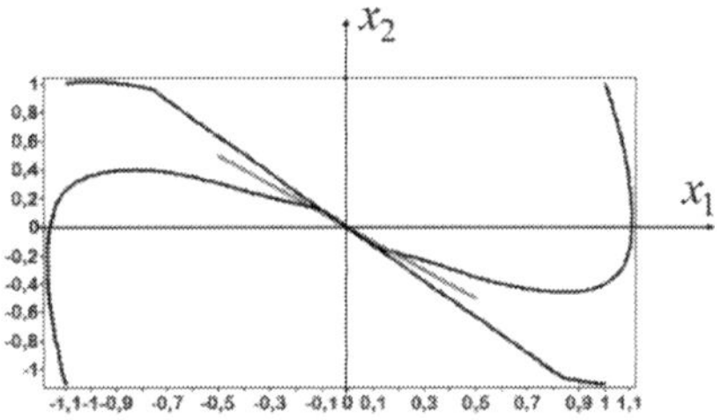

Fig. 1. Results of the 1st experiment.

In the second experiment we consider the following terminal manifold

$$x_2 = x_1, \quad x_1^- \leq x_1 \leq x_1^+,$$

where $x_1^- = -0.5$, $x_2^- = -0.5$, $x_1^+ = 0.5$, $x_2^+ = 0.5$.

The following control has been received

$$\tilde{u}_1 = (q_2+q_3)x_1\cos(q_1)+(q_3+1)x_2\sin(1) +$$
$$(q_3^2+1)x_2\sin(q_1)+q_2x_1\cos(q_2) +$$
$$q_2x_1\cos(q_2)+(q_3+1)x_2\sin(1),$$
$$\tilde{u}_2 = \exp((q_3+\sin(q_4)+q_1+\cos(1)) \times$$
$$\times(\arctan(q_3\operatorname{sgn}(x_1)\sqrt{|x_1|}) - (\ln|q_1|+1)) +$$
$$+\operatorname{sgn}((q_1+q_2+1-(q_2+1)^3) \times$$
$$\times(\arctan(x_2/x_1)-1-\arctan(x_1))) \times$$
$$\times\sqrt{|(q_1+q_2+1-(q_2+1)^3)|} \times$$
$$\times\sqrt{|(\arctan(x_2/x_1)-1-\arctan(x_1))|}),$$

$q_1 = 2.979$, $q_2 = 2.786$, $q_3 = 3.392$, $q_4 = 1.505$.

Fig.2 shows the received solutions for four initial values and the terminal manifold.

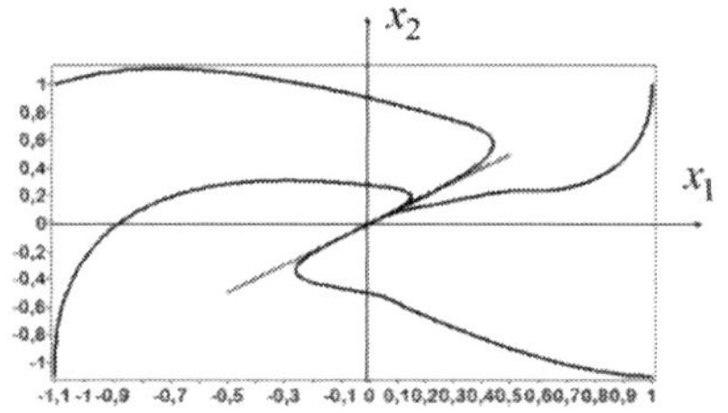

Fig. 2. Results of the 2nd experiment.

In the third experiment the following manifold was considered

$$x_2 = 0, \quad x_1^- \leq x_1 \leq x_1^+,$$

where $x_1^- = -0.5$, $x_1^+ = 0.5$,

As a result the following control has been received

$$\tilde{u}_1 = (q_2+q_2^2)x_1\cos(q_2)+(q_3+1)\sqrt[3]{\operatorname{sgn}(x_2)\sqrt{|x_2|}},$$
$$\tilde{u}_2 = (\vartheta(x_2)+q_3+1)^3(\pi/4-(x_2+\sin(q_1)))^3,$$

$q_1 = 1.472$, $q_2 = 2.530$, $q_3 = 2.157$, $q_4 = 1.213$.

Fig.3 shows the received solutions for four initial values and the terminal manifold.

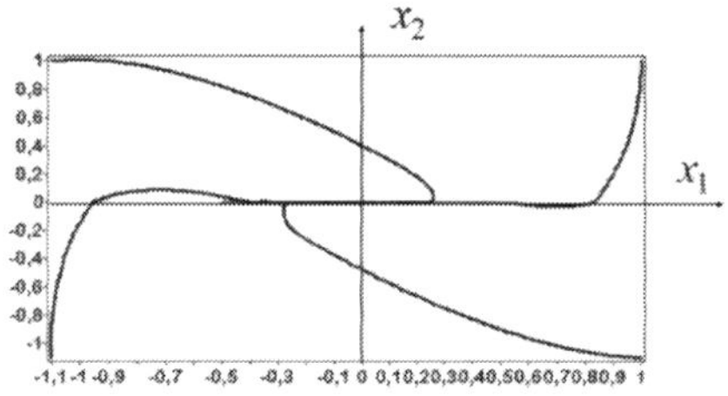

Fig. 3. Results of the 3rd experiment.

In the fourth experiment we considered the following terminal manifold

$$x_1 = 0, \quad x_2^- \leq x_2 \leq x_2^+,$$

where $x_2^- = -0.5$, $x_2^+ = 0.5$.

As a result the following control has been received

$$\tilde{u}_1 = -q_1x_1(q_2+q_1)+(q_3+1)\sqrt[3]{x_2}\sin(q_1) +$$
$$+\operatorname{sgn}((q_2+\exp(q_4))\cos(q_2)\arctan(x_1) -$$

$$-q_2 x_2 \arctan(q_3)) \times$$

$$\times(|(q_2+\exp(q_4))\cos(q_2)\arctan(x_1)-$$

$$-q_2 x_2 \arctan(q_3)|)^{0.5},$$

$$\tilde{u}_2 = (\arctan(x_2/x_1)-(q_1+1))(x_2+\sqrt[3]{q_4}+2)-$$

$$-q_1(\sqrt{q_4}+3)\arctan(q_2/x_1),$$

$$q_1 = 3.049,\ q_2 = 3.395,\ q_3 = 1.156,\ q_4 = 0.002.$$

Fig.4 shows the received solutions for four initial values and the terminal manifold.

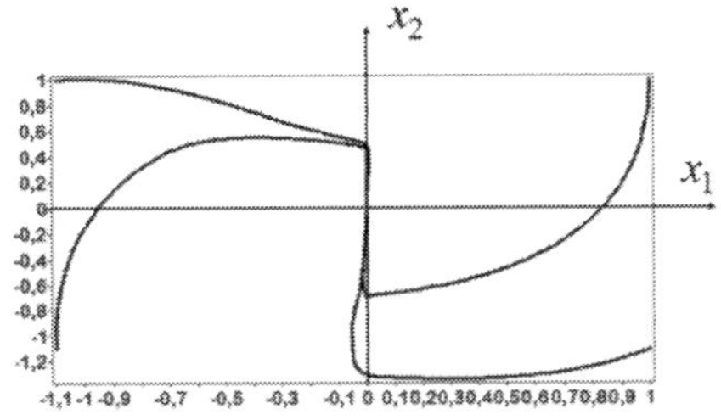

Fig. 4. Results of the 4th experiment.

In the fifth experiment we considered the following terminal manifold

$$x_2 = x_1^2 - 1,\ x_1^- \le x_1 \le x_1^+,$$

where $x_1^- = -1$, $x_1^+ = 1$.

The following control has been received

$$u_1 = \mathrm{sgn}(q_4 q_3(x_2+\sin(q_1)))\sqrt{|q_4 q_3(x_2+\sin(q_1)|}+$$

$$\vartheta(q_1+1+\exp(q_2^3\sin(q_1)))+$$

$$+(q_2+q_3)\cos(q_2)\sin(x_1)+$$

$$\left(\ln(q_3+1)\arctan\left(\frac{\sin(q_4)}{q_1}\right)\right)^2,$$

$$u_2 = \mathrm{sgn}(1-\exp(-\mathrm{sgn}(\vartheta(x_1)-$$

$$-\sin(q_4))\sqrt{|\vartheta(x_1)+\sin(q_4)|}))\times$$

$$\times\mathrm{sgn}(x_2-\sqrt{q_4\exp(q_2)}-\sqrt{q_1}-x_2)\times$$

$$\mathrm{sgn}(1+\exp(-\mathrm{sgn}(\vartheta(x_1)-\sin(q_4))\sqrt{|\vartheta(x_1)+\sin(q_4)|}))\times$$

$$\times\mathrm{sgn}\left(\ln\left|x_2^2+q_1^2+1+q_2^3\frac{1-\exp(-x_1)}{1+\exp(-x_1)}-q_4-\sqrt{q_3}\right|\right),$$

$$q_1 = 1.812,\ q_2 = 2.815,\ q_3 = 3.623,\ .\ q_3 = 2.251$$

Fig.5 shows the received solutions for four initial values and the terminal manifold.

As can be seen from the results of the experiments, the multipoint criterion (14) provides the possibility of obtaining an attractor and moving along it for a terminal linear manifold.

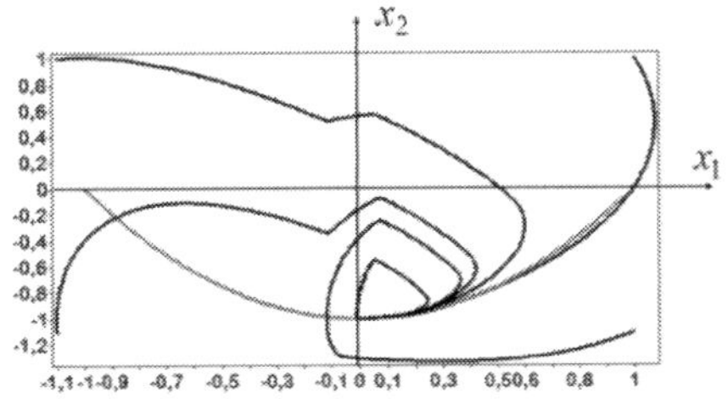

Fig. 5. Results of the 5th experiment.

6 Conclusion

For synthesis of system of synergetic control it is offered to use methods of symbolic regression. These methods allow to find needed mathematical expressions in the coded form by means of evolutionary algorithms. Criterion of search of the mathematical expression is the criterion of control system design. It is shown that for synergetic control it is insufficient to describe terminal manifold in the form of the system of algebraic equations. The multipoint criterion to check the properties of an attractor for terminal manifold is offered. By means of numerical examples it is shown that the offered multipoint criterion allows to receive controls with the necessary attractor properties of terminal manifold.

This research was supported by Russian Foundation for Basic Research (№ 17-08-01203-a and 16-29-04224-ofi_m).

References

1. H. Haken, M. Haken-Krell, *Erfolgsgeheimnisse der Wahrnehmung* (1992)
2. A.A. Kolesnikov, Synergetic control theory (Moscow, 1994)
3. A.A. Kolesnikov, TSURE News, **6**(61), 10 (2006)
4. A. Bezuglov, A. Kolesnikov, I. Kondratiev, J. Vargas, Synergetic Control Theory Approach for Solving Systems of Nonlinear Equations, *.Proc. of the 9th World Multi-Conference on Systemics, Cybernetics and Informatics*, pp. 121-126 (2005)
5. E.Y. Rapoport, J. Comp. and Sys. Sci. Int., **51** 375 (2012)
6. A.A. Kolesnikov, G.E. Veselov, A.N. Popov, A.S. Mushenko, et al. *Synergetics methods of complex systems control: Mechanical and Electromechanical Systems* (Moscow, 2006)
7. A.I. Diveev, G.I. Balandina, S.V. Konstantinov, Binary Variational Genetic Programming for the Problem of Synthesis of Control System, *ICNC-FSKD 2017*, pp. 165-170 (2017).
8. A.I. Diveev, E.Yu. Shmalko, ITM Web Conf. **10**, 02004 (2017)
9. S.I. Ibadulla, E.Yu. Shmalko, K.K. Daurenbekov, Procedia Computer Science, **103** 155 (2017)

Estimation of the flight thrust increment changing the operation mode of the engine

O.N. Korsun[1, *], *S.Yu.* Prihodko[2] and *S.A.* Sergeev[1,3]

[1] State Research Institute of Aviation Systems, Moscow, Russia
[2] Moscow Aviation Institute (National Research University), Moscow, Russia
[3] Moscow Automobile and Road Construction State Technical University, Moscow, Russia

Abstract. The paper presents a new method for flight test identification of the thrust increment when changing engine operation mode. It is known that the problem of separate estimation of the engine thrust and the aerodynamic drag force from the aircraft flight data belongs to a class of ill-posed. The idea of the presented method is to come out of the ill-posed class by changing the original problem formulation. To achieve this purpose we give up the absolute values of the thrust and proceed to estimating the thrust increment resulting from the change of the aircraft engine operation mode. The accuracy of the solution is improved by introducing the special flight test maneuver. The algorithm requires only a few on-board measured parameters, such as longitudinal and normal overload, airspeed and altitude, and angle of attack. The complimentary use of the engine gas-dynamic model may improve the estimates but is not obligatory. The proposed method also does not require a-priory estimates of the aerodynamic drag force.

1 Introduction

The paper presents a new method for flight test identification of the thrust increment when changing engine operation mode. It is known that the problem of separate estimation of the engine thrust and the aerodynamic drag force from the aircraft flight test data belongs to a class of ill-posed [1-3], in view of the collinearity of thrust and drag vectors at low angles of attack. There are several ways to deal with the problem, and all of them are their own constraints. The simplest way is to take one of above mentioned collinear vectors for known. Indeed, when drag is postulated the thrust may be estimated easily from flight data and vice versa [4,5]. Another variant is to insert special load sensors into the engine mounting system [6]. The most widespread approach is to calculate thrust using the engine gas-dynamic model and pressure and temperature measurements in the key sections of the flow [7]. The paper [8] discusses a method for drag and thrust absolute value separate identification from flight test data based on a specially designed test maneuver.

The idea of the method presented in this article is to extract the problem out of the ill-posed class by changing the original formulation. To achieve this purpose we give up the absolute values of the thrust and proceed to estimating the thrust increment resulting from the change of the aircraft engine operational mode. The new problem is correct from the mathematical standpoint. Moreover we may improve the accuracy of the solution by introducing the specific flight test maneuver. The idea of this maneuver is to compensate the change of the thrust by gravity force using dive or climb. In this case the principal flight parameters affecting the engine thrust, such as Mach number and angle of attack, keep constant with high precision, and the only parameter of significant variation is the engine operation mode. It allows us to estimate the corresponding increment of thrust. The duration of this test maneuver should not exceed 30…40 s, so the change of the altitude is not to be significant.

The detailed description is given further in the next part of the paper.

2 Flight test manoeuvres performance

The flight experiment is carried out as follows. As a first step the aircraft is balanced in straight and level flight at constant altitude, air velocity and angle of attack α (Fig.1).

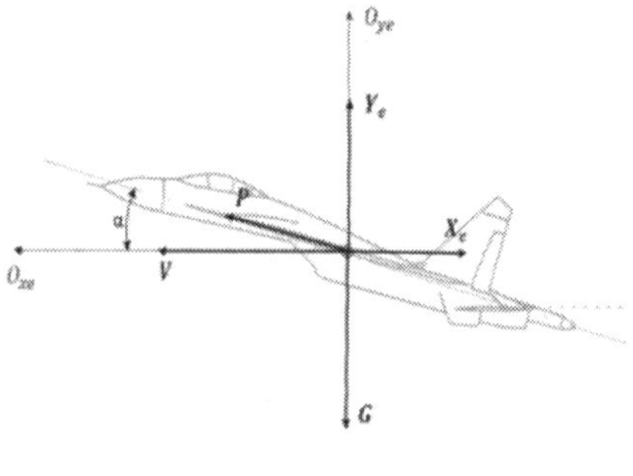

Fig. 1. Aircraft balanced motion in straight and level flight.

* Corresponding author: marmotto@rambler.ru

Then the pilot carries out the control stick stepwise symmetric deviations in pitch channel. It is required that the air velocity should be approximately constant and the fluctuations of the angle of attack amounted to ± (2 ... 3) degrees.

Next the pilot changes the engine operation mode, for example, to increase the thrust, and proceeds to straight climb in order to keep the air velocity and angle of attack approximately constant. The increased thrust is compensated by the climb, that is by the projection of the gravity force (Fig. 2).

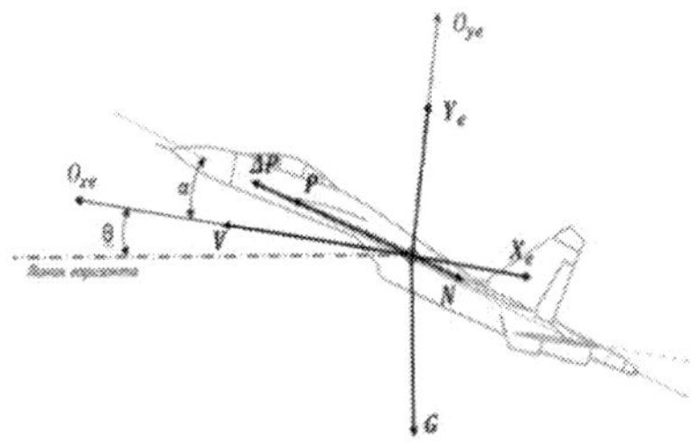

Fig. 2. Straight climb with constant velocity.

During the straight climb it is recommended to repeat the control stick stepwise symmetric deviations in pitch channel, but this is not obligatory. Next the pilot changes the engine operation mode, for example, to diminish the thrust, and proceeds to straight dive in order to keep the air velocity and angle of attack approximately constant. So, the dive is symmetric to the climb. One may chose several fixed engine modes. It enables to cover the full range of thrust at given Mach number and altitude.

In order to estimate all the admissible regimes we should choose Mach and altitude nodes through all the flight performance envelope of the aircraft.

Since the duration of this maneuver is small the altitude variations are limited and commonly do not affect the functioning of the engine.

It was confirmed that a qualified professional pilot performs testing regimes like that quite easily.

The example of pitch angle variation for a training aircraft is presented Fig. 3.

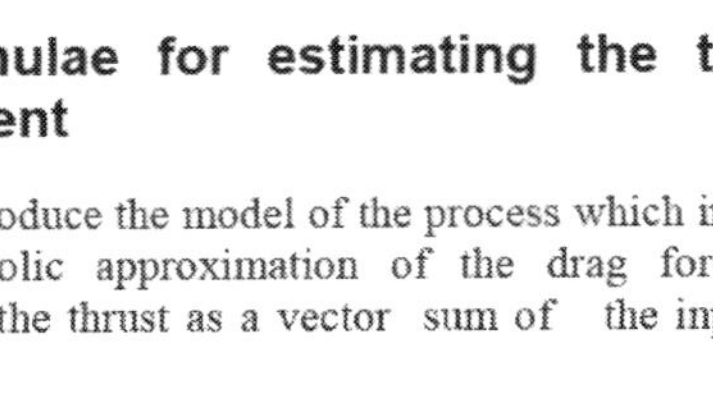

Fig. 3. The pitch angle variation during the flight test maneuver.

3 Formulae for estimating the thrust increment

Let us introduce the model of the process which includes the parabolic approximation of the drag force and considers the thrust as a vector sum of the input and output impulses. It is assumed that the input impulse P_{in} is directed along the axis Ox_e of the air velocity coordinate system, that is coincides with the direction of the air velocity vector. The output impulse P_{out} is directed along the engine axis, which is commonly deviated from the axis Ox, associated with the aircraft, by the engine installation angle ϕ_{inst}. The Ox_e axis force projections form the following equation

$$\begin{gathered} m\,g\,n_{x_e}(t) = -qSc_{x_0} - qSc_x^{\alpha}\alpha(t) - \\ -qSc_x^{\alpha^2}\alpha^2(t) - P_{in} + P_{out}\cos(\phi_{inst} + \alpha(t)), \end{gathered} \tag{1}$$

where $n_{x_e}(t)$ is the overload projection along the Ox_e axis; S – equivalent wing area; m – aircraft mass; g – gravity force acceleration; q – the dynamic pressure; $\alpha(t)$ – angle of attack; c_{x_0}, c_x^{α}, $c_x^{\alpha^2}$ - parameters for the drag force parabolic approximation.

To transform (1) the following trigonometric formula is used:

$$\cos(\phi_{inst} + \alpha) = \cos\phi_{inst}\cos\alpha - \sin\phi_{inst}\sin\alpha .$$

In the vicinity of zero angles of attack we get

$$\cos\alpha \approx 1 - \frac{1}{2}\alpha^2;\ \sin\alpha \approx \alpha .$$

Then at small angles of attack the equation (1) for force projections is:

$$\begin{gathered} m\,g\,n_{x_e}(t) = -qSc_{x_0} - qSc_x^{\alpha}\alpha(t) - qSc_x^{\alpha^2}\alpha^2(t) - P_{in} + \\ +P_{out}\cos\phi_{inst} - \frac{1}{2}P_{out}\alpha^2(t)\cos\phi_{inst} - P_{out}\alpha(t)\sin\phi_{inst} \end{gathered} \tag{2}$$

Let us write down the last equation for the initial stage of the flight test regime, that is straight and level flight. Let us also denominate input and output impulses for this initial stage P_{in_0} and P_{out_0} and regroup the equation's right part :

$$\begin{gathered} m\,g\,n_{xe}(t) = 1\cdot\left(-qSc_{x_0} + P_{out_0}\cos\phi_{inst} - P_{in_0}\right) - \\ -\alpha(t)\left(qSc_x^{\alpha} + P_{out_0}\sin\phi_{inst}\right) - \\ -\alpha^2(t)\left(qSc_x^{\alpha^2} + \frac{1}{2}P_{out_0}\cos\phi_{inst}\right). \end{gathered} \tag{3}$$

Taking into account that the sum of the input P_{in} and output P_{out} impulses form the so-called effective thrust P_{eff} [7, 8] we obtain:

$$P_{eff} = -P_{in} + P_{out}\cos\phi_{inst} \tag{4}$$

Let us substitute (4) into equation (3):

$$\begin{gathered} m\,g\,n_{xe}(t) = 1\cdot\left(-qSc_{x_0} + P_{eff_0}\right) - \alpha(t)\left(qSc_x^{\alpha} + P_{out_0}\sin\phi_{inst}\right) - \\ -\alpha^2(t)\left(qSc_x^{\alpha^2} + \frac{1}{2}P_{out_0}\cos\phi_{inst}\right) = a_0 + \alpha a_1 + \alpha^2 a_2 . \end{gathered} \tag{5}$$

The equation (5) corresponds to the flight test initial stage which includes the straight level flight and control stick stepwise symmetric deviations in pitch channel.

It is clear that the equation (5) fits the common multiple regression model with factors 1, $\alpha(t)$, $\alpha^2(t)$. The angle of attack α and overload n_{xe} may be taken from on-board measurements. So, out of the stepwise symmetric deviations interval we may obtain the following parameter estimates using the least square multiple regression:

$$\hat{a}_0 = \left(-qSc_{x_0} + P_{eff_0}\right);$$
$$\hat{a}_1 = \left(qSc_x^{\alpha} + P_{out_0}\sin\phi_{inst}\right); \qquad (6)$$
$$\hat{a}_2 = \left(qSc_x^{\alpha^2} + \frac{1}{2}P_{out_0}\cos\phi_{inst}\right).$$

Now to provide identification of the thrust increment we are to write the equation similar to (5) for time interval after the change of the engine operational mode. In this case we introduce that the input P_{in} and output P_{out} impulses are dependent of time:

$$m\,g\,n_{xe}(t) = 1\cdot\left(-qSc_{x_0} + P_{eff}(t)\right) -$$
$$-\alpha(t)\left(qSc_x^{\alpha} + P_{out}(t)\sin\phi_{inst}\right) -$$
$$-\alpha^2(t)\left(qSc_x^{\alpha^2} + \frac{1}{2}P_{out}(t)\cos\phi_{inst}\right). \qquad (7)$$

Finally, we may multiply the estimates (6) by proper factors 1, $\alpha(t)$, $\alpha^2(t)$ and subtract them from the equation (7). Thus we get the formula for estimating the the effective thrust increment:

$$\Delta P_{eff}(t) = m\,g\,n_{x_e}(t) - \hat{a}_0 + \hat{a}_1\alpha(t) + \hat{a}_2\alpha(t)^2 +$$
$$+\Delta P_{out}(t)\left(\alpha\sin\phi_{inst} + \alpha^2\frac{1}{2}\cos\phi_{inst}\right). \qquad (8)$$

The last term in the (8) right part is a systematic error. It is not considerable at small angles of attack and small ϕ_{inst}. Additionally, to reduce this error the estimates of ΔP_{out}, obtained from the engine gas-dynamic model, should be used. Errors of this model do not matter here, because of smallness of the whole term.

Effect of random errors can be significantly reduced by using more sophisticated identification methods [2,3] instead of the multiple regression. Systematic error of measurement of angles of attack and airspeed should be excluded at the stage of flight tests, using known identification techniques [2, 3].

Figure 4 shows the effective thrust increment estimates obtained by the proposed method (red line), and the values of the increments at the same flight regime, calculated independently from the engine gas-dynamic model described in [7]. The good enough coincidence of two unrelated assessments confirms performance of the proposed method.

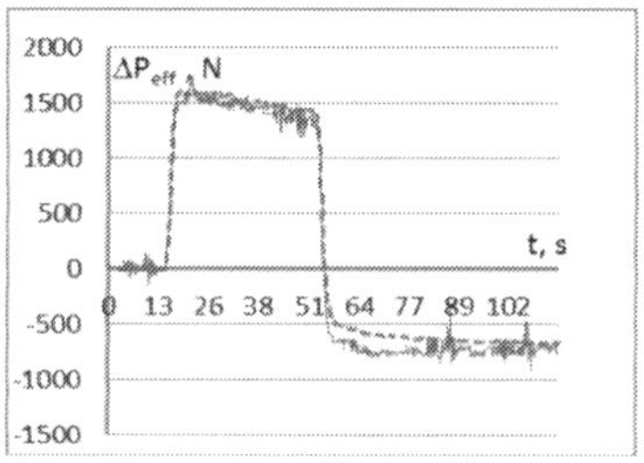

Fig. 4. Estimates increments effective (the proposed method) and internal thrust engines (model, made according to bench tests) on a test mode in flight

4 Conclusions

1. The proposed method improves the accuracy and stability of the thrust estimation by switching to mathematically correct problem formulation instead of ill-posed .

2. If necessary, to determine the absolute value of thrust, this method should be used in conjunction with a method of estimating the absolute value of thrust for the given Mach number and altitude [8].

3. The proposed method may be used for purposes of monitoring the engines technical state since the thrust increments at fixed changes in engine operating mode are strongly correlated with the deterioration of the engine.

This work is supported by Russian Foundation for Basic Research (RFBR), project 18-08-00921-a.

References

1. A.N. Tikhonov, V.Y. Arsenin, *Methods for incorrect problems solution* (Moscow, Nauka, 1986) *In Russian*
2. R.V. Jategaonkar, *Flight vehicle system identification: a time domain methodology* (American Institute of Aeronautics and Astronautics, Reston, 2006)
3. V. Klein, E.A. Morelli, *Aircraft system identification: theory and practice* (American Institute of Aeronautics and Astronautics, Reston, 2006)
4. G.Girija, V. Parameswaran, JR. Raol, S. Srinathkumar, *Journal of Aeronautical Society of India*, **43 (4)**, 285-292 (1991)
5. Hoff J.C., Barbarose J.R. Application of a Stochastic In-Flight Thrust Determination Process to Real Engine Data, *3rd CTA DLR Workshop on Data Analysis and Flight Control* (S.J. Campos, Brasil, 2009)
6. Muhammad H. Muhardi, Kuntjoro W., Sritjiono B.E. In-Flight Thrust Determination by Load Meassurement on the Engine Mounting System, ICAS- 2000 Congress, pp. 533.1–533.7 (2000)
7. O.N. Korsun, I.A. Leshchenko, M. Nemichev, Mechatronics, automation control, **11**, 50-54 (2011) [In Russian]
8. O.N. Korsun, B.K. Poplavsky, S.Ju. Prihodko, Procedia Computer Science, **103**, 82-87 (2017)

https://doi.org/10.1051/itmconf/20181801003

Methods for selecting the supporting curve for the model of hysteresis loop

O.N. Korsun [1] and *A.V.* Stulovskii [1,*]

[1]State Research Institute of Aviation Systems, Moscow, Russia

Abstract. The article deals with a model describing the dependence of aerodynamic coefficients on the angle of attack for post-stall conditions. This paper also discusses the choice of parameters for the calculating the lift coefficient in such cases. In addition, it also considers some methods used to choose the shape of a supporting curve. The article also provides arguments concerning the physical interpretation of the coordinate of flow separation point in the implementation of the model. The examples of processing the flight test data are presented.

1 Introduction

It is well known, that the aerodynamic processes at overcritical values of the angle of attack have fundamental differences if compared with similar processes occurring in the operational range of attack angles [1].

One of the most important features of this mode is the presence of hysteresis in the dependence of the aerodynamic coefficients on the angle of attack. Asymmetry of the flow disruption and its recovery during variation of the angle of attack explains this phenomenon. Since it takes place even with a very small value of the derivative of the angle of attack, such fact was named static hysteresis.

2 Mathematical model of hysteresis for the lift coefficient

Of considerable interest is the construction of models describing the behavior of the lift coefficient for the overcritical values of the angle of attack. The estimation of the coefficient itself was obtained through the identification methods described in [2], using the model [3] of forces and torques generated by thrust vector deviation.

One type of such model is given in [1, 4]. More detailed discussion concerning this topic may be found in [5–7]. This model includes additional parameter $\bar{x}$ – the coordinate characterizing the position of the flow separation point on the wing profile. Its units of measurement are the chord shares. Therefore, its value ranges from 0 to 1. The model itself is described by a system of two equations:

$$c_{ye}(\alpha) = c_{y0}(\alpha)\left(\frac{1+\sqrt{\bar{x}}}{2}\right)^2;$$
$$\tau_1 \frac{d\bar{x}}{dt} + \bar{x} = x_0(\alpha), \quad \bar{x}(0) = 1, \qquad (1)$$

where $c_{y0}(\alpha)$ – estimation of the lift coefficient values as the function of the angle of attack, with no account for hysteresis; $\tau_1 = const$ – model parameter; $x_0(\alpha)$ – static dependence of the co-ordinate of the flow separation point from the angle of attack.

The introduction of flow separation point makes possible the description of the asymmetry of the recovery and the disruption of the flow.

By the form of the expression itself it becomes clear that the model needs to be adapted for practical use – the function $x_0(\alpha)$ should be chosen. One of the possible function, according to [7], is

$$x_0(\alpha) = 0.5\{1 - \tanh[\lambda(\alpha - \tau_2 d\alpha/dt - \alpha^*)]\},$$

where $d\alpha/dt$ - time derivative of the angle of attack, rad/s; $\tau_1, \tau_2, \alpha^*, \lambda$ – parameters of the equation, which values are determined by the characteristics of the aerodynamic profile and the configuration of the wing, as well as by the dynamics of the flow process itself.

The physical sense of these parameters is discussed in more detail in [7]. Nonetheless, the question concerning choice of $c_{y0}(\alpha)$ remains actual, and the next section answers it.

3 Supporting curve

Physical sense of the $c_{y0}(\alpha)$ becomes clear after more detailed examination of the system (1). It could be seen that $c_{y0}(\alpha)$ function serves as a basic, or supporting, curve and values of $c_{ye}(\alpha)$ are derived from it by

* Corresponding author: avstlv2@gmail.com

addition of disturbances depending on coordinate of the flow separation point $\bar{x}$.

Cubic Hermite splines were used for specifying this curve, since they are capable of producing a sufficiently wide range of curves. Here we briefly give the formulas used for their construction. The reader can find more about them, as well as about the properties of these splines, for example, in [8].

Let us assume that for the certain interval $[x_1, x_M]$ M values of the independent variable are given, that is x_j, $j = \overline{1, M}$. Each such point is called spline node. Then the value of the spline for an arbitrary point $x \in [x_i, x_{i+1}]$ is obtained by the formula

$$S(x) = \varphi_1(t) f_i + \varphi_2(t) f_{i+1} + \varphi_3(t) h_i f_i' + \varphi_4(t) h_i f_{i+1}',$$

where

$$\varphi_1(t) = (1-t)^2(1+2t),$$
$$\varphi_2(t) = t^2(3-2t),$$
$$\varphi_3(t) = t(1-t)^2,$$
$$\varphi_4(t) = -t^2(1-t),$$
$$h_i = x_{i+1} - x_i,$$
$$t = (x - x_i) / h_i.$$

Now let us turn back to the model of aerodynamic hysteresis. Considering the system (1) mathematically it can be concluded that values of $c_{ye}(\alpha)$ will invariably be lower then $c_{y0}(\alpha)$ values.

This fact was additionally confirmed by building the supporting curve passing through the center of the hysteresis loop (Figure 1). Then the parameter identification of hysteresis model (1) was carried out. The results presented in Figure 1 show that the fits the lower branch of the loop with high precision, while the upper branch remains unreachable.

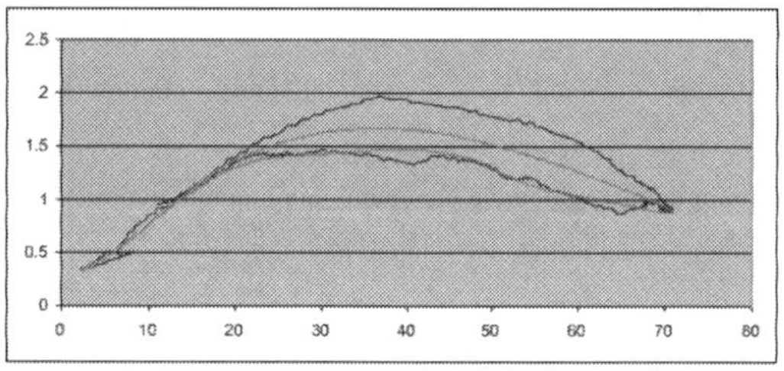

Fig. 1. The values of the lift coefficient (blue line) and the values obtained using the hysteresis model with the supporting curve passing in the middle of the loop (violet line), depending on the angles of attack.

Based on this observation, decision was made to use the upper branch of the hysteresis loop as the supporting curve. The resulting approximation proved to be excellent as it is shown in Figure 2.

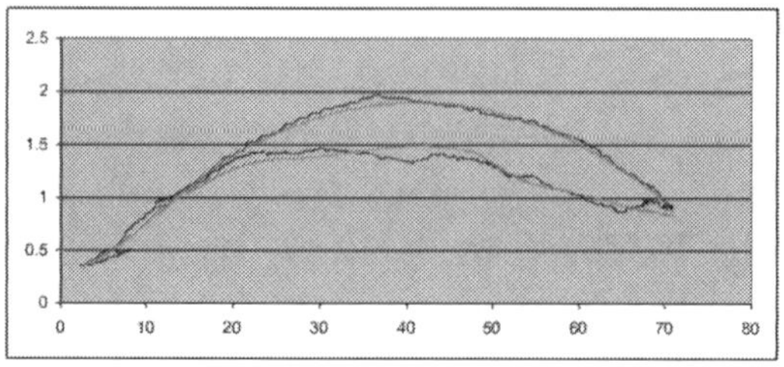

Fig. 2. The values of the lift coefficient (blue line) and the values obtained using the hysteresis model with the supporting curve passing on the upper branch of the loop (violet line), depending on the angles of attack.

4 Procedure of curve selection

As mentioned above, $c_{y0}(\alpha)$ is interpreted as the value of the lift coefficient for steady flow. But it is known in aerodynamics that a partial flow separation starts just when angles of attack exceed overcritical value.

As could be seen in Figure 2, choice of upper branch of hysteresis loop produces sufficiently good description of the experimental data. However, variation of the coordinate of the flow separation point in this case shows that separation of the flow starts at angles of attack far beyond critical value (Figure 3, blue line). This result is contrary to the nature of the process.

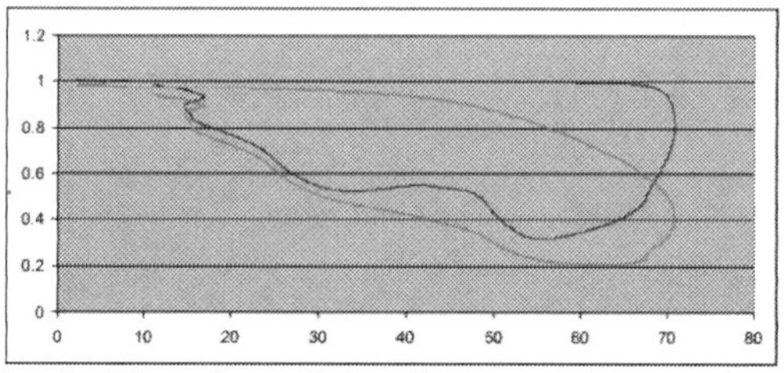

Fig. 3. The values of the flow separation coordinates depending on angle of attack for supporting curve from figure 2 (blue line) and figure 4(violet line).

Therefore, we can conclude that the supporting curve should pass higher than the upper branch of the loop. The bifurcation point should correspond to the angle of attack critical value. For example, let us consider the supporting curve passing as shown in Figure 4.

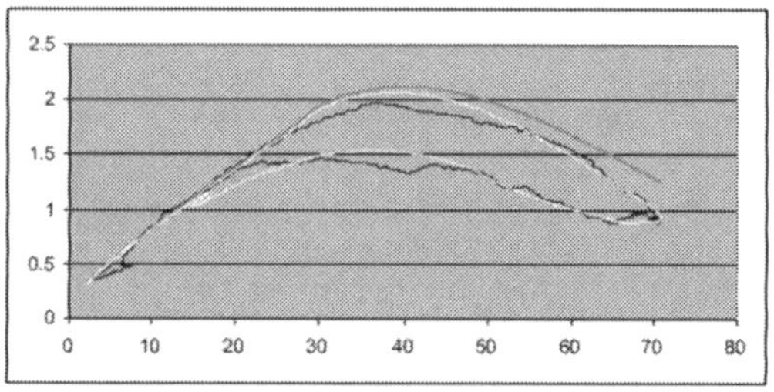

Fig. 4. The values of the lift coefficient (blue line) and the values obtained using the hysteresis model (yellow line) with the supporting curve (violet line) passing above the hysteresis loop, depending on the angles of attack.

https://doi.org/10.1051/itmconf/20181801003

In this case the variation of the flow separation point coordinate looks more natural, as shown in Figure 3, violet line. At the same time the loop approximation is still very accurate. Therefore, this kind of supporting curve provides good opportunities for tuning the hysteresis model parameters. It should be also noted that the supporting curve constructed above the upper branch of hysteresis loop is in certain sense virtual since it does not correspond to any actual aerodynamic dependency.

So, it is evident that considerable room for choosing a particular supporting curve exists.

5 Conclusions

The paper shows that there are two principal modes to choose the supporting curve in the aerodynamic hysteresis model.

The simplest way is to draw the curve following the upper branch of the hysteresis loop. In this case we obtain a good approximation of the loop, but the variation of the flow separation point coordinate contradicts the physical nature of the process. It may be acceptable when the flow separation point is not under consideration.

Another way is to construct the virtual supporting curve positioned above the upper branch of the loop. In this case both the loop approximation and the separation point variations are acceptable. The problem is that due to the considerable room for constructing the curve the choice is arbitrary to certain extent.

This work is supported by Russian Foundation for Basic Research (RFBR), project 17-08-00856-a.

References

1. G.S. Bjushgensa (eds) *Ajerodinamika, ustojchivost' i upravljaemost' sverhzvukovyh samoletov*, (Moscow: Nauka, 1998)
2. A.V. Kanyshev, O.N. Korsun, A.V. Stulovskii, *Mehatronika, avtomatizacija, upravlenie*, **19**, 201 (2018)
3. A.V. Kanyshev, O.N. Korsun, A.V. Stulovskii, *ITM Web of Conference*, **10**, 01004 (2017)
4. M.G. Goman, A.N. Khrabrov, Journal of Aircraft, **31**, 1109 (1994)
5. D.M. Luchtenburg, C.M. Rowley, M.W. Lohry, L. Martinelli, R.F. Stengel, Journal of Aircraft, **52**, 890 (2015)
6. R.V. Jategaonkar, *Flight vehicle system identification: A time domain methodology*, (Reston: AIAA, 2006)
7. V.N. Ovcharenko, *Identifikacija ajerodinamicheskih harakteristik vozdushnyh sudov po poletnym dannym* (Moscow: Izdatel'stvo MAI, 2017)
8. Ju.S. Zav'jalov, B.I. Kvasov, V.L. Miroshnichenko, *Metody splain-funkcyj* (Moscow: Nauka, 1980)

Improvement of specialized industrial manipulator movement control

Vladimir Kuvshinnikov[1,*] and *Evgeny* Kovshov[1]

[1]JSC «NIKIMT-Atomstroy», Moscow, Russia

Abstract. This article deals with the specialized portal manipulator motion control. The key features of the system are analysed, management efficiency improvement task is considered and formulated. An approach to the manipulator trajectory formation is proposed, based on existing mobile and industrial robotics solutions including artificial neural networks.

1 Introduction

Among the wide variety of industrial manipulators there is a separate class of large-dimensional massive portal manipulators. When managing such manipulators, the movement strategy and trajectory selection have a great impact on performance. Specialized manipulators, in turn, have a set of additional features, which often impose a significant imprint on the entire control system (CS).

The object of the operator control is a specialized portal manipulator (PM), located above the cooling pond (CP) and designed to perform the following technological functions: search and detection of leaks in the welds of the cooling pond coating; defects areas cleansing; identified CP coating defects mending by patch method, using glue; applied patches leakage detection; patches reapplying in case of need.

Inspection and control of CP walls is exercised step by step, as CP bottom and walls are freed from the stored fuel assemblies (FA).

Plant specific features are conditioned by following technical parameters: large linear dimensions of plant and work area: more than 14 meters length, 6.5 meters width and 20 meters deep (fig. 1); large manipulator structure weight: up to 20 tons; operating temperature up to 60 Celsius degrees; hydrostatic pressure operating conditions: up to 2 atm.; high radiation background: specific absorption rate 30 000 Gy. per hour;

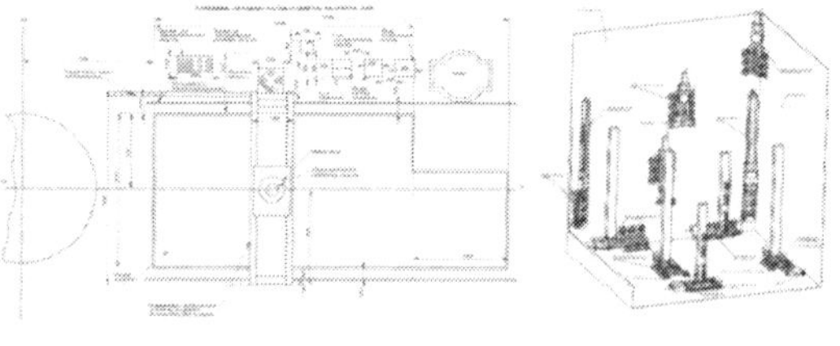

Fig. 1. Operating device position examples

work area scheme and dimensions changing within work space of the manipulator; replaceable highly specialized modules of the operating device (OD) of the manipulator; operator's camera surveillance restriction. The control is carried out by the operator from a specially equipped workplace using a personal computer with specialized software, as in others interactive non-destructive testing systems [1]. Portal manipulator control system (CS) is a distributed multicomponent system linked by local and controller area network. Control data exchange is performed via Ethernet, CAN, RS-485 bus interfaces and discrete sensor channels using Modbus TCP, CANOpen, FHPP and Modbus ASCII communication protocols.

During plant operating according to algorithm below shown on fig. 2, operator is responsible for OD strategic trajectory planning and motion regime. Optimal OD trajectory formation task is beyond operator strength due to human factor, man-machine interaction specifics [2] and operator view restrictions.

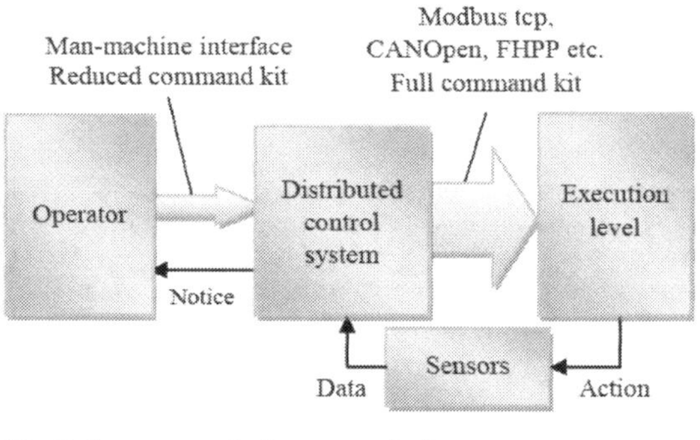

Fig. 2. Operator manipulator control scheme

Within the control process there will be trajectory deviations and overruns which results in extra motions to reach the end point. Described control scheme may cause following undesirable effects such as: motor winding overheat; the increased wear of PM mechanics;

* Corresponding author: Kuvshinnikov@ndtexpert.ru

excessive energy consumption; increased PM auxiliary time; increased OD service time.

Thus, it is required to solve a multicriteria optimization problem in order to reduce the negative effects of the PM operator management.

The problem is complicated by the fact that, unlike existing solutions [3], inadmissible manipulator configuration data is inaccessible in the considered CS. Periodic FS positioning change prevents unambiguous delimitation of work area, and OD is in no way sensitive to obstacles. In such conditions, the CS has the data obtained during manual control. Admissible manipulator configurations set is formed using executed movements data, from which optimized by the chosen criterion trajectory is selected. Such an approach is less effective than previously mentioned, but it allows to improve manipulator efficiency with no hardware changes, decreasing PM auxiliary time and service time of CP.

2 Structure and strategy

2.1. Structure of trajectory planning system

Trajectory planning is a multi-stage process of data processing, using current OD position data, work area shape and size data, and the endpoint data. It is proposed to use the structure based on three subsystems: neural network, trajectory generator and control signal generator to obtain the trajectory for auxiliary movement of the PM operating device. The developed architecture of the control system is shown in fig. 3.

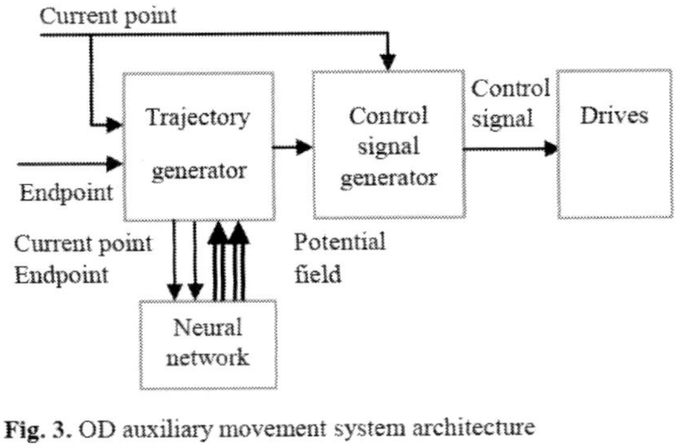

Fig. 3. OD auxiliary movement system architecture

There are solutions for the formation of trajectories and motion control of mobile robots based on similar architecture [4]. The differences between the presented solutions are based on the managed systems features.

On the one hand, as a control object, an industrial manipulator is simpler: it is not necessary to coordinate the trajectories of several simultaneously controlled objects, there is no need to dynamically adjust the trajectory due to volatile obstacles [5], and the simplicity of the working area makes the task of reaching an endpoint without getting into the local minima easier (fig. 4).

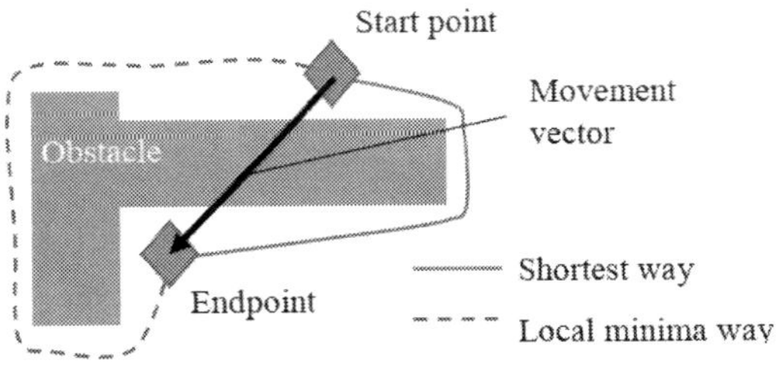

Fig. 4. Local minima trajectory example on surface

On the other hand, the task of PM control is complicated by the facts that it is necessary to form a three-dimensional trajectory; there is no sensory data to obtain information about the surrounding space during the OD movement; and working at greater depths under water requires the formation of a more complex potential transition cost field for each discrete configuration of the manipulator.

2.2 Movement planning stages

Determination of the manipulator OD position is achieved by absolute linear coordinates sensors data obtaining. The manipulator is equipped with sensors that provide information about the generalized X, Y and Z axes coordinates along the pool, across the pool and in the vertical plane, respectively. The work area of PM can be divided into several areas: the air area of free movement, the water area of free movement and the potentially inaccessible water area. The air area of free movement is above the water surface of the cooling pool. This area is distinguished by constant shape and the lowest travel costs due to the low viscous friction forces in the air compared to water. The water area of free movement is a vast volume located in a pool filled with water and limited by the speculative planes parallel to the walls and the bottom of the pool at some distance from them. This area is free from obstacles, but is completely filled with water, which forms a gradient of the transition cost along the horizontal plane depending on the depth of PM rod immersion. A potentially inaccessible water area is an area filled with water located between the free movement water area and the walls/bottom of the pool. The size of the most protruding technological structures, as well as the size of stored FA, determine the dimensions of this area. It is not possible to obtain sensory information about the shape and size of this zone for a number of reasons. It makes sense to use the recorded information on access to the inner surface of the pool, obtained during the manual control by operator, for trajectory formation.

Taking into account the mentioned peculiarities, the task of the movement planning should be decomposed into planning levels: strategic, tactical, detailed. This approach is used in mobile robotics as well [6] and is suitable for PM displacement planning. The shape of the work area either provides access to the part of the pool surface directly from the free movement area, or no access at all, which simplifies the potential paths to reach any available point of the CP surface. The main objective of the strategic planning level is to form a set of three-dimensional direction vectors that define the sequence of target endpoints movements. Tactical level planning involves finding the shortest path through a neural map, generated considering the weighting functions in terms of the specified discretization parameter. The detailed planning level is designed to smooth the movement trajectory.

2.2 Trajectory formation strategy

PM kinematic scheme includes three controlled translational joints and one unmanaged rotary joint. Unmanaged rotary joint intended for mounting specific modules in different orientations. It affects the size of the OD and determines the operating point coordinates.

If we discretize the configuration space of the manipulator with resolution N, then the coordinate in each of the joints j_1, j_2 and j_3 can take discrete values from the range $\mathbf{q}_{x_j}(x_j \in \{1, \ldots, N\})$, where q_{1j} and q_{Nj} are the lower and the upper constructive linear motion constraints of the joints. Let us name the set of all OD configurations, conditioned by a set of available modules and orientations, as a set of discrete options O. Then the coordinate in the joint j_4 can take on a values of $\mathbf{q}_{o4}(o_4 \in \{1,\ldots,O\})$. Then we can represent a discrete model of the manipulator configuration space as a set of $N^3 \cdot O$ vectors

$$DC=\{\mathbf{q}_a | 1 \ldots N^3 \cdot O\}, \quad (1)$$

where $\mathbf{q}_a = [q_{x1} \; q_{x2} \; q_{x3} \; q_{o4}]^T$ – discrete manipulator configuration $x_j \in \{1, \ldots, N\}$ where $j = 1, \ldots, 3$; $o_4 \in \{1, \ldots, O\}$; a – a one-dimensional index, taking a value of $a=N^2 \cdot O \cdot (x_1-1)+N \cdot O \cdot (x_2-1)+ O \cdot (x_3 - 1)+o_4$.

Due to the fact that the configuration of the j_4 joint is manually changeable in a dedicated area, the only joints to be controlled automatically and used for trajectory formation are j_1, j_2 and j_3. At the same time, taking into account the difference in the CP linear dimensions, in practice we better choose separate discretization value for each joint N_1, N_2 and N_3.

The system has no information about the set of obstacles $B=\{B_1, B_2, \ldots, B_m\}$, making it difficult to determine a set of free from a collision configurations, $DC_f=\{\mathbf{q}_a \in DC \mid M(\mathbf{q}_a) \cap B = \varnothing\}$, denoting manipulator in configuration $\mathbf{q}_a$ as $M(\mathbf{q}_a)$ [7]. Instead, a set of safe configurations DC_s is defined as a known subset of $DC_f \supseteq DC_s$. A set of dangerous configurations consisting of the configurations that do not belong to DC_s , including B and $DC_f \cap DC_s$, is

$$DC_d=B \cup (DC_f \cap DC_s); \quad (2)$$

Secure configurations set consists of the configurations sets corresponding to air and water areas of free movement ($DC_f \cap DC_{fw}$), and configurations of potentially unavailable water area, which are considered to be safe during the operator manual actions monitoring (DC_m)

$$DC_s=DC_{fa} \cup DC_{fw} \cup DC_m. \quad (3)$$

Key trajectory selection strategy implies avoiding potentially dangerous manipulator configurations and only bringing the manipulator into safe configurations.

3 Mapping and trajectory generation

3.1 Three-dimensional area representation

To simplify the presentation, to reduce the amount of stored data and the access time, certainly safe areas are specified by coordinate ranges. A potentially inaccessible water area is represented as a set of corresponding PM configurations. At the same time, to decrease the amount of filtering area cells calculations, adjacent configurations are initially combined into three-dimensional groups. Initially all the configurations in potentially inaccessible water area are considered dangerous. The size of the configurations groups is selected as a multiple of the linear size of the base group. Sample size for a cubic configuration group:

$$N_g=n_g^3; n_g=l^i, \quad (4)$$

where N_g – cubic group full size, n_g – cubic group linear size, l – base group linear size, i – group scale. At $i = 0$, a single configuration of the manipulator is considered. Configurations group is a three-dimensional convolution of the adjacent configurations, which stores information about the corresponding work area cell dangerousness. The convolution dangerousness is determined by the coefficient $d \in [0, \ldots, 1]$. Groups with $d = 0$ are completely safe and with $d = 1$ are completely dangerous. If the group contains only completely safe or completely dangerous groups of lower scale, it is also considered completely safe or dangerous correspondingly. The safety check of a cell comes down to sequential groups polling in descending order of scale to obtain sufficient or comprehensive information.

3.2 Trajectory generator

The manipulator OD motion trajectory formation is made by a sequential rise from the initial cell of the neural map to the final one in the direction of the maximum gradient. Initial cell is a cell, containing starting PM configuration. Final cell is a cell, containing endpoint configuration. The algorithm of trajectory generation is shown in fig. 5.

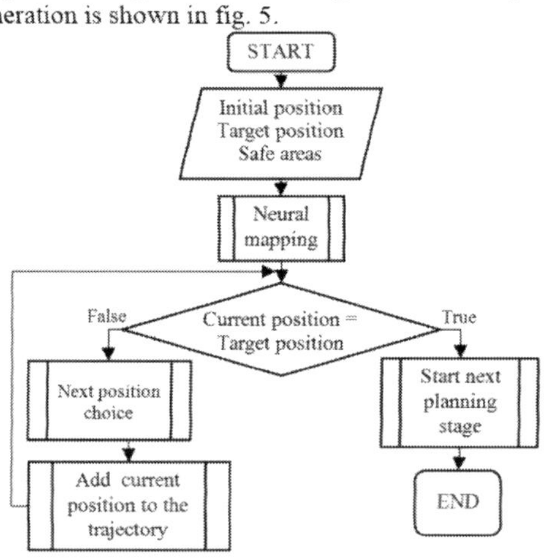

Fig. 5 Algorithm of trajectory formation

3.3 Neural mapping

A special representation of the manipulator configurations set - a neural map – is used for trajectory formation. Each group of configurations stands for a cell of work area and corresponds to one neuron. The choice of the neural network type is determined by the problem: filtering the work area cells by the cost of transition from each cell to adjacent cells, considering the weight function.

The Hopfield network is one type of network with filtering ability. We use neural network to filter configuration groups. The scheme of the elementary network neuron is shown in fig. 6.

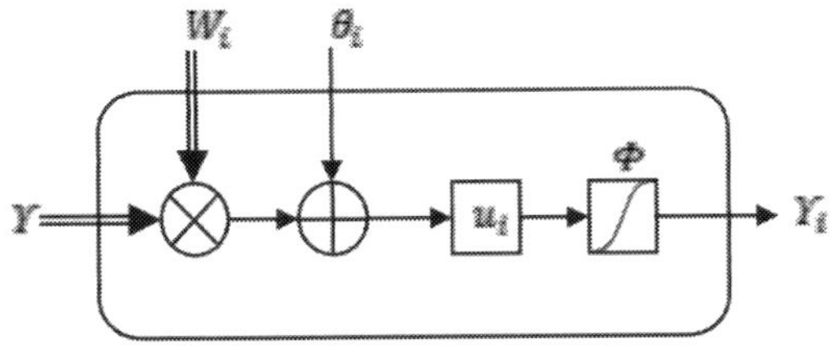

Fig. 6 Elementary nonlinear processing neuron unit

Neuron i is described by input vector **Y**, weight vector $\mathbf{W}_i$, displacement vector $\boldsymbol{\theta}_i$, that form a sum network signal

$$u_i = W_i \times Y + \theta_i = \sum_{j=1}^{n} w_{ij} v_j + \theta_i . \qquad (5)$$

The sum signal is processed by a nonlinear activation function Φ and formed the output signal of the neuron $\mathbf{Y}_i$. Hyperbolic tangent, sigmoidal function and others can be used as activation function.

Neural mapping requires determining the following parameters: the order of the considered configuration groups; the size of the considered area; the type of weight function, and the topology of the adjacent cells relationships. Considered configuration groups scale determines the linear dimensions of the working area cell, taken as a single position of the manipulator, which corresponds to one neuron. This parameter can be called the neural map resolution. The lower the scale, the more neurons will include a neural map, which will increase the trajectory sampling and allow better dangerous CP zone enveloping. Decreasing the scale increases the number of neural map neurons by a multiple of l^3, where l is the base configuration group linear size. The coverage of the map is determined by the initial and target trajectory points relative location.

Working area shape is simple and there is no need to move far beyond the parallelepiped, which includes movement direction vector to reach the endpoint. The map includes a sufficient part of the free movement zone to plot the trajectory, with a reserve of height (coordinate z) to take the gradient of the linear movement cost into account also. The size of that reserve depends on the aquatic environment viscous friction.

Piecewise given function is chosen as a weight function of the i-th and j-th neuron connection

$$w_{ij} = \begin{cases} 0 & \rho(q_i,q_j)\cdot k_f(z,\phi)=0 \\ f(\rho(q_i,q_j)) & 0<\rho(q_i,q_j)\cdot k_f(z,\phi)<r \\ 0 & r<\rho(q_i,q_j)\cdot k_f(z,\phi) \end{cases} \qquad (6)$$

where $\rho(\mathbf{q}_i, \mathbf{q}_j)$ – Euclidean distance between configurations, corresponding to i and j neurons; $k_f(z,\varphi)$ – function that counts how viscous friction forces affect the cost of transition at a given depth in a given direction; z – chosen configuration's depth; φ – the polar angle between the x-axis and the direction of travel from q_i to q_j measured in XOY plane; $f(\rho(\mathbf{q}_i, \mathbf{q}_j))$ – decreasing function of the form $f(x)=1/x$; r – the radius of the neutron region i.e. how far each neuron affects other neurons through weight functions [8].

Neural mapping may base on different topologies of connections between neurons. Hexagon (fig. 7a) and rectangular (fig. 7b) are the most common connections topologies for the plane. It is convenient to choose a parallelepiped form connection (fig. 7c) for a three-dimensional task. Each neuron has 6, 18 or 26 adjacent neurons connection depending on the selected neural region radius. This is because the distances between the nodes are different: along the edge (a), along the face diagonals ($a\sqrt{2}$) and along the three-dimensional diagonal ($a\sqrt{3}$).

After the scaling with the weight coefficients vector $\mathbf{W}_i$ operation, the i-th neuron bias vector $\boldsymbol{\theta}_i$ is applied.

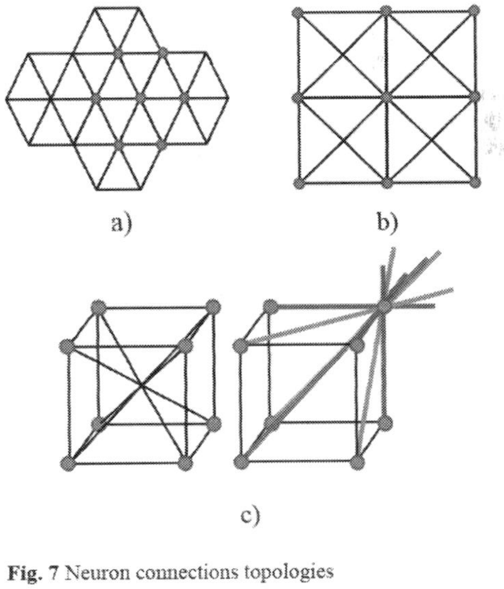

Fig. 7 Neuron connections topologies

The bias value is determined by the neural card input:

$$\theta_i = \begin{cases} +\infty & i-\text{th neuron is in target group} \\ -\infty & i-\text{th neuron is in group with } d > d_{max} \\ 0 & \text{other cases} \end{cases} , \qquad (7)$$

where d and d_{max} – i-th neuron corresponding configurations group danger coefficient and maximum allowed coefficient value.

The bias vector makes the target neuron always maximally activated, and neurons corresponding to potentially dangerous groups of manipulator configurations – always maximally deactivated. In other cases, it is possible to set the bias value as a function of parameter *d*.

Other neurons, which are not directly defined by external data, can be activated in several ways. One of the ways is spreading the activation from target neuron, which corresponds to the target configuration. Activation of neurons is distributed in all directions using the simultaneous activation method until either the activation signal reaches the initial neuron, which corresponds to the initial position of the manipulator, or all neurons are activated. Another method involves consecutive neurons activation with rasters, for example, cross-activation [8]. Activation does not extend through neurons with a bias $\theta_i = -\infty$ (neurons of potentially dangerous configurations), which allows to reach the target neuron by just climbing in maximum gradient direction starting from the initial neuron.

4 Results and conclusions

The trajectory generation method with neural mapping is expanded from two-dimensional into three-dimensional representation. Modern computers processing power has multiplied compared to previously used computers, which has been successfully used for trajectory calculations in two dimensions. In addition, modern computers support parallel processing of information at many levels, starting with the hardware. Special software and hardware-software tools have been developed to distribute computing power for parallel processing, such as CUDA [9, 10] and OpenCL [11]. No wonder that these solutions were previously used for the volumetric calculations that are associated with learning [12, 13], and activation of neural networks [14]. Thus, the possibilities of multidirectional neural network activation simultaneous calculations [15] are significantly increased. For better trajectory formation representation a computer simulation with flexible parameters is proposed. Currently, the NVIDIA GPU Cloud (NGC) provides an easy access to the full catalogue of software for deep learning and high performance computing, optimized for the GPU [16].

References

1. A. Kosach, E. Kovshov, ITM Web of Conferences, **10**, 01005 (2017)
2. E. Borisenko, P. Martynov, E. Kovshov, Collection of scientific papers on the materials of the international scientific-practical conference, **2** (2009)
3. V. Kuvshinnikov, E. Kovshov, "Rosatom" State Corporation innovation management unit. URL: http://innov-rosatom.ru
4. O. Darintsev, A. Migranov, Artificial intelligence, **3** (2009)
5. O. Darintsev, A. Migranov, Bulletin of RAS, **3** (2007)
6. A. Bolshakov, M. Stepanov, A. Stepanov, Bulletin of SSTU, **4** (2010)
7. L. Lobareva, M. Kozhevnikov, Bulletin of Polotsk state University, **11** (2017)
8. G. Michail, The Center for Advanced Computer Studies University of Southwestern Louisiana (1999).
9. CUDA Toolkit Documentation v. 9.1.85. URL: https://docs.nvidia.com/cuda/
10. NVIDIA Accelerated Computing. Deep learning. URL: https://developer.nvidia.com/deep-learning
11. The open standard for parallel programming of heterogeneous systems. URL: https://www.khronos.org/opencl/
12. E. Matkova, E. Kovshov, Informational technologies, **12** (2008)
13. J. Li, Q. Liu, 8th International Symposium on HEART, (2017)
14. S. Zoican, R. Zoican, D. Galatchi, Advanced Technologies, Systems and Services in Telecommunications (TELSIKS) (2017)
15. R. Glasius, A. Komoda, S. Gielen, Neural Networks, **8** (1995)
16. NVIDIA GPU Cloud. URL: https://www.nvidia.ru/gpu-cloud/

The approaches to developing the distributed information-control systems of organizational type

Victor L. Lyaskovsky[1], Igor *B.* Bresler[1], *Mihail A.* Alasheev[1,*]

[1]JSC "Research Institute of Information Technologies", Tver, Russia

Abstract. The article contains the results of research aimed at developing a scientific and methodological framework for justifying solutions for the development of distributed information-control systems of an organizational type. The structuring of the initial data is made, a formalized statement of the problem of justifying solutions for the development of distributed information-control systems of the organizational type is proposed. To solve this problem, a scientific-methodical approach is proposed, which includes methods for assessing the effectiveness of the solution and the individual indicators.

1 Statement of the problem

The management decisions in government departments, state corporations, integrated structures and enterprises of industry are implemented in the information processing and management systems specially created in the relevant other organizations. One of the main ways to improve the efficiency of the use of such systems is the integrated automation of information processing and management processes implemented in the process of creating (developing) the corresponding distributed information-control systems of the organizational type (DICS).

DICS are distributed automated information processing and management system created to automate the activities of the management bodies of the relevant ministries, agencies, agencies and other organizations in order to improve the effectiveness of the application of managed bodies (facilities). DICS, as a rule, is a multi-level system consisting of a set of functional subsystems (FS), each of which implements a number of interrelated functional processes (FP). In this case, individual FS are realized by performing complex functional tasks (FT), solved in the system at various levels of management.

The urgency of the tasks of creating, developing and modernizing complex information-control systems, some approaches and methods for their solution are given in the works [1-6].

The essence of the choice of solutions for the development of the DICS [1, 2] is that for each planned stage of forecasting (PS) system-based solutions for control centers (CC) automation should be selected by equipping the op amp with serial (equipment is possible at the current time) automation complexes (AC) or by developed AC (equipment is possible in the future after the end of the corresponding development work), taking into account the permissible (designated) resource of the use of AC within the DICS. At the same time, in the process of choosing the option for the development of the AC, the requirements for the integrated inter-level automation of the individual CC must also be taken into account, that is, the choice for the implementation in certain CC of such FT that constitute the FP under consideration.

As the initial data used to solve the problem under consideration, the following are accepted:

1. The organizational structure of the DICS, described as a set of CC and links of subordination and interaction between them. In this case, each CC can be equipped with no more than one AC of a certain type.

2. Functional structure of the DICS, described as a set of FS. Each of the FS consists of a set of FP, the constituent parts of which are FT.

Depending on the requirements for the timeliness of the implementation of the FP are divided into real-time FP and non-real-time FP. The main difference between these types of FP is that for real-time FP, there are requirements for probabilistic-temporal (PTC) or time (TC) characteristics of the duration of their performance, and for the non-real-time FP such requirements are not required.

Depending on the importance, which is determined by the degree of influence of the implemented FP on the overall efficiency of the DICS application for its intended purpose, all FP are divided into higher priority FP (FPh) and other FP (FPo).

3. Types of CC, each of them is characterized by a set of FT to be implemented in the AC.

4. Types of AC intended for automation of CC that, depending on the stage of the life cycle of the CC, are divided into operating (at the stage of operation in the CC), serial (at the stage of serial deliveries) and developed (at the stages of performing the relevant research or development works).

* Corresponding author: mihal81@mail.ru

5. The current version of the equipment of the CC by AC, including information on the types of AC, their resource and parameters implemented FT.

6. Requirements for PTC and TC of the FP.

7. Requirements for the design and reliability characteristics of the developed AC.

8. The list, organizational, production and financial characteristics of enterprises that perform works or can participate in the processes of development, production and supply of AC.

9. List of PS including their duration and amount of funding.

10. Initial data on standard project solutions, the application of which is possible in the development of the AC.

Taking into account the given initial data, the formalized statement of the problem of the formation of solutions for the development of the DICS in conditions of resource constraints can be written in the following form.

At each PS, it is necessary to determine the development variant of the DICS based on the choice of system engineering solutions $\mathbf{X}^*(u)$, $\mathbf{Y}^*(u)$, $\mathbf{Z}^*(u)$, which maximize the effectiveness of the implementation of FP $F(\mathbf{X}(u), \mathbf{Y}(u), \mathbf{Z}(u))$, with mandatory realization of FPh, with given maximum permissible PTC and TC of the FP implementation, with given requirements to information protection, constructive and reliability characteristics of AC ($\mho_{\text{тр}}$), with restrictions on the time $T_{\max}(u)$ and cost $C_{\max}(u)$ parameters of the process of development of the DICS:

$\{\mathbf{X}^*(u), \mathbf{Y}^*(u), \mathbf{Z}^*(u)\}=\text{Argmax } F(\mathbf{X}^*(u), \mathbf{Y}^*(u), \mathbf{Z}^*(u))$ (1)

with the constraints:

$\mathbf{\Omega}(\mathbf{X}(u), \mathbf{Y}(u)) \cap \mathbf{\Omega}_{\text{h}} = \mathbf{\Omega}_{\text{h}}$;

$\mathbf{\Omega}'_{\text{rt}} \cup \mathbf{\Omega}''_{\text{rt}} = \mathbf{\Omega}_{\text{rt}}$;

$\mathbf{\Omega}'_{\text{rt}} \cap \mathbf{\Omega}''_{\text{rt}} = \varnothing$;

$\forall\, i,\ i \in \mathbf{\Omega}'_{\text{rt}}$: $P_i(t_i(\mathbf{X}(u), \mathbf{Y}(u), \mathbf{Z}(u)) \leq t^{\max}{}_i) \geq P^{\min}{}_i$;

$\forall\, i,\ i \in \mathbf{\Omega}''_{\text{rt}}$: $\tau_i(\mathbf{X}(u), \mathbf{Y}(u), \mathbf{Z}(u)) \leq \tau^{\max}{}_i$;

$\mho(\mathbf{X}(u), \mathbf{Y}(u), \mathbf{Z}(u)) \subseteq \mho_{\text{req}}$;

$T(\mathbf{X}(u), \mathbf{Y}(u), \mathbf{Z}(u)) \leq T_{\max}(u)$;

$C(\mathbf{X}(u), \mathbf{Y}(u), \mathbf{Z}(u)) \leq C_{\max}(u)$;

where $u \in \{1, \dots U\}$, U – the number of PS;

$\mathbf{X}(u)$ – decisions on development of AC;

$\mathbf{Y}(u)$ – decisions on AC manufacturing and CC equipment;

$\mathbf{Z}(u)$ – decisions to extend the operation of the AC;

$\mathbf{\Omega}(\mathbf{X}(u), \mathbf{Y}(u))$ – set of realized FP;

$\mathbf{\Omega}_{\text{h}}$ – set of FPh;

$\mathbf{\Omega}_{\text{rt}}$ – set of real-time FP;

$\mathbf{\Omega}'_{\text{rt}}$ – set of real-time FP with the requirements to PTC of the implementation;

$\mathbf{\Omega}''_{\text{rt}}$ – set of real-time FP with the requirements to TC of the implementation;

$P_i(t_i(\mathbf{X}(u), \mathbf{Y}(u), \mathbf{Z}(u)) \leq t^{\max}{}_i)$ – probability of timely execution of i-th FP;

$P^{\min}{}_i$ – required probability of timely execution of i-th FP;

$\tau_i(\mathbf{X}(u), \mathbf{Y}(u), \mathbf{Z}(u))$ – average execution time of i-th FP;

$\tau^{\max}{}_i$ – the required average execution time of i-th FP;

$\mho(\mathbf{X}(u), \mathbf{Y}(u), \mathbf{Z}(u))$ – set of implemented requirements for information protection, constructive and reliability characteristics of AC;

$\mho_{\text{req}}$ – a set of requirements for information security, design and reliability characteristics of AC;

$C(\mathbf{X}(u), \mathbf{Y}(u), \mathbf{Z}(u))$ – cost of implementation of decisions on the development of DICS;

$T(\mathbf{X}(u), \mathbf{Y}(u), \mathbf{Z}(u))$ – duration of DICS development.

2 Scheme of the scientific-methodical approach to the solution of the problem

The general scheme of the scientific and methodological approach to solving the problem of selecting system-technical solutions for the development of the DICS includes the following main blocks:

- input of initial data and constraints;
- formation of decision options;
- evaluation of decisions;
- obtaining the results of solving the problem.

The composition of these blocks and the sequence of their application are shown in figure 1.

3 Methods for solving the problem

The analysis of the algorithmic complexity of the solution of the problem posed showed that it is NP-hard. Moreover, as shown in [2], even with the use of high-performance computing, it is possible to obtain an exact solution of such a problem by the exhaustive search method only for relatively small dimensions of the initial data. The use of other precise methods of discrete optimization also will not allow to achieve appreciable advantages, since in the general case, the number of analyzed variants of the solution can be close to the number of variants of the solution by the exhaustive search method [1, 2, 7].

We estimate the algorithmic complexity of the solution of the problem by the most labor-intensive exact method – the exhaustive search method. To do this, we introduce the following notation:

N – number of CC;

K_n – number of AC for each CC, $n \in \{1, \dots N\}$;

M_n – number of FT for each CC.

Then the total number of options for developing the AC, which must be formed and evaluated in the decision process, will be calculated in accordance with the following expression:

$$Q_1 = \left(\prod_{n=1}^{N} (K_n + 1) 2^{M_n} \right)^U . \qquad (2)$$

The total number of options for AC manufacturing and CC equipment will be calculated in accordance with the following expression:

$$Q_2 = \left(\prod_{n=1}^{N} (K_n + 1) \right)^U . \qquad (3)$$

The total number of options for extending the operation of the AC will be calculated in accordance with the following expression :

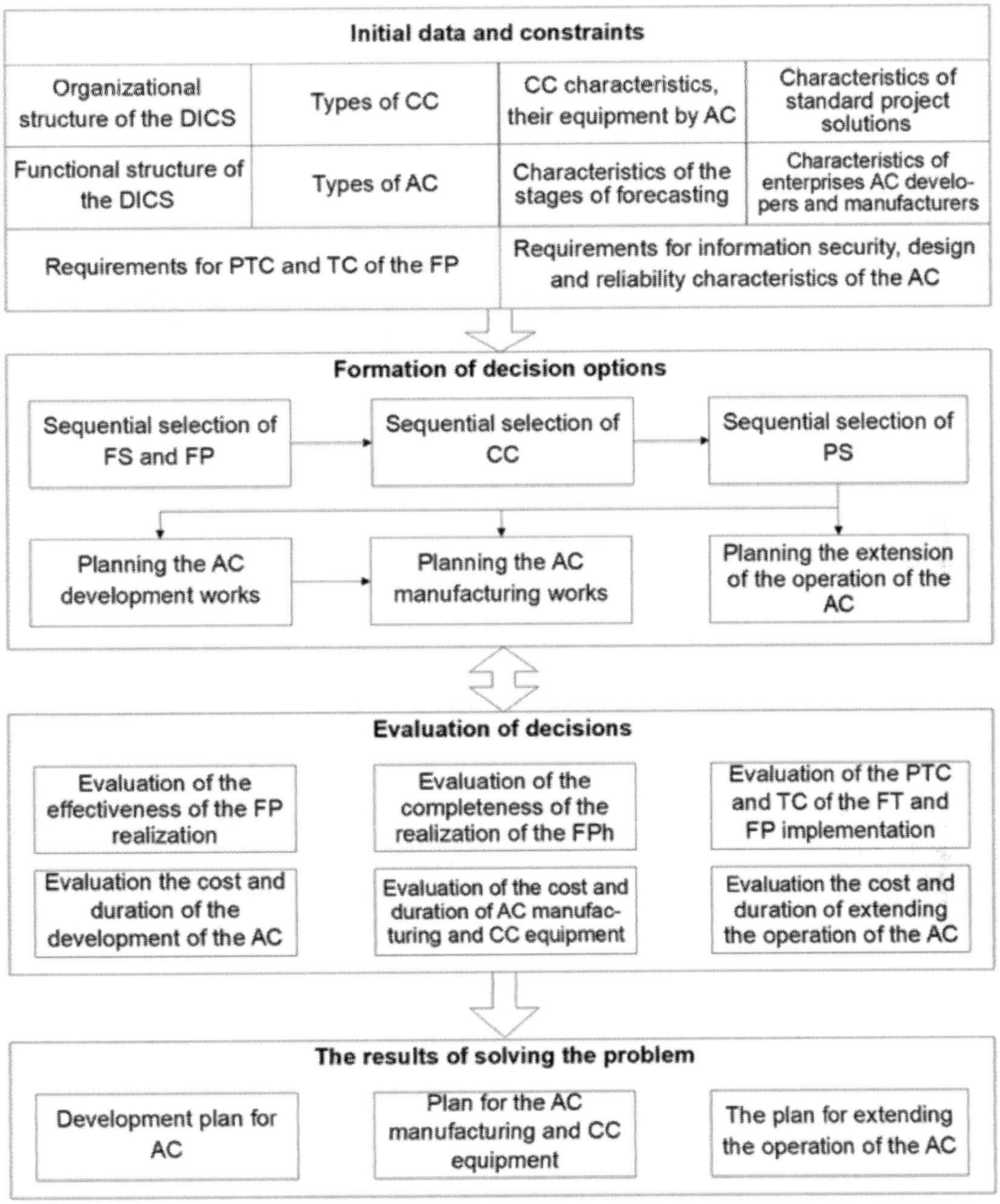

Fig. 1. Scheme of the scientific-methodical approach to solving the problem of choosing system and technical solutions for the development of the DICS

$$Q_3 = 2^{NU}. \quad (4)$$

Accordingly, the total number of solutions to the problem will be equal to:

$$Q = Q_1 \cdot Q_2 \cdot Q_3. \quad (5)$$

To estimate the practical possibility of solving the problem by the exhaustive search method, we set the following values of the initial data:
$U = 5$, $N = 8$, $K_n = 3$, $M_n = 200$.

Then the total number of solutions is equal to $2^{1800} \approx$ $\approx 7.14 \cdot 10^{541}$. This allows us to conclude that it is practically impossible to solve the problem posed by the exact method for given dimensions of the initial data.

In [1, 2], the possibility of solving problems of a similar class on the basis of approximate optimization methods was considered and justified. It was shown that at the initial stage of the DICS design, when the input data for solving the problems of the choice of system-technical solutions for the development of the DICS are determined inaccurately, it is expedient to apply selection methods based on the "greedy" algorithm.

In this regard, to solve this problem, a complex "greedy" algorithm is proposed that consists in choosing the best of the many solutions obtained by particular "greedy" algorithms. Each of the particular "greedy" algorithms is a sequential choice of the solution based on the estimation of the parameters of the objective function and the constraints in the initial problem.

4 Methods to evaluate the effectiveness of the solution and private indicators

As an objective function for the solution of the problem it is expedient to choose a complex indicator [8], reflecting the degree of automation of the required FP, with the necessity to perform a number of FP on a real-time scale. For this we shall use below two particular indicators:

1. The indicator for estimating the realization of the FPh.

2. The indicator of the degree of automation of all FP.

The first indicator can be written as a vector discrete Boolean function that takes the value "1" if all of FPh are realized, "0" otherwise.

The second indicator can be estimated in accordance with [8].

The estimation of the PTC and TC of the FP implementation can be performed using the following types of models:

- analytical models;
- simulation models;
- combined analytical and simulation models;
- metamodels;
- semi-full-scale and full-scale models.

It was shown in [1] that at the initial stages of the design of a AC, the use of analytical and combined models is most expedient.

When obtaining estimates of cost and time indicators in the initial stages of the development of the AC, expert assessment methods, normative-calculating and analog-comparative methods can be applied [9]. The most appropriate is the joint use of these methods. In this case, we assume that the projected AC has a AC-analog, developed and manufactured for one of the CC from the DICS structure, with similar characteristics for the FT being implemented. This condition is usually satisfied in the development practice. At the same time, all estimations of cost and time indicators for the development of a projected AC will be carried out for the enterprise - developer of AC-analog. Recalculation for other enterprises that have differences in basic economic standards for the performance of design work is not difficult.

5 Conclusion

In this paper, we propose an original formulation of the problem of choosing system-technical solutions for the development of a DICS and a new approach to its solution, which consists in evaluating the algorithmic complexity and applying the solution method on the basis of a complex "greedy" selection algorithm. The methodological provisions of the proposed approach can become the main one for the formation of an automated decision support system for the justification of plans and programs for the development of automated systems for various purposes.

References

1. V.L. Lyaskovsky, *System-technical basis for automation of information processing and control processes in hierarchical military systems* (Tver: Military academy of aerospace defense, 2014)
2. V.L. Lyaskovsky, I.B. Bresler, M.A. Alasheev, Programmnye produkty i sistemy, **2**, 165-171 (2017)
3. Khaled M. Khan, Yan Zhang, *Managing Corporate Information Systems Evolution and Maintenance*. (Idea Group Inc, 2005)
4. John Krogstie, *Model-Based Development and Evolution of Information Systems: A Quality Approach*. (Springer Science & Business Media, 2012)
5. N. Gorla, T.M. Somers, B. Wong, Journal of Strategic Information Systems. **19**, 207 (2010).
6. Y.E. Malashenko, I.A. Nazarova, Journal of Computer and Systems Sciences International, **55**, 83 (2016)
7. V.A. Kostenko, Journal of Computer and Systems Sciences International. **56**, 48 (2017).
8. V.L. Lyaskovsky, Jelektronnye informacionnye sistemy, **4**, 15 (2015)
9. V.L. Lyaskovsky, I.B. Bresler, M.A. Alasheev, M.V. Deikina, Jelektronnye informacionnye sistemy, **1**, 41 (2018)

https://doi.org/10.1051/itmconf/20181801006

Investigation of wear of insulation of traction engines of locomotives in operation

Roman Nefedov [1] and *Elena* Loginova [2, 3, *]

[1]Russian Railwas (RZD) Moscow, Russia
[2]Moscow Technological Institute, Moscow, Russia
[3]Russian University of Transport (MIIT), Moscow, Russia

Abstract. The article analyzes reliability of traction electric motors in operation. It is shown that the greatest number of failure falls on the winding of the armature. Investigation of the causes of increased wear of the armature winding insulation was carried out using the dynamic thermal model of the electric motor. The model is represented by 150 final elements and takes into account the conditions of thermal conductivity between the nodes and heat transfer to the cooling air. Verification of the model was carried out by comparison with the results of thermal tests of electric motors of the series НБ-406 and ЭД-118. The field of temperatures in the traction motor under various loads was investigated. It is shown that in stationary mode the temperature change along the armature winding can reach 60C. Modeling of thermal dynamic processes in the engine during its operation on the locomotive allowed to identify the most stressed nodes. It is shown that the resource of the electric motor is determined by the wear of the insulation of the frontal part of the armature winding on the side of the traction drive of the locomotive.

1 Introduction

The traction electric motor is the main aggregate of the power chain of the locomotive. Its reliability determines the reliability of the entire locomotive [1]. The manufacturer determines the planned mileage of traction motors 1.2 mln km. But in practice the mileage of traction motors is much smaller. The experience of the depot Gorkovskoye showed that the maximum value of the failure flow of traction engines corresponds to a mileage of 0.42 mln km (Fig. 1) [2]. The main flow of failures occurs at the motor armature (Fig. 2) [3].

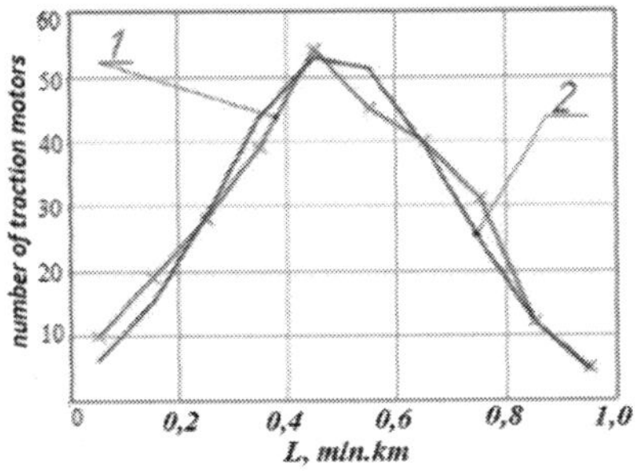

Fig. 1. The failure flowof traction engines of lokomotives in 2011-2012: 1- experimental data; 2 - theoretical curve of the normal distribution

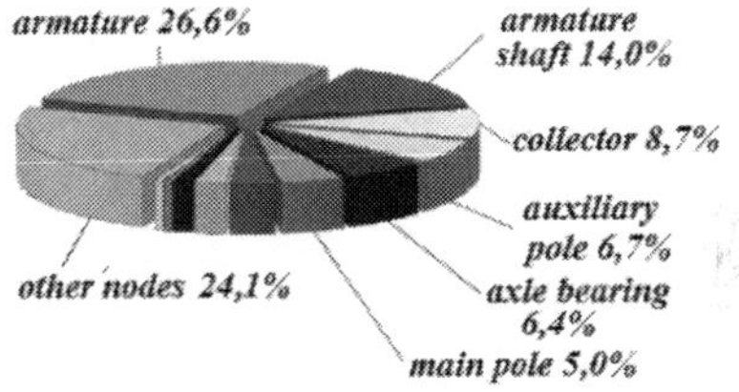

Fig. 2. Malfunctions of traction electric motors of ED118 in 2014.

2 Study and modelling

To study the processes in the traction motor was created its dynamic thermal model. The model is represented by 150 final elements and takes into account the conditions of thermal conductivity between the nodes and heat transfer to the cooling air.

The basis of the model consists of differential equations of the form:

$$\frac{dT_k}{d\tau} = \sum_{l=1}^{b} \alpha_{kl}(T_k, T_l)\cdot(T_k - T_l) + \sum_{k=1}^{m} W_k(T_k) \quad (1),$$

where $\alpha_{kl}(T_k,T_l)=\Lambda_{kl}(T_k,T_l)/C_k(T_k)$, $W_k(T_k)=P_k(T_k,\tau)/C_k(T_k)$ – parameters of adiabatic heating of the k-th node, due to heat transfer to the heat carrier and heat exchange with adjacent nodes of the machine; $\Lambda_{kl}(T_k,T_l)$ – coefficients of the heat transfer matrix from the *k*-th node to the heat carrier and thermal radiations; $C_k(T_k)$- reduced heat capacity of the *k*-th node.

* Corresponding author: ejy-loginova@mail.ru

 https://doi.org/10.1051/itmconf/20181801006

The model of aerodynamic processes in the electric motor was represented by a discrete system of distribution of air flows through cooling channels. The collector channels of the cooling system were represented (n_1 + n_2) by discrete sections with aerodynamic tees, where **n1** and **n2** are the number of tees to the right and left of the collector along the course of the airflow. The aerodynamic model had a nonlinear formulation. The aerodynamic resistance of the cooling system was determined by the value of the air speed taking into account the effect of rotation of the air ducts of the armature [2–3].

Comparison of the calculated and experimental temperature field in the armature winding НБ-406 showed their good convergence (Fig. 3).

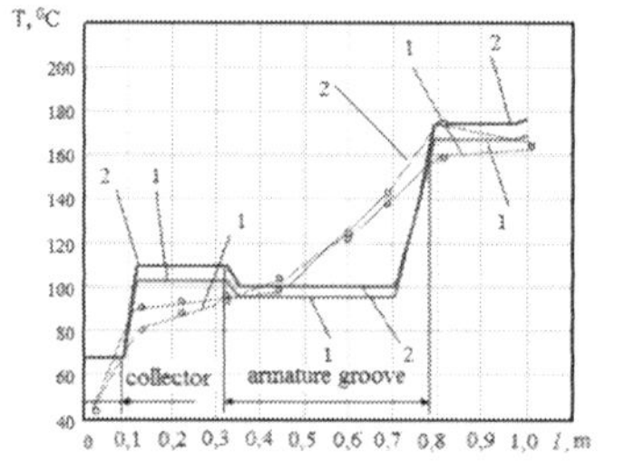

Fig. 3. Temperature distribution in the winding of the motor armature of the НБ-406 in the rated operating mode.

The error in calculating the heating curves of the armature winding at the rated power of the traction motor did not exceed 7% for the whole range of the load current (Fig. 4). To calculate the steady-state temperature distribution in the windings of the electric motor, we used the model of its thermal state, in which the left-hand sides of all the differential equations (1) vanish.

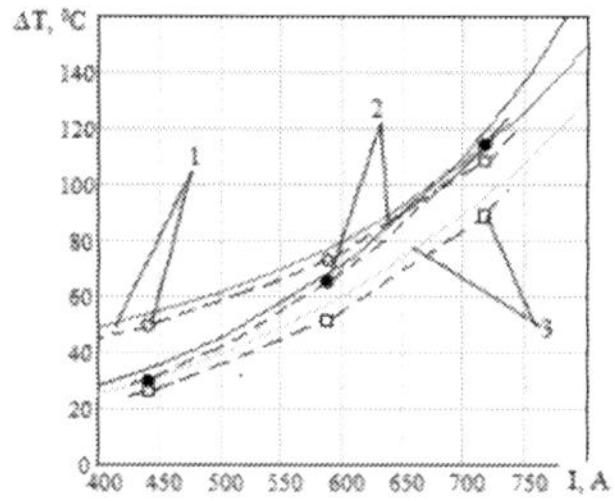

Fig. 4. The calculated (___) and experimental (- -) dependences of the excess of the mean temperature of the armature windings (1), the main poles (2), the additional poles (3) on the load current ED118A for the continuous operation mode and t_{HB} = 260.

The calculation of the mode of motion of the locomotive 2TE116 for the given section was carried out taking into account the kinetic energy of the train. The basis of the model was the traction characteristic of the locomotive at various operating modes of the power plant and the modes of weakening excitation of traction motors (Fig. 5).

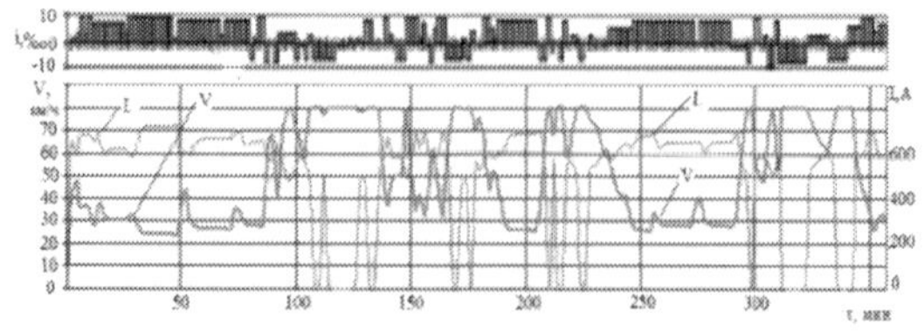

Fig. 5. Simulation of the movement of the diesel locomotive 2ТЭ116 with the composition of the estimated weight for the section of the railway of the type III: i - the current slope value, V - train speed; I - traction motor current.

When modeling traffic processes at a train speed of 80 km / h (speed limit of freight cars), the diesel generator was switched to idling. The air consumption for cooling the traction motors was set in accordance with the condition of the problem being solved.

When modeling the resource tests of traction motors on the thermal factor and the search for rational principles of cooling control, methods of non-linear programming, in particular, variational methods, were used.

All software modules for calculating non-stationary thermal processes of traction motors, including for calculating the values of cooling management evaluation criteria, are developed for Windows in the Borland C ++ integrated environment with the organization of streaming input / output of source data in the Microsoft Excel.

When solving management tasks related to operating modes of locomotives, a minimax approach was used to select traction engine loading regimes and a stochastic approach to account for operating conditions.

To calculate the insulation of the winding of the traction motor under various operating conditions and the selection of the cooling modes, the traction motor model as a non-stationary object is used, supplemented with a traction problem solution module, winding insulation wear calculation modules, and energy costs for cooling the engine.

Wear of insulation by thermal factor is defined as a value that is inverse to the insulation resource at a given temperature:

$$q = \frac{1}{L(\Theta)} = \frac{1}{A} \cdot e^{-((B/\Theta)-G)},$$

where $L(\Theta)$ is the resource insulation by thermal factor; A, B, G – coefficients characterizing the properties of the insulating material; Θ – value of the absolute temperature of the winding.

Or when going to discrete welsh:

$$q = \sum_{i=1}^{n} \frac{q_i \cdot \Delta\tau}{\tau} = \sum_{i=1}^{n} \frac{1}{\tau} \cdot \frac{1}{A} \cdot e^{-((B/\Theta)-G)} \cdot \Delta\tau,$$

where $\Delta\tau$ is the integration step; τ is the current time. The results of modeling the temperature of the windings of traction motors during the movement of the locomotive by profiles of different types showed that with the full use of the power system's power, the armature winding has the greatest temperature throughout the entire driving regime (Fig. 6, 7).

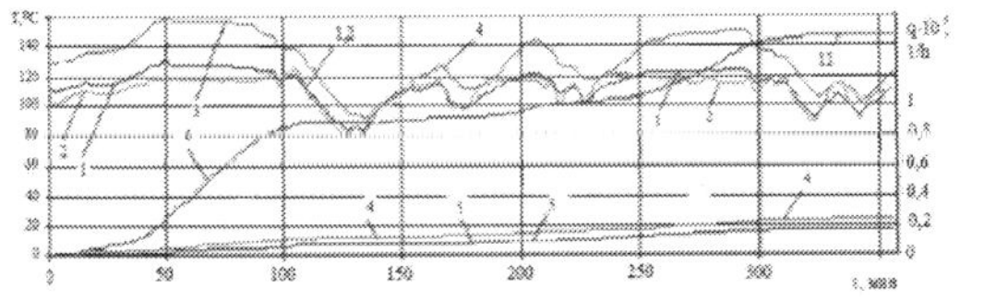

Fig. 6. The Changes of temperature of windings, wears insulation and energy consumption for cooling of winding ЭД118А operating in the energy circuit of the diesel locomotive 2ТЭ116 while moving along the III type profile with full use of the power at the outdoor air temperature of 25 C: 1) average temperature of armature winding; 2) temperature winding of the armature in groove; 3) temperature of the front part of the armature winding from the drive side; 4) wear of the armature winding, determined by the average temperature of the winding; 5) wear of the armature winding, determined by the temperature of the groove; 6 - wear of armature winding, determined by the temperature of the frontal part.

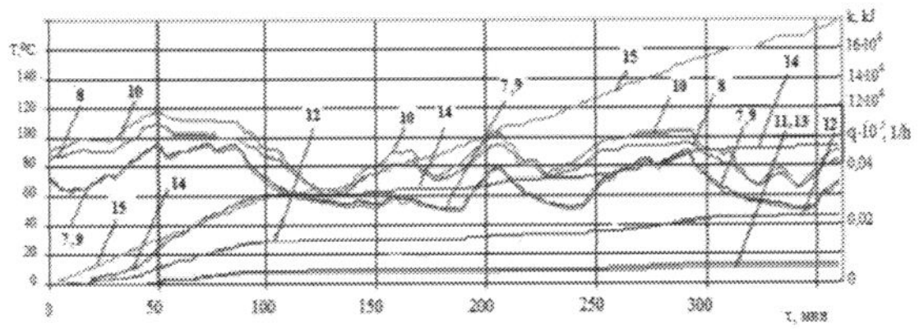

Fig. 7. The Changes of temperature of windings, wears insulation and energy consumption for cooling of winding ЭД118А operating in the energy circuit of the diesel locomotive 2ТЭ116 while moving along the III type profile with full use of the power at the outdoor air temperature of 25 C: 7) average temperature of the winding of the main pole; 8) average temperature of the winding of the additional pole; 9) temperature of the middle part of the winding of the main pole, 10) temperature of the middle part of the winding of the additional pole; 11) wear of the winding of the main pole determined by the average temperature; 12) wear of the winding of the additional pole determined by the mean temperature; 13) wear of the winding of the main pole determined by the temperature of the middle part; 14) wear of the winding of the additional pole determined by the temperature of the middle part; 15) energy consumption for cooling the engine.

3 Conclusions

The average temperature of the armature winding only approximately shows the process of temperature variation of its individual nodes.

The actual temperatures of the elementary units of the armature winding during the operation of traction motors on unsteady conditions may differ from the average value by 10 ... 30 C.

The frontal part of the armature winding on the drive side always have of the maximum temperature (t_{YK}^{LP}).

Therefore, the actual wear of the insulation of the frontal parts of the armature winding from the drive q_{YK}^{LP} is 3...5 times greater than the wear of the winding q_{YKSR} determined by the average temperature. This result is in good agreement with the operation data (Fig. 1).

The actual wear of the insulation of the coils of the main and additional poles by the thermal factor is almost 10 times less than the wear of the armature winding insulation.

Obviously, the frontal part of the armature winding on the drive side will determine resource of insulation of the traction motor in operation.

References

1. E.Y. Loginova, Buren-Itgel Gantumur, Cloud of science **2**, 89 (2015)
2. I.R. Nefedov, E. Loginova, Analysis of reliability of traction electric motors of locomotives, *In Proceedings of the XVIth Scientific and Practical Conference "Safety of Train Traffic"*, pp. II-94-II-95 (2016)
3. O. Podlesy, E. Zenina, Bulletin of Volgograd State University. Series 10: Innovative activity, 2, 149 (2013)

The representativeness of the statistical data frame in the quantitative image analysis

Vladimir N. Petrushin [1,*], *Yuriy V.* Rudyak [2], and *Georgy O.* Rytikov [2]

[1] Institute of Contemporary Arts, 121309 Moscow, Russia
[2] Moscow Polytechnic University, 107023 Moscow, Russia

Abstract. In the article the concept of representativeness of the statistical data frame is discussed. Also the statistical measure of representativeness and a method for the quantitative assessment of the degree of representativeness of the general population are proposed. To demonstrate the techniques and methods of application, we consider a case of identifying the amount of statistically reliable sampling in the analysis of polymer composite surface's SEM-images.

1 Introduction

Use A4 paper size (210 x 297 mm) and adjust the margins to those shown in Table 1. The final printed area will be 172 x 252 mm.

Affiliations of authors should be typed in 9-point Times. They should be preceded by a numerical superscript corresponding to the same superscript after the name of the author concerned. Please ensure that affiliations are as full and complete as possible and include the country.

In the description and modeling of the scientific and industrial research results, the statistical approach is one of the best known and most widely used. The combination of quantitative methods of the statistical approach relies primarily on the conceptual apparatus and many techniques to apply elements of probability theory and mathematical statistics, combined with the concept of "applied statistics". The basic concepts of applied statistics are general population and data frame [1-4].

Due to the classic epistemological problem (the inability of the formal definition of basic concepts), the unified and generally accepted definitions of General population and statistical data framing, apparently, do not exist. However, many researchers of the subject area successfully understand each other intuitively in the use of the discussed concepts. The general population is usually understood as all the "target" set of objects about which some insights or predictions on the results of statistical research should be received. The data frame is the set of objects which it is possible to measure and/or calculate and on the basis of that to draw certain statistical models. With the help of these models the conclusions are drawn and the predictions are made about the general population's «behavior».

Thus it is implicitly assumed that the models successfully describing the frame will also be effective to describe the population. All the criticism of the applied statistics' methods generally and these of the parametric statistics specifically is based on the impossibility of proving or disproving this assumption. In order to remove the problem under discussion, when statistically analyzing the data in different ways, the concept of "evaluation of the data frame representativeness» is introduced. It postulates that in the process of the quantitative statistical models formation a data frame is used which is so similar to the general population that the results of the predictions for the frame and the population should be the same. Obviously, it is impossible to test this claim if the general population is not known. If the general population is known, it is not often necessary to use the statistical methods to describe it. However, predictions for the general population (the set of elements of which is not known) are not actually made, because the verification of predictions and models is always carried out only on a sample from the general population. In fact, the problem of quantitative statistical modeling and predicting in the most general form is as follows: it is required to obtain a model based on the results of some primary data frame analysis (or some aggregate thereof); the model is also expected to be sufficiently reliable from the point of view of the researcher, and efficient to describe the validation data frame (or some aggregate thereof) in case of randomness of frames and independence of measurement results from each other.

Thus, for the effective usage of applied statistics methods of data analyzing and predictions building, it is possible to formulate the concept of relative representativeness (as measured quantitatively on an interval [0;1]) of statistical data frame: primary data frame from the general population is representative, according to some criterion, relative to the validation frame, if the value of the corresponding criterion,

* Corresponding author: petrushinvn@mail.ru

calculated on the basis of statistical analysis of the primary and validation frames, takes the extreme value.

With that, the more powerful is the aggregation of validation frames for which the underlying frame is representative, the higher the quality of the statistical models generated on the basis of the primary frame is, on condition of minimizing the cost of obtaining the primary frame (minimize the amount of the primary frame and the power of the aggregation of the primary frames analyzed to determine the statistical model).

It is important to note that the above concept as presented relates mainly to the analysis of stationary random variables. In random processes' analysis (in particular, non-stationary), it requires the significant additions and refinements (for example, you may need to evaluate the results of dynamic statistical analysis of a large number of repeated experiments), considered by the authors as the problems for further research.

There are a lot of approaches and criteria [5–12], used to evaluate the representativeness of the data frame relative to the general population (we will call this theoretical representativeness «absolute» one). All the existing criteria require statistical calculation on the frame. It is obvious that the power of the criteria based on this principle, is substantially less than the power of the criteria based on the comparison of the empirical density functions and the empirical functions of probability distributions, as for all additional calculations of statistical indicators the number of degrees of freedom decreases significantly. The main advantage of the approach associated with the comparison of empirical distributions is that there is no need to justify the choice of theoretical distribution, presumably characterizing the general population.

The result of the comparison of empirical distributions is a quantitative assessment of the relative representativeness of the sample. The concept of relative representativeness application allows to combine the advantages of private and general criteria of representativeness, because no assumption is done on the nature of the general population data distribution, no values of any "alleged" criteria are calculated, but the empirical distributions of the primary and validation data frames are built and compared according to the criteria .

From our point of view, one of the "closest to reality" criteria of representativeness is the overlap area of the histograms of the base and validation data frames' empirical distributions. However, for simplicity of calculations it is traditional to apply the sum of squares of relative frequencies deviations to find the volume of a representative frame, in fact, using the method of the least squares. It is obvious that the maximum overlap of the areas of the histograms of empirical distributions corresponds to the minimum of the sum of the squares of their mutual deviations.

2 The data for the computational experiment

For a generalized description of the structure of the experimental data involved in the statistical analysis and processing, in most cases, the model of multidimensional tensor is ample, projected onto the space of variables in which the problem is stated and the results of the statistical analysis are formulated. Since visualization of more than a three-dimensional space causes some difficulties, we will consider an example of data analysis described within the traditional three-dimensional Cartesian coordinate system.

As a test data we consider the table of values of the image pixels brightness formed by a scanning electron microscope in the study of the sub-micro relief (topographic morphology) of low density polyethylene membrane surface modified by the method of gas phase sulfonation (see Fig. 1).

Fig. 1. The investigated fragment of a SEM-image of sample surface of LDPE modified [13] with the method of gas phase sulfonation [14].

When you visualize this data in the Cartesian coordinate system, along the axes of abscissa and ordinate the coordinates of the pixel will be plotted , and its brightness will be along the axis of the applicat. Despite the fact that when describing a real surface there is no reason to suppose that the corresponding coordinates take only integer values, the measuring procedure using the scanning electron microscope automatically discretizes the measurements. As a result, when visualizing, along the axes of the coordinate system only natural numbers (numbers of columns and rows of the data table on the axes of abscissa and ordinate, and the values of the brightness levels of the pixels range from 0..255 on the axis of the applicat) are plotted. One of the features of this example is that it is a typical situation when in order to describe continuous variables a limited number of discrete values of these variables are used (results of experimental measurements or observations).

It is also convenient that the main objective of the statistical analysis of these SEM images is the identification of submicrometer structures (regular or stochastic [15, 16]) on the investigated surfaces; these structures are obviously smaller than the entire field of view of the device, but they provide typical values of those or other physics-chemical and/or functional properties of the tested materials (What is a "molecule" according to the original definition? It's such a tiny part of matter that is characterized by the same set of chemical properties, as the substance in general. With the modern refinements, in our case it is more about something like a domain or macromolecules, as for individual molecules there are many size effects arising in the analysis of chemical reactions on monomolecular

https://doi.org/10.1051/itmconf/20181801007

level, but "large" (tens of thousands or more) conglomerates of molecules "behave" like the substance in general).

In terms of the definition proposed in the Introduction, the General population is the totality of all possible SEM-images of surfaces of the investigated class materials (i.e., as expected, unattainable large amount of measurements); the validation data frame is the table of values pixels' brightnesses describing one specific analyzed SEM-image, and possible primary data frime is made up of a subset of the validation frame (i.e., they are fragments of the investigated SEM-image). Identification of the primary data frame volume, characterized by the same empirical distribution of pixel brightness as the verifying data frame, allows us to estimate the characteristic sizes of the regular or stochastic structures, making a decisive contribution to the formation of those or other physics-chemical and functional properties of all the studied material. Thus, an abstract mathematical problem about finding the way to assess the degree of representativeness of data frames is correlated with a specific area of application in chemistry and materials science (an important problem is solved in the formation of structural-functional model of the material associated with the assessment of the characteristic dimensions of the structural domains of the material surface).

3 The results of the computational experiment

For the SEM-images presented in Fig.1 we built the histograms of the empirical pixels' brightnesses distributions for a series of 40 primary data frames (Fig.2 shows a typical histogram in integral and differential forms of representation) and the histogram of the empirical pixels' brightnesses distribution for the all analyzed image (see Fig.3).

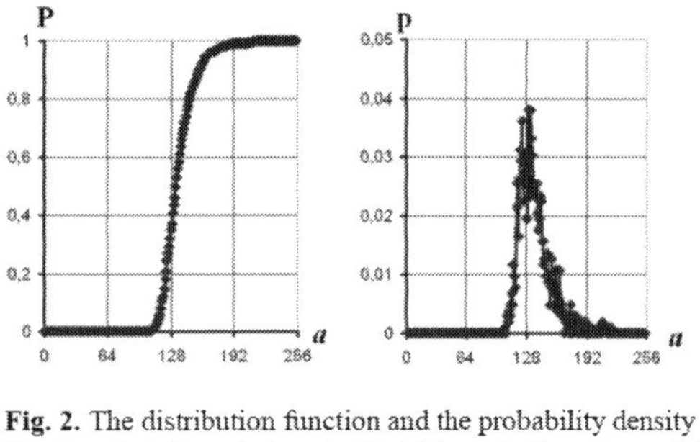

Fig. 2. The distribution function and the probability density function that characterize pixel brightness in the primary data frame of 32x32 elements.

The integral functions of the empirical distributions, in this case, seem to be preferable due to the fact that they make it possible to use the traditional parametric mathematical statistics approaches like minimizing the sum of squared deviations (or the sum of absolute deviations) in the representativeness analysis. Although it is also possible to carry out the appropriate calculations requiring the statistical proximity for the probability densities if it is necessary.

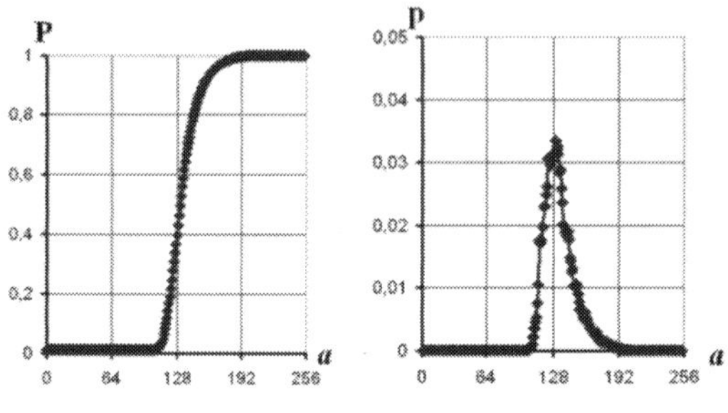

Fig. 3. The distribution function and the probability density function that characterize the pixel brightness in the validation data frame of 220×152 elements.

Let us consider, for example, the sum of the squares of mutual deviations for the empirical distributions that characterize various primary and validation data frames.

A trivial solution for the squares sum minimizing is to match the primary and the validation data frames, which guarantee the zero value for the sum. However, this decision does not answer our purpose, because we want to find such subsets of the considered set that the distributions would coincide as much as possible and the capacity of the subsets would be minimal.

As the empirical distribution for the validation data frame is known, and the empirical distributions for the primary data frame is calculated numerically, we present (Fig. 4) the fragment of a chart based on the sum of the squares of the empirical distributions deviations for the primary and the validation data frames as function of the volume of the primary data frame. (The low volume zone is clipped because there is absolutely no sense to talk about the distribution for the sample if it is less than 4×4 elements, and the high volume zone is clipped because it is clear that there will be 0 «at the end». And what we need to find is the local extrema corresponding to the smallest possible sample size).

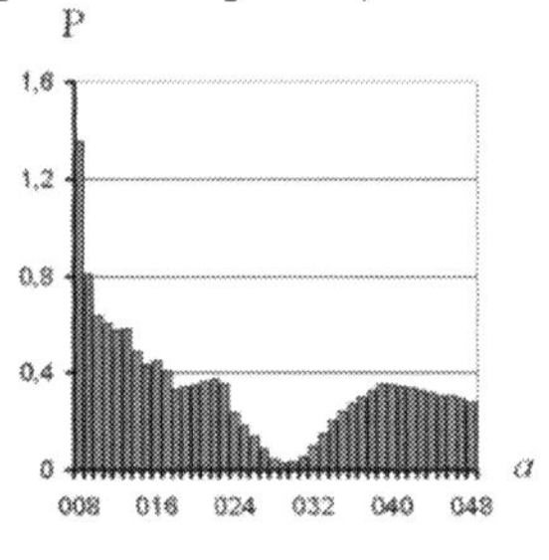

Fig. 4. The sum of squared deviations for the probability distribution functions of the primary and the validation data frames as function of the frame size (in pixels).

In our example, the primary data frame is formed in the shape of a square, as the method of the source material processing does not imply any anisotropy, which is confirmed by the preliminary experiments in wettability and other physics - chemical properties of the surface studied.

In this case it is convenient to enumerate the sample size with the number of pixels forming the side of the corresponding square.

It is clearly seen that the selected criterion of representativeness reaches a local minimum when the amount of the primary data frame is $29(\pm1)\times29(\pm1)$, i.e. the 29×29-frame is representative for minimizing the differences in distribution functions relative to the 220×152-frame, which estimates the structural domain dimension of the studied surface. The presence of the local minimum can be interpreted as a sign of similarity of the empirical distributions of the primary and the validation samples. And we can consider it to be prerequisite for the fractal surface structures observation.

The observation of a local minimum at approximately 4-fold increasing of the primary data frame volume ($56(\pm1)\times56(\pm1)$) and the observation of the corresponding local maxima when assessing the representativeness according to the Kolmogorov-Smirnov criteria (similar to [17]) (see Fig. 5.) are the indirect confirmation of the need for special methods for fractal structures detecting. These are also the direct evidence that the evaluation of the characteristic size of the structural domain is not random.

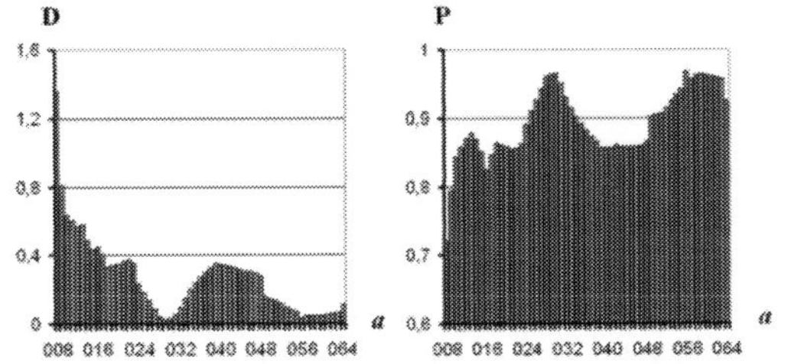

Fig. 5. The illustration of testing the hypothesis about the possibility of the fractal surface structures observation. The left figure illustrates the function of the sum of distributions' squared deviations for the primary and validation data frames. The right figure shows the primary data frame reliability (determined on the basis of the Kolmogorov-Smirnov test) relative to the validation one, as function of the frame volume parameter.

The numerical experiment results analysis (based on the application of Kolmogorov-Smirnov criteria) shows that the accuracy of the primary data frame relative to the validation one varies from 0.73 to 0.96 (when changing the data frame's size parameter in range of [8;64]) and reaches local maxima when the size is $30(\pm1)\times30(\pm1)$, $56(\pm1)\times56(\pm1)$, which indicates the coincidence, within the statistical error, of the interval values of the representative data frame size calculated with two different ways.

The incongruence of the representative data frame double volume value and the 4-fold increased relative data frame is due to the errors in digitizing the images and the applied statistical criteria peculiar properties. The corresponding function and distribution density of pixels' brightnesses are shown in Fig.6.

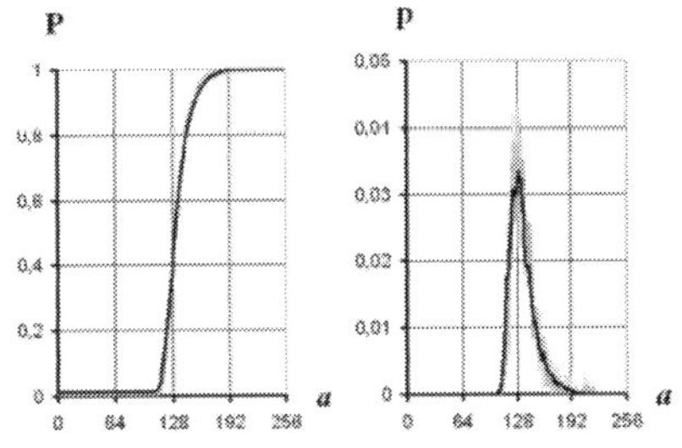

Fig. 6. The comparison of the pixels brightness distributions for the representative ("light grey line" - 29×29, "dark grey line" - "56×56"), and validation ("black line" - 220×152) samples.

To remove the problem under discussion, apparently, it is required to reconsider the structural domain on SEM-images with a larger zoom.

Generally speaking, there are several ways of primary data frame shaping. We have considered the square "from the upper left corner"; it is possible to choose the rectangles, the squares in various "locations" for a validation data frame; it is also possible to introduce the average distribution in the ensemble of samples of the same size, etc.

In the general case, the "shape" of the studied subarea of the image must be determined according to its physical aspects (for example, based on the consideration of symmetries, or on the basis of a priori information about any anisotropy) and (in multi-dimensional tasks) after the sham elimination of anisotropy with the help of scaling it can be considered as a hypercube. But this issue is not the subject of this article and will be investigated in future works.

It is important that we perform a tool for the quantitative evaluation and selection of the relative representativeness of data frames, and that a side effect is the estimation of the characteristic size of the structural domains in the analyzed images.

4 Conclusions

In this article the concept of relative representativeness of data frames is presented, as well as the method for its quantitative estimation. As the criterion of representativeness it is proposed to use the overlap areas of the histograms of probability functions empirical distributions of the primary and validation data frames, which will make it possible to assess the degree of representativeness of the base frame relative to the validation one by our proposed numerical criterion.

The example of application and demonstration of the physical meaning of the presented concept is the analysis of the gas-sulfonated membrane of low density polyethylene (LDPE) surface's SEM- images obtained by scanning electron microscopy. It is shown that the subset of $29(\pm1)\times29(\pm1)$ pixels (with the value of the assessment of representativeness $0.96\pm0{,}02$) is the relatively representative data frame of the analyzed image, which allows us to estimate the characteristic sizes of the structural domain of the surface.

In the considered example, the maximum overlap area of the empirical distributions histograms for the primary (29×29 and 56×56) and the validation (220×152) data frames (in both cases) was 0.96(±0,02), indicating a high degree of relative representativeness of these primary data frames. The minimum overlap area of the histograms for the primary (8×8) and validation (220×152) samples amounted to 0.73, which is interpreted as a relative lack of representativeness of this (8×8) sample.

Evaluation of the characteristic dimensions of the sub-regions of images featuring the empirical distribution of pixels' brightnesses close to the pixel brightness distribution of all the considered images, suggests the possibility to observe the fractal structures, and points to the need for specialized, more sensitive and resource-intensive methods of identifying such structures in further research.

The work was performed with financial support from the RFBR grant 16-03-00540. The authors express their deep appreciation to the referees, the interpreter (M.V. Pluzhnik) and the editor for helpful and significant suggestions and tips.

References

1. M.J. Kendall, A. Stuart, *The theory of distributions* (Nauka, 1966)
2. M.J .Kendall, A. Stuart, *The statistical inference and communications* (Nauka, 1973)
3. M.J. Kendall, A. Stuart. *The multivariate statistical analysis and time series* (Nauka, 1976)
4. V.N. Petrushin, M.V. Ulyanov, *Information sensitivity of computer algorithms* (PhisMatLit, 2010).
5. A.I. Urazbahtin, I.G. Urazbakhtin, Information and communication technologies, **4**(3), 10 (2006)
6. V.A. Banakh, I.N. Smalikho, E.L. Pichugina, A. Brewer, Optics of atmosphere and ocean, **22**(10) 966 (2009)
7. B.F. Melnikov, S.V. Pivneva, O.A. Rogova, Stochastic optimization in informatics, **6**, 74-82 (2010)
8. F.N. Ilyasov, Sociological studies, **3**, 112-116 (2011)
9. O.A. Rogova, N.V. Sofonova, Heuristic algorithms and distributed computing, **1**(6), 58-75 (2014)
10. G.O. Rytikov, M.V. Ulianov, V.N. Petrushin, Double smoothing in time series formalization, *In 2014 International conference on computer technologies in physical and engineering applications (ICCTPEA)*, pp. 150-151 (IEEE, 2014)
11. T.P. Svetlova, Proceedings of the Main geophysical Observatory named by A.I. Voeikov, **579**, 115-128 (2015)
12. E.Yu. Ivanov, M.S. Kosyakov, Software products and systems, **4**(112), 198-202 (2015)
13. V.G. Nazarov, *Surface modification of polymers* (Moscow state University of Printing Arts, 2008)
14. V.G. Nazarov, V.P. Stolyarov, S.P. Molchanov, G.A. Jurassic, M.N. Artemenko, Polimer Science. Series A, **55** 1343 (2013)
15. E.S. Kopachev, S.A. Nozdrachev, V.N. Petrushin, Yu.V. Rudyak, G.O. Rytikov, V.G. Nazarov, Physical Mesomechanics, **18** 98 (2015)
16. V.N. Petrushin, Y.V. Rudyak, G.O. Rytikov, The holistic method of the surface structure characterization, *In 14th International Baltic Conference on Atomic Layer Deposition, BALD 2016 – Proceedings*, pp. 15-19 (2016)
17. V.N. Petrushin, S.A. Drozdov, G.O. Rytikov, Cloud of Science, **2** 247-264 (2015)

Fuzzy logic controller for stabilization of biped robot gait

I.V. Ryadchikov [1], *S.I.* Sechenev[1,*], and *A.A.* Gusev[1]

[1] Kuban State University, 350040 Krasnodar, Russia

Abstract. The article centers round the problem of stabilization of biped robot gait through smoothing out the jumps of first and second order derivatives of a biped robot control vector using the fuzzy logic approach. The structure of a composite Takagi-Sugeno fuzzy logic controller developed by the authors is presented. The simulation study of a robot gait with climbing an obstacle is carried out and the results provided in the article showed that the developed controller performed significantly better than the analytical formula model in terms of smoothing out the derivatives of the control vector.

1 Introduction and statement of the problem

The smoothness of the curves of the control vector of the robot legs, as well as their derivatives is important for stabilization of a robot gait. Using the Simscape Multibody Contact Forces package, we previously developed a Simulink model of the leg of a bipedal walking robot [1, 2]. The structure of the leg is shown in Figure 1.

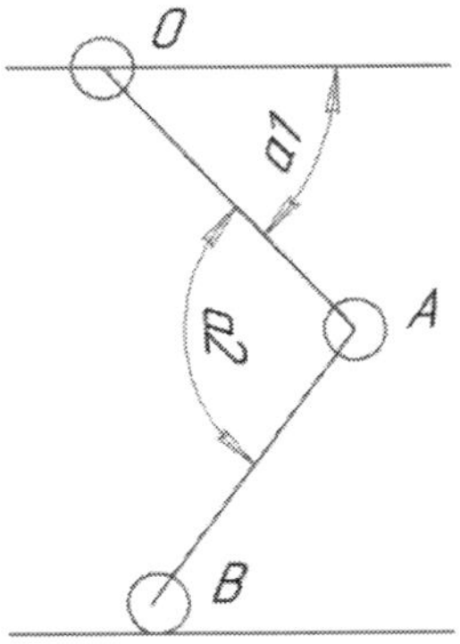

Fig. 1. The biped robot leg.

The center of mass of the leg is at point O. The leg is controlled by setting the angle vector (a_1, a_2). Earlier, we created a MATLAB-function that performs the assignment of angles for the coordinates (x, z), using the geometric relationships between the elements of the foot.

The use of formula calculation for vector values (a_1, a_2) led to jumps and discontinuities in the graphs of the first and second derivatives of the control vector, which negatively affected the stability of the gait. To stabilize leg control, it was decided to create a Takagi-Sugeno (TS) fuzzy logic controller.

2 Solution

The structure of the fuzzy controller we've created is shown in Figure 2: the composite controller consists of two TS-controllers performing separate tasks for a_1 and a_2. A triple of values consisting of the current value of the linear Ramp signal, the previous value of a_1 and the previous value of a_2 are given to the input of both TS controllers.

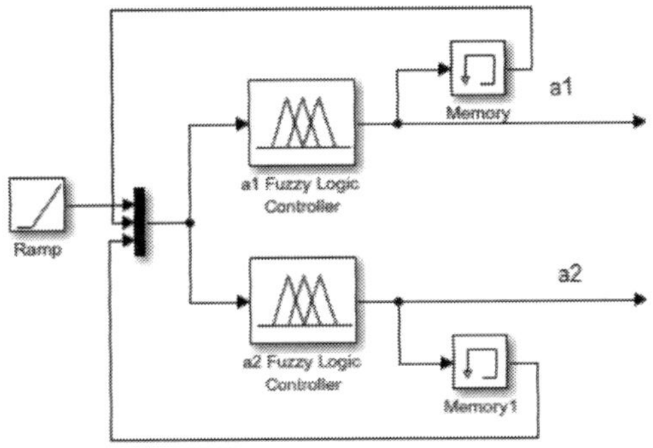

Fig. 2. The structure of the robot leg fuzzy controller.

The training of the TS-controllers was carried out using the ANFIS method on a data sample generated using the previously developed formula model for one step of the robot's leg. The sample contained 2910 values of the input triple. The ANFIS method was chosen due to the success of the neuro-fuzzy approach in the tasks of mobile robotics [3-6].

* Corresponding author: sechenev.semen@gmail.com

For each TS-controller, the three generalized bell-shaped membership functions were selected. The learning error was of the order of 10^{-5} after 3 epochs of training.

3 Results and discussion

Figure 3 compares the graphs of the first time derivative for the angle a_1 (left) and for the angle a_2 (right) for one step of the robot, obtained using the original formula model and using a fuzzy model.

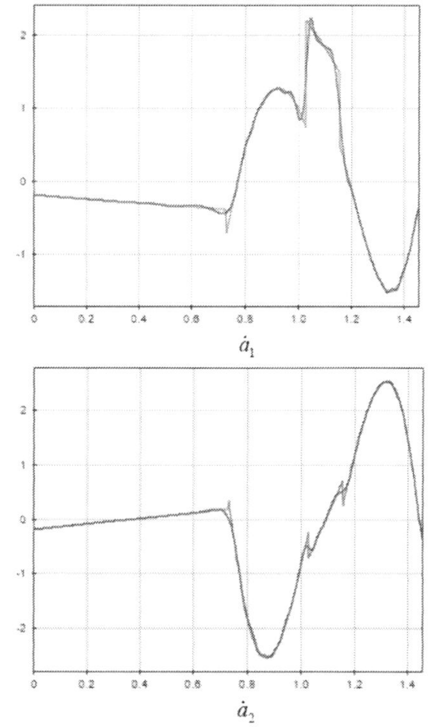

Fig. 3. The first derivatives of angles, obtained with the formula model (blue) and with the fuzzy inference (violet).

To smooth out the jumps of the second derivatives, we envisaged the use of a filter (Figure 4). However, even with this filter, a smoother control over the second derivatives is noticeable when using a fuzzy controller (Figure 5)

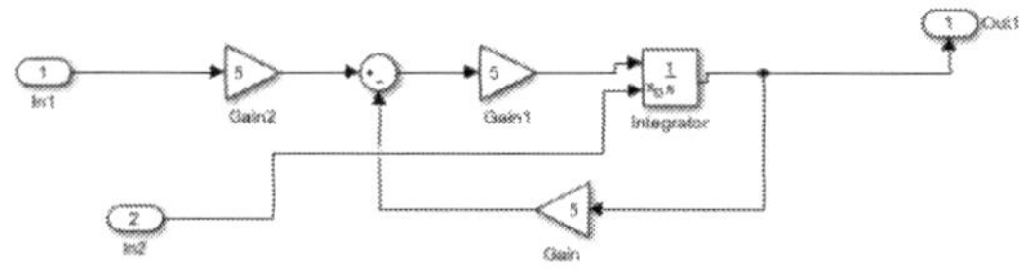

Figure 4. Structure of the filter used to smooth out the jumps of the second derivatives of the control vector.

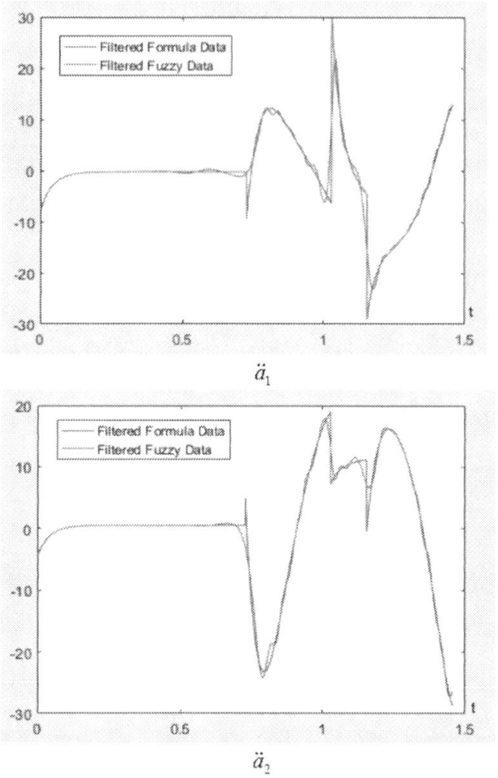

Fig. 5. The comparison of the filtered formula (blue) and filtered fuzzy (brown) second derivative for the angles.

As can be seen in the graphs presented in Figure 3 and Fig. 5, the use of the fuzzy logic controller has made it possible to substantially smooth the oscillations of the control signal, which is especially noticeable in the graphs of the second derivatives. This effect should have a significant positive impact on improving gait stability, as well as reliability of the electronic mechanical components of the robot legs.

Based on the one-step fuzzy data, we modeled a 10-step walk of the robot with climbing an obstacle - a stair 10 cm high (Figure 6).

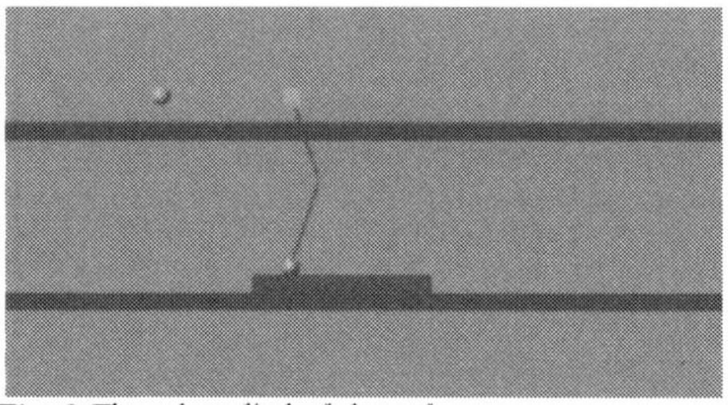

Fig. 6. The robot climbed the stair.

The results of the simulation is shown in Figures 7–10.

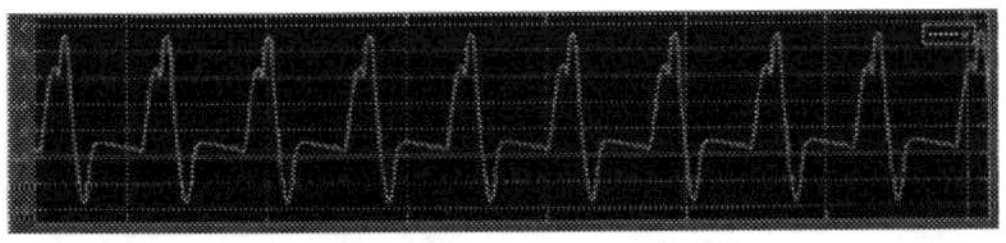

Fig. 7. $\dot{a}_1$ **during 10 step walk.**

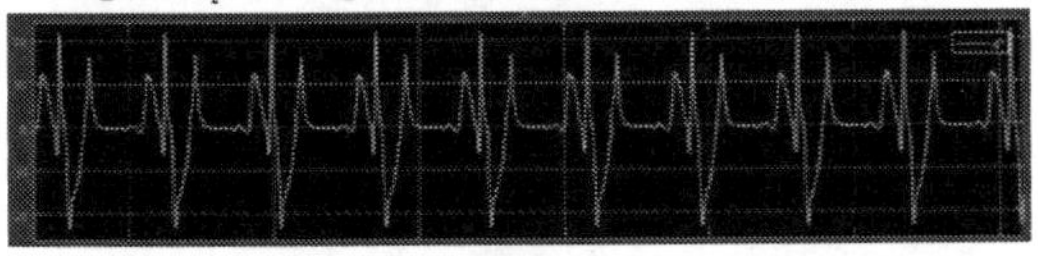

Fig. 8. $\ddot{a}_1$ during 10 step walk.

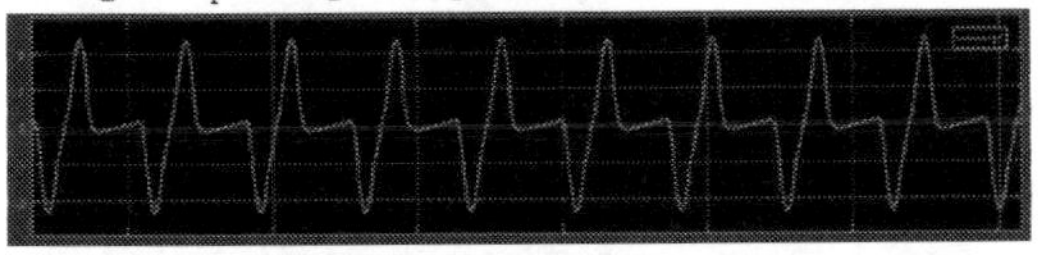

Fig. 9. $\dot{a}_2$ during 10 step walk.

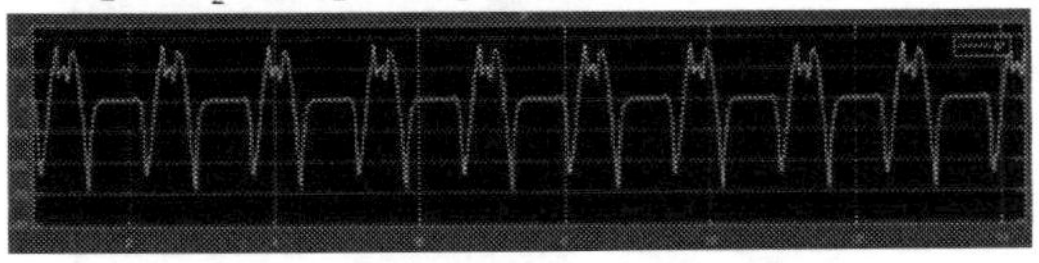

Fig. 10. $\ddot{a}_2$ during 10 step walk.

As can be seen from the results of the simulation, the data obtained with the fuzzy logic controller has made it possible to carry out the robot walk with climbing the obstacle without bursts and discontinuities in the graphs of the first and second derivatives of the control vector.

4 Conclusion

We have created a composite Takagi-Sugeno fuzzy logic controller to stabilize the gait of the biped robot. Training of the controller was carried out using the ANFIS method.

In the simulation and comparative analysis of the control with the analytical formula model and with the help of the developed fuzzy controller, we discovered a much smoother control over the first and second derivatives using the fuzzy controller. The significant advantage of the fuzzy controller is also preserved when the filter is used to smooth out the jumps of the second derivatives for the formula model.

Further researches will be directed on improvement of the fuzzy controller, new samples of training data and genetic algorithms for automation of training of the controller will be applied.

The work was carried out within the framework of the state task of the Ministry of Education and Science, project No. 8.2321.2017 "Development and adaptation of control systems for compensation of dynamic deflecting effects on mobile objects in a state of dynamic equilibrium".

References

1. Ryadchikov, I.; Sechenev, S.; Sinitsa, S.; et al., International Journal of Advanced Computer Science and Applications, Volume:, **8**, 29 (2017)
2. Ryadchikov, I.; Sechenev, S.; Svidlov, A.; et al. MATEC Web of Conference, **99**, 02007 (2017)
3. A. Ranasinghe, N. Sornkarn, P. Dasgupta et al. IEEE Transactions on Cybernetics, **46**, 568 (2015)
4. M. Njah, M. Jallouli, Wheelchair obstacle avoidance based on fuzzy controller and ultrasonic sensors, *In Proceedings of the International Conference on Computer Applications Technology (ICCAT '13)* (2013).
5. T. T. Mac, C. Copot, R. De Keyser, T. D. Tran, T. Vu. Journal of Automation and Control Engineering, **4,** 65 (2016)
6. S. Armah, S. Yi, T. Abu-Lebdehet, American Journal of Engineering and Applied Sciences, **7**, 149 (2014)

Algorithms for classification of a single channel EMG signal for human-computer interaction

Andrei Lukyanchikov [1], *Alexei* Melnikov[1] and *Oleg* Lukyanchikov [1, *]

[1] Moscow technological university, 119454 Moscow, Russia

Abstract. One of the most accurate and effective ways to control gestures is to control muscle activity, which occurs with any movement. Electromyography (EMG) is used to record such activity. This article compares SVM classification algorithms, perceptron, random trees and the method of density of probability in relation to the EMG signal. Arduino Leonardo with a single-channel Shield EMG is used to record the signal. The aim of this paper is to prove the possibility of creating a cheap and accessible biointerface based on EMG signal.

1 Introduction

Since the beginning of the development of computer technology, the main interface of human-computer interaction has been dialog boxes controlled by keyboard and mouse. However, with the development of hardware and software, for example, with the advent of mobile phones, augmented reality helmets, IoT, more intelligent interaction interfaces were required, which can be classified as follows: (1) Voice control [1, 2]; (2) Control gestures (with video cameras [3], special gloves [4] or special sensors, such as Kinect); (3) The brain-computer interface [5,6].

The use of these interfaces provides convenience in situations where there is no possibility or need to interact with external physical devices.

One of the most accurate and effective ways to control gestures is to control muscle activity, which occurs with any movement. Therefore, the use of signals of bioelectrical activity of muscles to control a device is an urgent task for today. Electromyography (EMG) is used to record this activity. In addition, the scope of EMG signals is very wide: they can be used in medicine to study muscle activity abnormalities; when evaluating the effectiveness of rehabilitation measures; for monitoring the human condition, etc.

When analyzing the bioelectrical activity of different muscles, one can understand which muscles were involved, and, therefore, with the best classification method, determine the movement that is made with their help.

2 Hardware

2.1 Signal nature

After the arrival of a nerve impulse from the spinal cord to the terminal plate of the nerve attached to the muscle fiber, the post-synaptic membrane of the muscle fiber depolarizes. The depolarization is caused by the movement of Ca++ ions inside. The depolarization process extends to both sides of the end plate. The electrodes located in this field register the voltage (electrical potential) of the muscle fibers. The range of amplitudes of the electromyographic signal lies in the range of one microvolt to several tens of millivolts. The frequency of the signals varies from 0.5 Hz to several hundred hertz, but the individual components of the EMG spectrum can have a frequency of 10-20 kHz.

2.2 Electrodes

Electrodes for removing muscle biopotentials are subdivided into surface and needle. In this paper, the surface electrodes shown in Figure 1 are used.

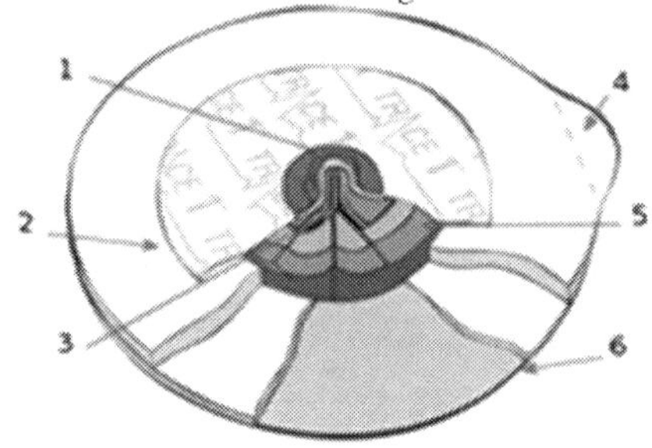

Fig. 1. Structure of the electrode. (1) Metal cone, (2) Foam lining, (3) Ag / AgCl sensor, (4) wing, (5) Electrolyte gel, (6) Adhesive protective film.

With the help of the surface electrode, only total muscle activity can be recorded, representing the interference of the action potentials of many hundreds and even thousands of fibers.

To record the action potentials of muscle fibers or their groups, needle electrodes inserted into the muscle

* Corresponding author: luk-it6@yandex.ru

are used. Such electrodes will make it possible to classify more qualitatively similar movements, but such electrodes cannot be used in everyday life, but only in the laboratory with the participation of medical specialists.

2.3 Equipment for EMG signal removal

In the research work for testing, the Arduino Leonardo microcontroller and the EMG shield from OLIMEX were required, the advantage of which is the general availability and cheapness of relatively expensive medical equipment.

Figure 2 shows the Arduino microcontroller and the shielded EMG shield.

Fig. 2. Device for fixing EMG signal.

3 Classification of signals

In [7], four channels and the maximum likelihood method were used to classify eight gestures based on entropy probability densities. In this regard, it was decided to try to get the same result with only one channel and other hardware, but with the same method.

The location of the electrodes for one channel was chosen the same as the second channel in [7], since in this channel there is the most powerful useful signal. Figure 3 shows the location of the electrodes.

Fig. 3. Location of electrodes.

There are three gestures shown in Figure 4.

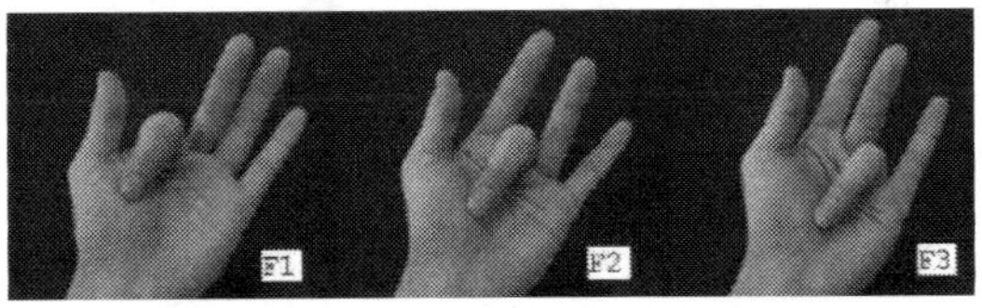

Fig. 4. Three finger gestures: F1– flexing of the index finger, F2 – bending of the middle finger, F3 – bending of the ring finger.

The signal recording lasted 5 seconds, of which 2 seconds – inactivity, then compression, and again inactivity.

Figure 5 shows the recorded signals of each of the three gestures.

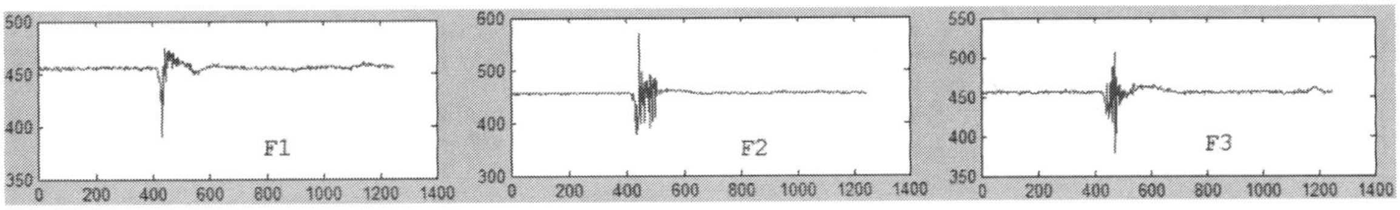

Fig. 5. Signals EMG of three gestures.

The essence of this classification method lies in the search for entropies of signals for each gesture. Based on the entropies obtained, the probability density for each gesture is calculated

$$H(x)=\sum_{m=1}^{M}p(x_m)log_2\frac{1}{p(x_m)}, \quad (1)$$

where **x** is the row vector of the long M signal of the moment of flexion and extension of the finger selected by the window; H(**x**) is the entropy of the signal vector; $p(x_m)$ is the probability of hits of counts **x** in the grid of amplitudes equally divided into n parts (the choice of n will be described later);

$$f(h)=\frac{1}{\sqrt{2\pi\sigma^2}}\exp\left(-\frac{1}{2\sigma^2}(h-\mu)\right); \quad (2)$$

where f is the probability density; $\mu=E[H]$ is the expected value; $\sigma^2=E[(\mu-H)^2]$ is dispersion.

Consider an example: there are 60 experimental compression signals of the index finger, for each signal is calculated the entropy (1), resulting in a vector of 60 entropies. Further, based on these entropies the probability density (2) is calculated. This algorithm is applied to the rest of the gestures in the same order.

For training 45 measurements were taken for each gesture, and for testing 10 for each gesture and $n = 220$.

The result is the result of the probability densities shown in Figure 6 and the test result shown in Figure 7.

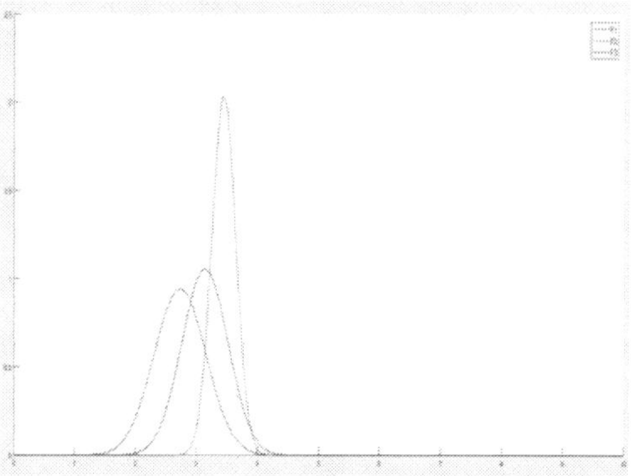

Fig. 6. Density of entropy probabilities on the training sample.

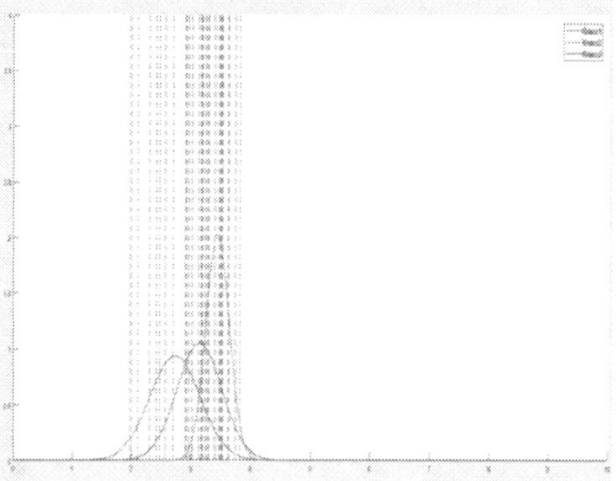

Fig. 7. Hits of the test sample.

Vertical lines show the locations of the test sample. Thus, the result of the misclassification:

- the probability of misclassification for F1 = 40%
- the probability of misclassification for F2 = 20%
- the probability of misclassification for F3 = 60%

In total, the probability of an misclassification for this method is 4 misclassifications of 10 for the first movement, 2 for the second movement, and 6 for the third. The total probability of incorrect classification is 12/30 = 40%.

4 Discussions

This method showed a poor result on one channel, and it was not possible to obtain such a good result as in [5], it is possible for this method that the number of channels for removing the EMG signal is important, as well as the high accuracy of the equipment.

Consider other classification methods: SVM, perceptron, and random tree method. For each of these methods, the signs indicated in [8] are distinguished from the signal:

- The algorithm for classifying three classes is the "one against all" method. Three classifiers are under construction.
- In training perceptron, 6 errors occurred (perceptron parameters: three hidden layers of 50 neurons in the first, 20 in the second and 5 in the third layer).
- Linear SVM was trained with one error (so that there was no retraining, SVM was allowed to err).
- The trees were trained without errors (100 random trees were used).

The results on the test data is given in Table 1.

Table 1. The results on the test data

Method:	SVM	Perceptron	Trees
Probability of misclassification:	3.3%	6.6%	3.3%

You can try to improve the result by selecting only significant features from the signal; this can be done using feature_importances_ method in Python.

Order of features:
1) IEMG; 2) MV;
3) MAV; 4) MAV1;
5) MAV2; 6) TM4;
7) RMS; 8) V;
9) LOG; 10) DASDV;
11) MYOP; 12) WAMP;
13) MAVSLP; 14) SSI;
15) VAR; 16) STD;
17) WL; 18) AAC;
19) X; 20) ff;
21) PKF; 22) MNF;
23) MDF; 24) MNP;
25) FR; 26)SM1;
27) SM0; 28) VCF;
29) SSC; 30) FMD_vec;
31) FMN_vec; 32) MFMD_vec;
33) MFMN_vec; 34-44)LPC

The calculation of these characteristics can be seen in the open-source code [8].

In LPC is stored not one feature but a vector of 10.

In Figures 8-10, important features for three gestures, respectively:

```
[ 0.00921421  0.00497849  0.00578273  0.02360915  0.01663195  0.00437406
  0.00300479  0.00410594  0.00526003  0.00374392  0.03046298  0.02148194
  0.00543951  0.01042253  0.01814929  0.01524105  0.09151464  0.00993092
  0.06897916  0.0243665   0.0074655   0.00131414  0.01717347  0.0090273
  0.00210581  0.02310525  0.0117797   0.0042108   0.15111523  0.01769872
  0.04441073  0.03228979  0.00382383  0.          0.03285823  0.06604691
  0.0059778   0.00558217  0.00447066  0.00235993  0.00332311  0.00214678
  0.00493034]
```

Fig. 8. Important features for the F1 movement.

We chose a threshold equal to 0.02 and took the features above the preset threshold. Features: MAV1; DASDV; MYOP; WAMP; WL;AAC; X;ff; SM1; SSC; FMN_vec; MFMD_vec; LPC (2,3). Feature numbers: (4; 10; 11; 12; 17; 18; 19; 20; 26; 29; 31; 32; 35; 36)

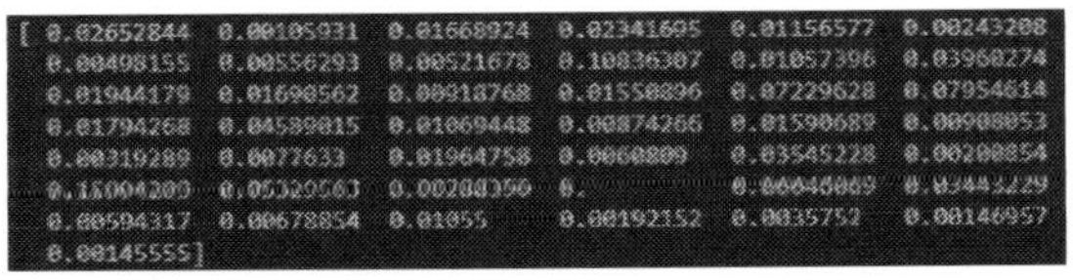

Fig. 9. Important features for the F2 movement.

Feature numbers: (1; 4; 10; 12; 13; 17; 18; 19; 20; 29; 31; 32; 35; 36)

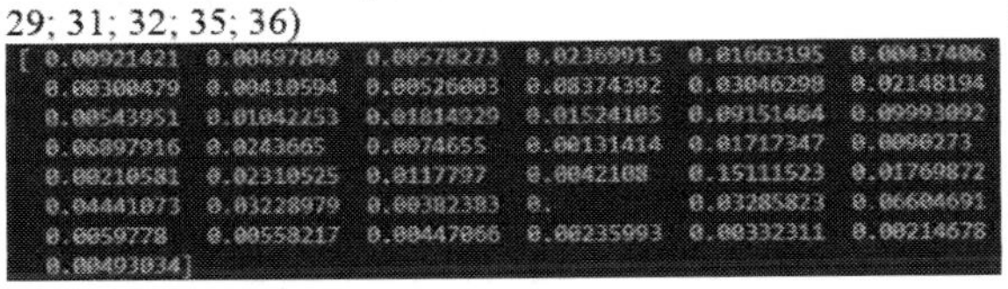

Fig. 10. Important features for the F3 movement.

Feature numbers: (4; 10; 11; 12; 17; 18; 19; 20; 26; 29; 31; 32; 35; 36)

This set of features is tested on three classification methods. As a result, the probability of misclassification is shown in Table 2.

Table 2. The probability of misclassification

Method:	SVM	Perceptron	Trees
The probability of misclassification	3.3%	3.3%	0%

Having eliminated unnecessary signs, the probability of classification has improved, but it is necessary to allocate for each method its set of features. In the end, it is better to select the characteristics of the method and apply to other than not to provide the signs at all.

5 Conclusions

This study, using a single channel and cheap hardware, showed a good result on a test sample for three movements, thereby showing the ability to manufacture affordable, cheap and simple biointerfaces.

This simple and affordable hardware allows the expansion of the definition of the maximum number of well-classified gestures to increase the number of controlled impacts.

References

1. J. Yamagishi, T. Kobayashi, IEICE TRANSAC. on Information and Systems **90** 533 (2007)
2. J.A. Bilmes et al., The Vocal Joystick: A voice-based human-computer interface for individuals with motor impairments, *In Proceedings of the conference on human language technology and empirical methods in natural language processing. Association for Computational Linguistics* (2005)
3. A. Kapur, , A. Kapur, , N Virji-Babul et al., Gesture-based affective computing on motion capture data. *In International conference on affective computing and intelligent interaction* (Springer, Heidelberg. 2005)
4. V. Buchmann, S. Violich, M. Billinghurst, A. Cockburn, FingARtips: gesture based direct manipulation in Augmented Reality. *In Proceedings of the 2nd international conference on Computer graphics and interactive techniques in Australasia and South East Asia*, pp. 212-221 (ACM, 2004)
5. T.O. Zander, C. Kothe, Journal of neural engineering, **8** 025005 (2011)
6. J.R. Wolpaw, N. Birbaumer, D.J. McFarland, G. Pfurtscheller, T.M. Vaughan, Clinical neurophysiology, **113** 767 (2002)
7. K.J. You, K.W. Rhee, H.C. Shin, Experimental neurobiology, **19** 54 (2010)
8. A. Phinyomark, P. Phukpattaranont, C. Limsakul, Expert Systems with Applications, **39** 7420 (2012)

The experimental testing of semi-authomated process of degraded DNA extraction and reading on ancient samples from Baltic area

Vsevolod Merkulov [1], *Vladimir* Kulakov [2] and *Alexander* Semenov [3, 4, *]

[1] International scientific journal Historical format, Moscow, Russia
[2] Institute of Archeology of the Russian Academy of Sciences, Moscow, Russia
[3] Moscow Technological Institute, 38a Leninsky prospect, Moscow, Russia
[4] Deep Dive Group, Moscow, Russia

Abstract. The extracting the genetic information from old and degraded DNA now become a serious and promising direction of biotechnology. In Russia, this kind of technological systems is fully developing only recent years, so building and testing the processes for degraded DNA extraction and reading is still important, as it makes Russia independent from foreign laboratories. Below we outline the authomated process designed and performed in Russia, and mainly the result of the experiment on Y-DNA haplogroup defining of two ancient burials from Kaliningrad Area. The obtained data allows defining the Y-haplogroup R1a with a certain probability. The paper outlines the experiment, testing process, and the obtained results for both samples in form of precise but scarce data. The experiment showed that the developed system manages with 1000-1500 year old samples preserved in acid soils prevailing in Russia. The technology mentioned and used in the test was developed in Moscow Institute of Physics and Technology by the Laboratory of Historical Genetics, Radiocarbon Analysis, and Applied Physics and was used in the project according to the agreement.

1 Introduction

The paleoDNA testing becomes one of the challenging branches of modern biotechnology. Modern technology processes allow high-quality DNA extracting and testing by various number of methods including Y-chromosome and mitochondrial DNA haplogroup defining. The results are used in forensic, archaeological, and criminalistics needs. In archaeology they can give a valuable insight for defining the affinity of an ancient population to other ancient and modern population groups. In criminalistic and forensic works it can be a good tool for kinship and in some cases person's origin estimation.

The field of study of ancient DNA (aDNA) extracted from museum specimens and archaeological and paleontological samples began about 30 years ago [1]. The main aim was to determine the nucleotide sequence of short mitochondrial DNA (mtDNA) fragments. The development of new DNA extraction techniques and subsequent bioinformatics analysis has made it possible to reconstruct the complete full-scale genomes of ancient organisms [2]. These techniques have helped researchers to draw conclusions about the organisms that became extinct tens to hundreds of thousands years ago as well as also about the population structure of those species. Nowadays, studies of aDNA have become an important tool for testing evolutionary hypotheses and allowing the complex reconstruction of the history of biota changes. Special attention has been paid to the study of nucleic acids extracted from human remains, as this helps researchers to answer many important questions.

Despite these technological advances, certain technical and methodological problems exist that are specific to aDNA, arising primarily from its high degree of degradation and the presence of the so-called postmortem modifications of nucleotide bases, as well as the small quantities of authentic DNA normally available to be studied. One of the most noticeable changes in the aDNA structure is the deamination of nucleotides, which leads to substitutions of bases in the polymerase chain reaction (PCR) process: cytosine to uracil, 5-methylcytosine to thymine (both variants lead to incorporation into the growing chain of thymine instead of cytosine), and, more rarely, adenine to hypoxanthine (causing inclusion of guanine instead of adenine) [3–5]. Another very serious obstacle to studying aDNA is the contamination of ancient samples by the DNA of other organisms [6–9]. To manage these issues, researchers over the years have developed several guidelines to ensure the quality of aDNA data and the reliability of conclusions drawn, which resulted in the nine "gold criteria" outlined by Cooper and Poinar in "Ancient DNA: do it right or not at all" [10]. These criteria include points such as a physically isolated work area to prevent intra-laboratory contamination, multiple negative controls to reveal contamination, if it occurs, and a molecular behavior test to detect whether characteristics of the sample DNA match the degradation pattern or not.

* Corresponding author: semyonov1980@mail.ru

In Russia a successful work of building an authomated genetic testing system and process of old degraded DNA was done in Moscow Institute of Physics and Technology by the Laboratory of Historical Genetics, Radiocarbon Analysis, and Applied Physics (headed by Dr. Kh.Kh. Mustafin).

In the Laboratory it was introduced an approach for aDNA extraction and sample preparation that helps minimize intra-laboratory contamination. The only way to avoid intra-laboratory contamination of aDNA samples is to physically isolate them from other samples that are prepared in a laboratory and from each other during the sample preparation procedure [11]. To manage this issue, in the ideal case, the laboratory should have several extremely clean rooms connected by transmission locks and to be used only for works with ancient samples, which is difficult to afford in general. The sterile box system is located in a single room but offers four independent sterile areas isolated from the environment, which can be completely cleaned after processing of each sample. Thus, it is much easier to maintain such small "laboratories" under sterile conditions. Using the glovebox, it is possible to conduct all stages of sample preparation, including modern human DNA samples.

To test its possibilities a series of experiments of testing ancient degraded samples was undertaken.

The method was also used earlier and results were described in work [12] (test was done in 2016), but the previous sample was not as old as current (300-400 years old), and the process was then still in design. The aim of the current experiment was to test whether the existing process manages with much older samples, to test the current technical kit, and to design more precise process in the near future taking into account the results obtained.

The two ancient samples for this experiment were excavated in Kaliningrad Area of Russia by the Baltic archaeological expedition lead by V.I. Kulakov [13]. The sample Do-367 (Dollkeim-Kovrovo) was extracted from the oval urn pit. The urn contained small fragments of calcined bones of Do-367 male burial (described in [15]). The preliminary date is late Roman time (IV-VI century) (fig. 1).

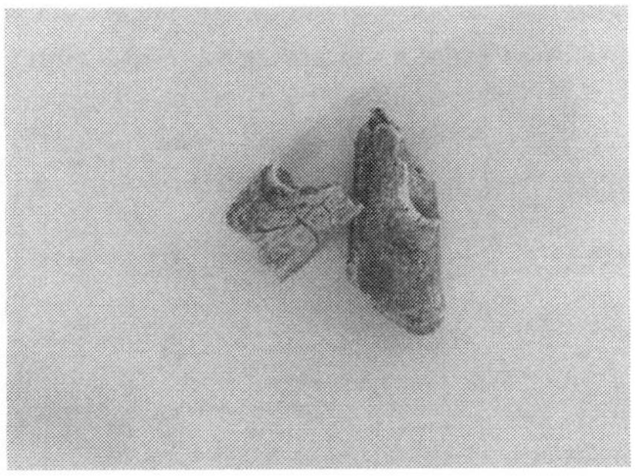

Fig. 1. The photo of the sample 1 (Do-367).

The sample 2 Y-68 from Yrzekapinis/Klinstovka-1 is a two-level burial in oval tomb, oriented from north-east to south-west [14]. The preliminary date is Early Middle Ages (XI century) (fig 2). It is younger than the sample 1 but it was less preserved (in absence of better samples in the available collection).

Fig. 2. The photo of the sample 2 (Y-68).

It was decided to use these calcined samples to test the technology in complicated environment, where DNA would certainly be degraded. Nevertheless, to mitigate risk, a sample rather large by size were taken.

2 Experimental Design, Materials, and Methods

The DNA was extracted by means of the commercial kit PrepFiler BTA Forensic DNA, what is used in criminalistics and forensic medicine for the extraction of degraded DNA from complicated objects. So, a partially authomated process was developed and the system was assembled by the Laboratory of Historical Genetics, Radiocarbon Analysis, and Applied Physics headed by Dr. Kh.Kh. Mustafin as the unique complex containing the glove boxes (fig. 3). The main part is a specially designed glovebox module that maintains a high purity nitrogen atmosphere, allowing DNA extraction in ultra-clean conditions.

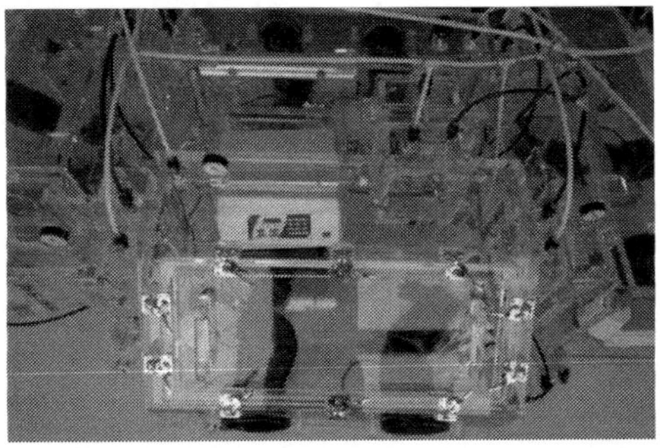

Fig. 3. The system (glovebox_ used in the experiment) [15].

Below we outline the resulting process.

The work contained the following stages:

- preparing of equipment and tools;
- the cleaning of the sample from contamination;
- grinding the sample to a powdery state;
- extraction of DNA from a ground sample;
- measuring the concentration of DNA;
- carrying out PCR and capillary electrophoresis of PCR products to determine the STR loci of the Y chromosome (27 STR loci).

All stages of work with the archaeological sample were carried out in glove boxes, in which the atmospheric air was replaced by an inert gas of high purity. That included the following stages (for the sample 1):

1. Sterilization of all instruments and working space in the boxes with the help of chemicals and hard UV-irradiation within 24 hours.

2. The primary mechanical cleaning of the ancient bone from the surface layer of impurities on specialized equipment with milling cutters and secondary cavitation cleaning with ultrasound.

3. Grinding of the purified bones in a ball mill. As a result, a bone powder weighing 3.40 g. was obtained.

4. DNA extraction from the bone material was carried out 2 times by 2 different methods - the phenol extraction method and the method based on silicone.

5. The resulting DNA concentration was 0.9 ng / μl. This concentration contained DNA fragments from 20 to 180 bp in length. During the PCR reaction, STR fragments of the Y chromosome from 90 to 180 bp in length were successfully amplified. Fragments of greater length did not survive due to DNA degradation in the sample Do-367.

6. As a result of electrophoresis of PCR products on the capillary sequencer AB3500xl and analysis of phoreogram (Fig 4), 7 STR loci of the Y chromosome with the values of the alleles indicated in Table 1 were reliably detected.

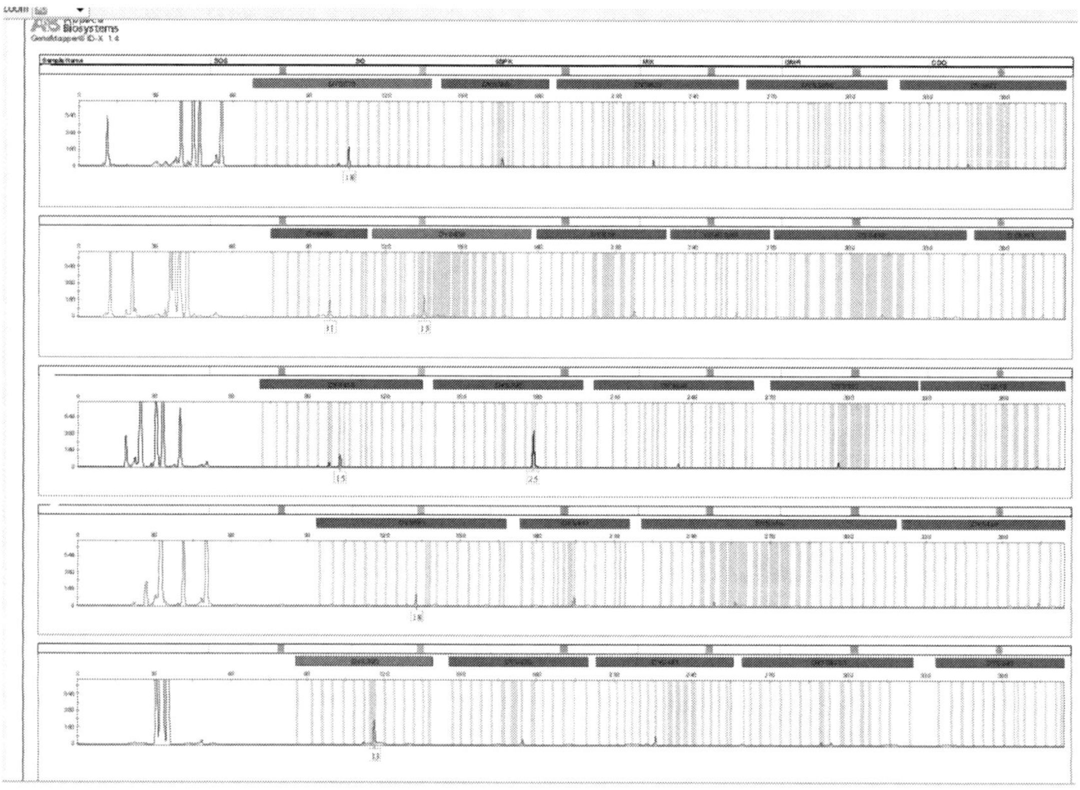

Fig. 4. The phoreogramm of the experiment for the sample 1

Analogically, the same procedure for the sample 2 yielded the following results, less impressive than for the sample 1 due to the worse preservation. Mass of obtained bone powder was 0,7g (> 1,0 g required to assure the robustness). The resulting DNA concentration was 0.3 ng / μl. (> 0,5 g required) The small concentration makes the result to be only of preliminary character, but 2 loci were firmly estimated. The result on sample 1 can be considered as robustly estimated.

3 Data and interpretations

The experiment resulted in following data (table 1).

Table 1. STR loci of the Do-367 sample

STR loci obtained							
	393	390	458	460	456	576	570
Do-367	**13**	**25**	**15**	**11**	**15**	**18**	**18**

The definition of Y-haplogroup with 7 loci according to the predictor HPRG.com http://www.hprg.com/hapest6/files/hapest6.htm?order=orig) gives a very high probability (83%) of R1a haplogroup. The full list of haplogroups and probabilities is given below in the table 2.

Table 2. The prediction of Y-haplogroup according to the experimental data for the Do-367 sample.

Haplogroup	Probability (%)
E1a	0.0
E1b1a	0.0
E1b1b	1.2
G1	0.0
G2a	0.0
G2b	0.0
I1	0.0
I2a	0.2
I2b	0.1
J1	0.0
J2a	0.0
J2b	0.0
L	0.0
N	0.0
O	0.0
Q	0.1
R1a	83.0
R1b	15.5
R2	0.0
T	0.0

For the sample 2 the definition of Y-haplogroup with 2 loci (**DYS392=11, DYS438 =11**) according to the predictor HPRG.com http://www.hprg.com/hapest6/files/hapest6.htm?order=orig) gives a high probability (66%) of R1a. The full list of haplogroups and probabilities is given below in the table 3.

This correspond to the proposed affinity of ancient population of Kaliningrad district to other Eastern European populations.

Table 3. The prediction of Y-haplogroup according to the experimental data for the Y-68 sample.

Haplogroup	Probability (%)
E1a	0.0
E1b1a	11.6
E1b1b	16.3
G1	0.0
G2a	1.5
G2b	0.1
I1	2.3
I2a	0.9
I2b	0.0
J1	0.5
J2a	0.2
J2b	0.0
L	0.0
N	0.0
O	0.1
Q	0.1
R1a	66.2
R1b	0.1
R2	0.2
T	0.

4 Discussion

In this study, we outline the result of the experiment for a novel approach to work with aDNA, which consisted of isolating the sample in a specially designed module system that maintains a high purity nitrogen atmosphere, allowing DNA extraction in ultra-clean conditions. Furthermore, the collective of the Laboratory designed a sample preparation protocol for massive parallel sequencing using non-standard modified sequencing adaptors, enabling us to obtain a library of fragments from extremely low amounts of starting degraded material.

The DNA was isolated from the remains that were found in the Baltic Region; soils in this region are highly acidic. The bones were calcined and seriously older than in previous experiment (300-400 years ago, Central Russia).In addition, severe weather conditions in this region do not contribute to the preservation of genetic material in the remains. Seasonal fluctuations causing high/low temperatures and increased humidity destroy bone tissue enabling chemicals and microorganisms to damage DNA. It was compared the level of DNA damage in the two samples with that mentioned in published data and it was found that the level corresponds to that in much older remains, which were stored in more favorable conditions.

The experiment showed that the technical process and semi-authomated system for genetic testing is working for much older samples that were tested before (more than 1200 years in difference).

For the previous sample [12], 23 markers were obtained. The current result is less informative due to higher degree of degradation which is stronger with respect to the age and conditions of preserving. Of course, 7 of 27 tested loci seems far from compete test, so the direction of the future work of the Laboratory will be the further improvement of the accuracy what may result in newer architectures, reactive kits, and processes. The sample 2 was more seriously degraded and the 2 loci obtained are considered to be rigid but incomplete result. So, of course we see that highly-degraded samples yield serious loss in quality what signals for a need to improve the technology.

The problem is really important for Russia as much of the both old and recent burials quickly degrade due to high acid soils, and it is often hard to obtain accurate result either for archaeological or forensic and criminalistics needs. That problem is existent even for «new» 100-200 years old samples.

Another challenge is to learn to extract more information from the lesser amount of DNA as in practice often only lesser parts of bones are available for research and DNA analysis.

5 Conclusions

We can conclude that the experiment was proper and the positive result was obtained. Nevertheless we see that even in the improved conditions the capacity of the system falls drastically so for the needs of solving tasks for Russian acid soil the system and process should be still improved. As a conclusion, the experiment showed that the method developed in Moscow Institute of Physics and Technology is working in degraded samples and can be a good base for future development. The technology of a glovebox and new technological processes proved to be a good solution for an old and destructed DNA research.

All the technical information about the system and technology itself are described by its authors Dr. Kh.Kh. Mustafin and his team in the paper [15].

The authors appreciate E. Loytsker, S.Senicheva, E. Shcherbinina, I. Rylshikov, E.Payor, D.Votrin, A.Zubko, Andr. Semenov for financial contribution for the research.

The reseach was done by the Laboratory of Historical Genetics, Radiocarbon Analysis, and Applied Physics according to the agreement №DNA-CA/12-17 dated 26.12.2017.

References

1. S. Paabo, Proc Natl Acad Sci USA, **86**, 1939 (1989)
2. J. Krause, L. Orlando, D. Serre, B. Viola, K. Prufer, M.P. Richards, J.J. Hublin, C. Hanni, AP. Derevianko, S. Paabo, Nature, **449**, 902 (2007)
3. M.T. Gilbert, A.J. Hansen, E. Willerslev, L. Rudbeck, I. Barnes, N. Lynnerup, A. Cooper, Am J Hum Genet, **72**, 48 (2003)
4. M.T. Gilbert, A.J. Hansen, E. Willerslev, L. Rudbeck, I. Barnes, N. Lynnerup, A. Cooper Am J Hum Genet, **72**, 32 (2003)
5. M. Hofreiter, V. Jaenicke, D. Serre, A. von Haeseler, S. Paabo, Nucleic Acids Res, **29**, 4793 (2001)
6. J.J. Austin, A.B. Smith, R.H. Thomas, Trends Ecol Evol, **12**, 303 (1997)
7. G. Gutierrez, A. Marin, Mol Biol Evol, **15**, 926 (1998)
8. H Nicholls, PLoS Biol, **3**, e56. (2005)
9. H. Zischler, M. Hoss, O. Handt, A. von Haeseler, A.C. van der Kuyl, J. Goudsmit, Science, **268**, 1192 (1995)
10. A. Cooper, H.N. Poinar, Science, **289**, 1139 (2000)
11. T.L. Fulton, Methods Mol Biol, **840**, 1 (2012)
12. Kh.Kh. Mustafin, I.E. Alborova, A.S. Semenov, V.I. Vishnevsky, RUSIN, **1**(47) (2017)
13. V.I. Kulakov, *Dollkeim-Kovrovo. Research of 1992-2002* (Minsk, Historical Institute of Belarusian National Academy of Sciences, 2007).
14. V.I. Kulakov, Stratum plus: Archeology and cultural anthropology, **5**, 211 (1999)
15. A.D. Matsvay, I.E. Alborova, E.V. Pimkina, M.L. Markelov, K. Khafizov, K.K. Mustafin, *Experimental approaches for ancient DNA extraction and sample preparation for next generation sequencing in ultra-clean conditions* (Conservation Genetics Resources, 2018)

Review puzzles and construction sets falling under the category of augmented reality games

Ilya V. Osipov [1,*] and *Evgeny* Nikulchev [2]

[1] Study Inc, San Francisco, CA, USA
[2]Moscow Technological University MIREA, 119454 Moscow, Russia

Abstract. In this article, the authors review puzzles and construction sets falling under the category of augmented reality games and, at the same time, serving as the elements of TUI interfaces. The review does not include games based on jigsaw puzzles (dissection puzzles, where the player has to put together a set of fragments of variously shaped images). Transreality puzzles are electronic-mechanical puzzles (usually three-dimensional), where the gameplay takes place both in the domain of a virtual game, and in that of a mechanical device.

1 Introduction

For almost forty years, the keyboard and the mouse have been the main means of the human-computer interaction. They are supplemented by the graphical user interface called the windows, icons, mouse, pointer (WIMP model) [1]. Almost all TUI projects contain some of the innovations listed below: touchscreen, accelerometer, computer mouse, computer vision, or various sensors. As they are adapted, simplified, and introduced into general practice, such interface devices and methods become mundane and start to be used in conventional graphical user interfaces.

The evolution of user interfaces started with the command-line interface invented in the 1960-70s. The first versions of the graphical interface (GUI) were developed at the Xerox Palo Alto Research Center in 1970. Now, GUIs are used everywhere in personal computers and mobile devices. User interfaces are developed further as a series of interconnected designs and concepts called conventionally tangible user interface, kinetic user interface, natural user interface, touch user interface, organic user interface, natural language user interface, kinetic user interface, gesture recognition, and even brain-computer interface.

The tangible user interface falls under the "tangible interaction" category. It is a variety of the user interface, in which a human being interacts with electronic devices by using material objects and structures [2].

The advantages of tangible interfaces were first recognized by manufacturers of video games, specifically, electronic arcade machines. Special TUI-style devices were used in such machines already in the 1980s. Toy guns, steering wheels, pedals, joysticks provide much better interaction with video games. Additionally, game manufacturers started to build sensors into their products. For example, Boktai for Game Boy Advance was equipped with an ultraviolet photo sensor, and real sunlight was required to charge the "weapon" in order to shoot vampires. Nintendo produced WarioWare: Twisted with a piezoelectric gyroscope. In addition to using buttons, players were supposed to shake, twist, and jiggle the console. Nonstandard controls imitating natural interaction with material subjects became a standard for Nintendo DS games: for example, in Zelda for DS, players should blow at the screen to propel the sails of windmills.

Gradually, TUI elements appear in unspecialized devices. Specifically, the iPhone interface is based partially on the principle of direct interaction with objects. "People do not understand that we invented a new class of interfaces," Steve Jobs said in 2007, and explained that "the matter is that the iPhone interface lacks verbs almost entirely." This peculiarity, which the head of Apple emphasized, is really very important. A user of the traditional graphical interface first chooses an object, and then chooses an action to perform from a menu (that very verb Jobs was talking about). A TUI user does not need a "verbal" menu: user picks an object and does what needs to be done. This is how multitouch gestures understood by the Apple phone work, it also works with browsing and map viewing in iPhones, as well as with inertial scrolling [3].

TUI techniques are also widely used in robotics, especially in those kinds of robots, which are designed to interact with humans [4].

In this article, the authors review puzzles and construction sets falling under the category of augmented reality games and, at the same time, serving as the elements of TUI interfaces.

* Corresponding author: ilyavosipov@gmail.com

2 Transreality puzzles, similar devices and construction sets

1. *Frazer's Intelligent Beermats* and *Three-dimensional Modelling System*, were among the first cubes, where the physical shape was augmented by an electronic game. From the authors' viewpoint, they approach the mixed reality category, but do not enter it, since the virtual space of the games is weakly manifested. This is what Kelly Heaton, the Physical Pixels developer, tells about this project in her doctorate thesis: "John Frazer and his colleagues at the London Architectural Association have been innovating alternate representations of computation since the late 1960s. For thirty years, Frazer's research has been motivated by an "evolutionary architecture", or one in which the computer contributes generative rules, responsive behavior and other life-like qualities to building structures. Not surprisingly, he finds the two-dimensionality of monitors and plotters restrictive for his exploration of a three-dimensional material space, and his background in architecture naturally leads him to physical modeling systems" [5].

TangledCube. Within the framework of this project, designers from the Faculty of Environment and Information Studies, Keio University in Japan created a Rubik's Cube, which serves as a computer interface and displays positions of its sides on a computer monitor in real time. The virtual space of the game is represented only on the display, which turns TangledCube into the interface of an entirely virtual reality game, rather than a self-sufficient instrument [6].

Triangles. This construction set was designed at the MIT Media Laboratory, shown in Fig. 5. It allows one to use triangles to build sophisticated shapes and review the results displayed on a computer monitor. The physical computer interface is a construction set consisting of identical plane plastic triangles, which are joined both physically and digitally, by means of magnetic conductive junctions. As in the previous case, the virtual space of the game is displayed on a computer monitor, which also makes Triangles an interface to an entirely virtual game, rather than a self-sufficient instrument [7].

ActiveCube. This project was developed at the Osaka University in Japan. Cubes can be assembled to form any shape, similar to LEGO. However, since each cube is equipped with a microprocessor and a parallel data transmission interface, the block of cubes "understands" the current configuration in real time. A computer receives the information about the collective set of blocks via the main block connector and shows the entire group on its display. If the operator moves blocks, the display shows the final configuration in real time. This project is similar to Triangles. The two projects, however, were designed by two design groups independently [8].

Peano is a set, which consists of fifty cubes, which, when joined, form a modular full-color 3D display. Each cube made of colorless diffuse plastic has an LED installed in the center. The LED illuminates the entire cube volume, and its color may vary. The cubes are combined in a modular network, which supports direct and software control of the structure color. Although the network topology is linear, its geometry is three-dimensional, which is possible due to the use of the Peano curve. This curve (as well as its variant, the Hilbert curve) is a linear structure turning at an angle of 90 degrees to determine three-dimensional space in Cartesian coordinates. Magnetic mechanical connectors are designed to maintain connection in four directions and form a linear peer-to-peer network. Peano cubes can be animated by using a digital palette. Since the cubes are sensory and "are aware" of the network topology, they can be controlled by touching them [5].

Constructed Narratives. This construction set consists of 3D Pentomino tiles, which interact with each other and a PC via wireless channels and allow several people to play various games simultaneously. The PC displays show their virtual representation and additional information, e.g., colors and owners of the tiles, or letters for playing. According to the Jennings, the author of the project, Constructed Narratives is the first experiment in the field of studies of social tangible interfaces [9-10].

Siftables/Sifteo. In the authors' opinion, this is the first full-scale device falling under the transreality puzzles category. The elements of Siftables (Sifteo is the commercial name of this project) are both physical objects and virtual game elements at the same time. No external computers or displays are required. Thus, this is the first construction set or puzzle, which is a mixed reality object. Siftables elements look as toy bricks. The top of an element is a small-size LED display. Inside each tile, an accelerometer, four IR sensors (one per each side), and a microprocessor are installed. The tiles interact with each other and a PC. By means of the sensors, they "perceive" contacts with other tiles and can "feel", when they are lifted, shaken, or tilted. Test applications developed by the Siftables inventors at the MIT Media Laboratory demonstrate the familiar set of gestures used in tangible interfaces. A set of such tiles can be used as a platform for child's games [11-12].

Cubelets. The Cubelets game was developed by Modular Robotis. It is a toy set replaying the functionality of the ActiveCube and Triangles projects. However, its elements can be equipped with motorized units, as well as with sensors and other additional equipment. All this allows players to build toy robots, cars, and other items making the game more entertaining. From the authors' viewpoint, this project has few features in common with transreality puzzles. Rather, it is a computerized and motorized construction set and is presented here for illustration purposes only [13].

3 Wawcube transreality puzzle

The author (Osipov) has designed and made a prototype of an entirely "transreal" puzzle: a set called Wawcube. The main purpose of this puzzle is to join physical representation and virtual gaming environment in a common indivisible gameplay scenario [14].

According to Paul Milgram's concept of mixed reality, illustrated in Fig. 1, the proposed puzzle will fit in the middle of the scale, between augmented reality

(AR) and augmented virtuality (AV), since the gameplay will require elements of the physical and virtual world equally. The gameplay lies at the boundary of the two media. Comparing it with the Siftables/Sifteo project, one can state that the latter is closer to augmented virtuality, since all Sifteo cubes can move around on a plane freely, and during the game, players focus mainly on what is happening in virtuality (see Fig. 1).

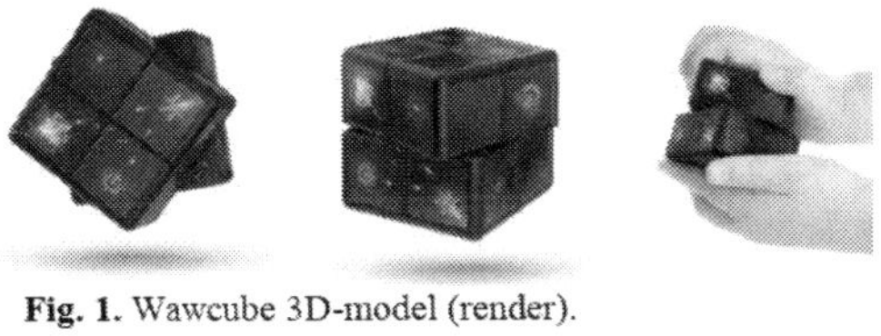

Fig. 1. Wawcube 3D-model (render).

Has been developed a prototype of the Wawcube set, shown in Fig. 2 and 3. The software was written in the C programming language, electronics was assembled on the basis of an ATmega328 and STM32 microprocessors, and bodies and electromagnetic connectors were printed on a 3D printer. In future versions, displays will occupy all possible space on side surfaces, and the frames around them, as well as the gaps between them will be minimized.

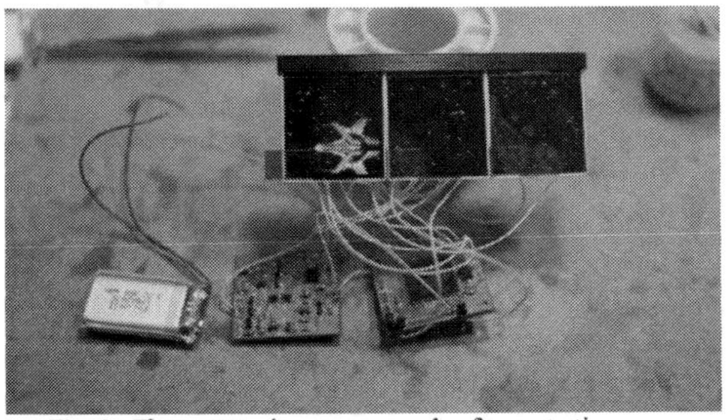

Fig. 2. The prototyping process and software testing

Fig. 3. Assembled and functional prototype Wawcube of 8-elements

.

4 Discussion and conclusions

The main question for such projects is how potential users will receive it. To find this out, it is planned to manufacture several full-scale prototypes, develop several full-scale games, and offer them to participants of test groups, who will play and study the device.

The test methods will be questionnaire surveys, test games, and contests (e.g., who will be the first to lead Pac-Man from one side to another without running into an obstacle, or who will be the first to make up ten words playing in the Scrabble regime). Test groups will include pre-school kids, schoolchildren, teenagers, as well as retired population. Testing by representatives of puzzle fan communities would be most welcome, as well as running tests with random adults in places, where people have to wait for a long times and would not object to being offered an interesting pastime, e.g., in airports. In addition, using the focus groups, it will be determined what construction is better for users, demountable or not. The tests will be finalized by questionnaire surveys, both direct and comparative ones (i.e., comparing the project with other puzzles or game consoles). The authors are planning to publish the results in a separate paper.

In conclusion, a review of mixed reality puzzles is conducted and the device called Wawcube, as an illustration of a mixed reality puzzle, is presented

References

1. R. J. Jacob, A. Girouard, L. M. Hirshfield et al. Reality-based interaction: unifying the new generation of interaction styles. *In CHI'07 extended abstracts on Human factors in computing systems*, pp. 2465-2470 (2007)
2. O. Shaer, E. Hornecker,. Foundations and Trends in Human-Computer Interaction, 3, 1-137. (2010)
3. J. Markoff, *As Apple Gains PC Market Share, Jobs Talks of a Decade of Upgrades* (New York Times, 2002) http://www.nytimes.com/2007/10/22/technology/22apple.html
4. C. Guo, E. Sharlin. Exploring the use of tangible user interfaces for human-robot interaction: a comparative study. *In Proceedings of the SIGCHI Conference on Human Factors in Computing Systems*, pp. 121-130 (2008)
5. K. B. Heaton, *Physical pixels* (Doctoral dissertation, Massachusetts Institute of Technology, 2000).
6. Y. Kamada, Y. Kakehi, *TangledCube: A Proposal on an Electronic Puzzle Using a Rubik's Cube-typed Tangible Interface* (Faculty of Environment and Information Studies, Keio University, 2010) http://www.interaction-ipsj.org/archives/paper2010/demo/0140/0140.pdf
7. M. G. Gorbet, M. Orth, H. Ishii, Triangles: tangible interface for manipulation and exploration of digital information topography. *In Proceedings of the SIGCHI conference on Human factors in computing*

systems, pp. 49-56 (ACM Press/Addison-Wesley Publishing Co., 1998)

8. Y. Kitamura, Y. Itoh, T. Masaki, F. Kishino. ActiveCube: a bi-directional user interface using cubes. *In Proceedings. Fourth International Conference on Knowledge-Based Intelligent Engineering Systems and Allied Technologies*, vol. 1, pp. 99-102 (IEEE, 2000)
9. P. Jennings, Tangible social interfaces: critical theory, boundary objects and interdisciplinary design methods. *In Proceedings of the 5th conference on Creativity & cognition*, pp. 176-186 (ACM, 2005)
10. P. Jennings, A Theoretical Construct of Serious Play and the Design of a Tangible Social Interface. *In Shared Encounters*, pp. 153-172 (Springer, 2009)
11. S. Hunter, J. Kalanithi, D. Merrill, Make a Riddle and TeleStory: designing children's applications for the siftables platform. *In Proceedings of the 9th International Conference on Interaction Design and Children*, pp. 206-209 (ACM, 2010)
12. P. Milgram, H. Takemura, A. Utsumi, F. Kishino Augmented Reality: A class of displays on the reality-virtuality continuum, *In SPIE 2351, Telemanipulator and Telepresence Technologies*, pp. 282–292 (1995)
13. E. Schweikardt, Modular robotics studio. *In Proceedings of the fifth international conference on Tangible, embedded, and embodied interaction, Portugal* (2011)
14. I.V. Osipov, International Journal of Virtual and Augmented Reality, **1**(2), 1-17 (2017)

Using cloud computing technologies in IP-video surveillance systems with the function of 3d-object modelling

Kirill Zhigalov [1,*], *Karen* Avetisyan [2]

[1]V.A. Trapeznikov institute of Control Science of Russian Academy of Sciences, Moscow, Russia
[2]Moscow University of the Ministry of Internal Affairs of the Russian Federation n.a. V. Ya. Kikotya, Moscow, Russia

Abstract. This article is devoted to the integration of cloud technology functions into 3D IP video surveillance systems in order to conduct further video Analytics, incoming real-time data, as well as stored video materials on the server in the «cloud». The main attention is devoted to «cloud technologies» usage optimizing the process of recognition of the desired object by increasing the criteria of flexibility and scalability of the system. Transferring image load from the client to the cloud server, to the virtual part of the system. The development of the issues considered in the article in terms of data analysis, which will significantly improve the effectiveness of the implementation of special tasks facing special units.

1 Introduction

Video surveillance as a service based on cloud storage systems is one of the most important trends of modern security systems. Currently, Video Surveillance as a service in infrastructure is used at both government and commercial facilities.

Software as a service. Access to the application is carried out by means of the network, and most often through an Internet browser. In this case, the main advantage of the VSaaS model for the client is the absence of costs associated with the installation, updating and maintenance of equipment and software running on it. In the model VSaaS there are:

- application is adapted for remote use;
- multiple clients can use the same application;
- payment for the service is charged either as a monthly subscription fee or based on the total volume of transactions;
- application support is included in the payment;
- application upgrades can be performed by service personnel smoothly and transparently for customers.

2 Three types of cloud services

From the point of view of software developers, the SaaS model allows you effectively combat unlicensed use of the software, because the client can't store, copy or install the software.

The software within the SaaS can be seen as a more convenient and cost-efficient alternative to internal information systems.

The development of SaaS logic is the concept of WaaS (Workplace as a service). That is, the client gets at his disposal, fully designed software with everything necessary for work on a virtual workstation. According to recently published Soft Cloud data, the following SaaS applications are in demand: mail; communications (VoIP); anti-spam and antivirus; helpdesk; project management; remote education; Customer Relationship Management; data storage and backup.

All three types of cloud services are interconnected and represent a nested structure. In addition to the various ways of providing services, there are several options for deploying cloud-based systems.

Private cloud is used to provide services within the same organization, which is both the customer and the service provider. This option is implementation of the «cloud concept», when the company creates it to perform its internal tasks. Public cloud is used by cloud providers to provide services to other organizations. Mixed or hybrid cloud is a mixed model of private and public deployment models.

3 Implementation of 3d camera systems

Advanced data storage, intelligent 3D modeling functions, data retrieval using a set of approaches, tools and methods for processing structured and unstructured data of huge amounts of information, all these tasks can be implemented in cloud video surveillance systems using 3D cameras. Development of mobile device access services opens new perspectives in ensuring the security of controlled objects. In recent years 3Dcamera systems in IP video surveillance are integrated in large international corporations such as Google, Apple and others.

Speaking about the advantages of 3D IP-video surveillance systems, we will highlight one of their key criteria that is scalability and flexibility of building a video surveillance system, i.e. the ability to include in the 3D IP-video surveillance system the required number

* Corresponding author: kshakalov@mail.ru

of cameras with a sufficient number of channels, combining 3D video cameras into clusters, using of frame-by-frame or stream video compression standard, the possibility of creating hybrid systems, the flexibility of which allows forming a geographically distributed video surveillance system, expanding it to the size of the city, territorial subject or the whole state.

Cloud data storage. Storage of 3D IP video surveillance data on «Cloud» is becoming increasingly popular [1]. This approach allows you to avoid the cost of purchasing and maintaining equipment for storing large volumes of high-quality video received from security IP-systems [2]. In its turn, it promotes the development of the services like video Surveillance services (VSaaS).

Data protection in the network video surveillance system. IP-video surveillance of security systems imposes high requirements on the security and confidentiality of the resulting video information. The question of unintentional receipt of information relating to personal data is acute. Such a threat takes place in view of the wide range of cyber-attacks, since the components of IP-based surveillance systems are network devices. From the legal point of view,all the requirements of the

Reliable data protection against unauthorized access is provided by the use of encryption mechanisms, and the main criteria that increase the cryptographic stability will be not only the encryption algorithm itself, but also the length of the key (bit), as well as the frequency of its replacement [3].

As for the password protection and the establishment of a multi-level system of user rights, for the purpose of increased security a multi-factor approach should be used for authentication, including the analysis of biometric data system, i.e. the retina, fingerprints, voice parameters of the recipient and other characteristics of an object. 3D IP camera before sending a video message over the network may encrypt it, create a cryptogram with the aim of preventing from viewing and alteration of the information. The IP system may be configured to authenticate the connection by means of encrypted certificates perceived by a particular network camera, which prevents an outsider from implementing a man in the middle attack.

In addition, the developers of specialized software systematically upgrade algorithms and means of protection against possible cyber threats. Implementation this integrated approach to face identification of the user significantly increases the security data storage.

Modern video surveillance systems provide wide opportunities for video Analytics. The ability to use data obtained both in real-time mode and to use the accumulated resource in storage systems allows you to set goals such as early detection of an event or an object.

Video Analytics is widely used as an effective tool necessary to systematize the segment of information or data according to certain criteria. In its turn, 3D IP video surveillance, in the future, has the highest potential for video analysis. The software approach allows you to combine a video surveillance system with multiple cameras, ensures easy video search on key criteria and making use of video analytics. Less often, it is an integral part of the platform, providing an integrated approach to solving the company's problems through the effective integration of various components.

Thus, the client receives information at any time and through the mobile device in which the above function takes place.

In order to highlight the additional features provided by the provider of video surveillance, even a special term was created - MVaaS (Managed Video as a Service).

Video Analytics may be implemented through the integration into existing video surveillance systems, where the compatibility of IP cameras, defined by RTSP/ONVIF protocols, as well as with web and analog cameras of standard resolution. Encryption of video streams for the standard SSL and multi-level redundancy. Open APIs and SDKs for integration with third-party applications IFTTT.

Intelligent video Analytics: calculating the number of people who passed through the zone of control – checkpoint (Element, Counter), integration with control systems and control accesses. The placement of cameras on the map for easy navigation.

In addition to software and operator analysis of video and the subsequent formation of analytical reports, the management of some functions of the access control system based on data obtained through video surveillance systems has proved to be quite popular in the market of services.

Subject-subject interaction. The need for the use and management of consolidated data, also in the framework of "smart cities" and other projects of the Internet of Things - IoT, the development of cloud services creates the opportunity of mobile access to video surveillance systems and video analytics functions.

In addition, VSaaS drivers include innovative technologies in the field of video surveillance, reducing the cost of video surveillance equipment and increasing the needs for video Analytics make it possible to argue that the development of the market of 3D IP video surveillance is the main direction in Video-Surveillance-as-a-service. Cloud, on-premises, and hybrid video storage defines a range of topical issues, including:

- about the systematization of the required number of cameras and objects in a single personal account;
- about implementation of flexible management of access rights to cameras and their groups;
- about possibility of remote configuration of the cameras in the personal account;
- about grouping cameras according to the structure of a particular organization;
- about rapid organization of public events.

4 Security problems in ip video systems

A number of positions on security issues in the implementation of the 3D IP video surveillance system remain dispositional [4].

Threats to the security of cloud computing are associated with potential damage to resources, such as information, processes and systems, and therefore – organizations [5]. They may be of natural or fabricated origin and may be accidental or intentional; may arise inside or outside the organization, divided into casual or intentional, or active or passive. Specific threats detected depend heavily on the specific cloud service you choose. Security risks for CSC are loss and leakage of data, unprotected access to the service, internal threats. Security threats for CSP are unauthorized administrative access, internal threats [5].

Security concerns include those related to the nature and work environment of cloud services. An indirect threat occurs if it creates risks not only in carrying the data of one object, but also for other users. Security challenges for CSC are due to the complexity of the environment, or indirect threats that can cause more immediate threats to the interests of the consumer of cloud services. The uncertainty in respect of liability, loss of trust, loss of control, loss of privacy, lack of services, adherence to one provider of cloud-based services, misappropriation of intellectual property loss of software integrity [6].

Security problems for CSP are uncertainty about responsibility, shared environment, inconsistency and conflict of protection mechanisms, conflict of jurisdictions, associated with changes in the risks of unsuccessful transition and integration (transition to the cloud often involves transferring large amounts of data and major configuration changes). The other may be named as Disruptions in activities, binding to the partner cloud services, the vulnerability of the supply chain, and the interdependence of software.

Security challenges for cloud partners services (CSN) are uncertainty regarding liability, misappropriation of intellectual property loss of software integrity. A common trust model is needed for any system in which multiple suppliers work together to provide a credible service. Due to the extremely distributed nature of cloud computing, accompanied with the presence of several participants, it is necessary that the cloud-computing environment is included into a General trust model. This trust model will enable the creation of Islands and/or federations of trusted entities so that the disparate elements of the system can authenticate the identity and sanctioned rights of other entities and components. Each island of the Federation of trust is based on one or more trusted public key infrastructure (PKI) certificate authorities. Today, there are many trust models available for use in a cloud-based and cloud-based environment.

In a cloud-computing environment, network security enables you to isolate physical and virtual networks and ensure secure communications between all participants. This capability makes it possible to partition the security domain, access controls on the network boundary (such as a firewall), intrusion detection and prevention, and network traffic separation based on security policy. It also protects your network against attacks in physical and virtual network environments. Data isolation, data protection and privacy protection address common data protection issues that often have legal implications. As different cloud computing service means different ways of implementing security controls, the usage of this feature coordinates actions of diverse security mechanisms toprevent conflicts of protection mechanisms.

5 Conclusions

In addition to the above, it should be noted that the IP camera technology itself, and in particular the use of the 3D scanning function, are widely used. In particular, the functions of modular integration of this type of means technically open new opportunities in the field of not only the control and search of persons in public places and on concrete objects, but also their application on unmanned aerial vehicles.

It is a modular function and cloud technology that will allow you to transmit information in real time, whether it is the operational headquarters or the management of a certain level in the performance of any operational, tactical or strategic tasks (Figure 1).

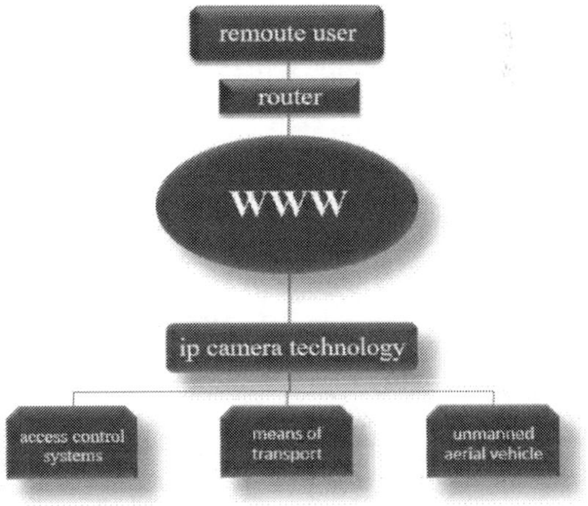

Fig. 1. An example of cloud technology structure

The 3D identification function, including 3D scanning, will allow you to simulate the probed sector in order to make it more responsive for further analytical work and action planning.

Development of cloud technologies, and 3D technologies-identification, given the possible implementation of all kinds of threats come to the fore in effective problem-solving search and identification (including the simulation objects).

References

1. N. Sultan, International Journal of Information Management, **34**, 177 (2014)
2. E. Nikulchev; E. Pluzhnik, D. Biryukov et al., International Journal of Advanced Computer Science and Applications,, **6,** 22 (2015)
3. *Security Guidance for Critical Areas of Focus in Cloud Computing V2.1. Cloud Security Alliance,*

https://cloudsecurityalliance.org/csaguide.pdf (2009)

4. Ch. Hoff, *Security guidance for critical areas of focus in cloud computing*, pp. 12–20. https://cloudsecurityalliance.org/guidnce/csaguide.v3.0.pdf (2011)
5. C. Hewitt, IEEE Internet Computing, **12**, 96 (2008)
6. A.V. Brednik, *Security issues of cloud computing. Analysis of methods of protection of the clouds from cloud security alliance* (Tambov, 2013) [In Rus]

UML class diagram object-oriented metrics: algorithms of calculation

Olga Deryugina [1, *]

[1]Moscow Technological University (MIREA), 119454 Moscow, Russia

Abstract. The paper proposes algorithms of the object oriented UML class diagram metrics calculation. Metrics include Average CBO, Average DIT, Average NOC, Average DAC, Average NLM, Average NOM, DAC2, SIZE2, and DSC. The proposed algorithms have become a part of the UML Refactoring tool providing UML class diagram analysis and transformation.

1 Introduction

Model-Driven Architecture (MDA) approach [1], which was developed by the Object-Management Group (OMG), introduces a new software development paradigm. This paradigm proposes a design process, which starts with the creation of the PIM (Platform Independent Model). Then the PIM is automatically transformed into the PSM (Platform Specific Model).

MDA approach proposes a set of standards including MOF (Meta-Object Facilities) [2], UML (Unified Modelling Language) [3], XMI (XML Metadata Interchange) [4], etc., which provide model design, transformation, validation and exchange.

The problem of model refactoring is tightly connected with the MDA approach: model refactoring is less time consuming than code refactoring. In addition, models can help a developer to look at the software system from a perspective view.

In the MDA approach, software models are designed using UML diagrams. UML class diagrams describe main classes, interfaces of the system and the relations between them.

With the software systems of the large size, it becomes harder to analyze UML class diagrams manually. Software tools of the automated UML class diagrams refactoring have been developed: Dearthóir [5], Darwin [6], CODe-Imp [7], Bunch tool [8], UML Refactoring [9], etc.

These tools use a fitness function for the refactoring process. Nowadays a number of studies have investigated several means of the object oriented metrics [10-14]. Some of them can be calculated for the UML class diagrams too [15] (see Fig. 1).

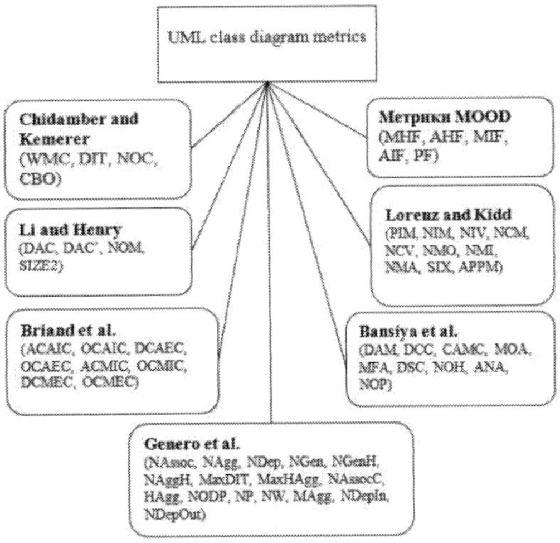

Fig. 1. UML class diagram metrics

The aim of this paper is to propose algorithms of several object oriented UML class diagram metrics calculation based on the abstract data structure UML Map [9].

The rest of this paper is organized as follows: First, the UML Map abstract data structure, which stores elements of a UML class diagram in hash maps, is introduced in Section 2. In Section 3, the algorithms of object oriented UML class diagram metrics calculation including Avg. CBO, Avg. DIT, Avg. NOC, Avg. DAC, Avg. NLM, Avg. NOM, DAC2, SIZE2, and DSC [9] are proposed. In addition, the experimental results of applying these algorithms to class diagrams of different size are presented. In Section 4, the role of the proposed algorithms in the UML Refactoring software tool is introduced before concluding in Section 5.

* Corresponding author : o.a.derugina@yandex.ru

2 UML Map abstract data structure

UML Map abstract data structure provide UML model storage, analysis and transformation. It is based on the hash maps of UML model elements. The reduced UML class diagram of the UML Map abstract data structure is shown in Fig. 2.

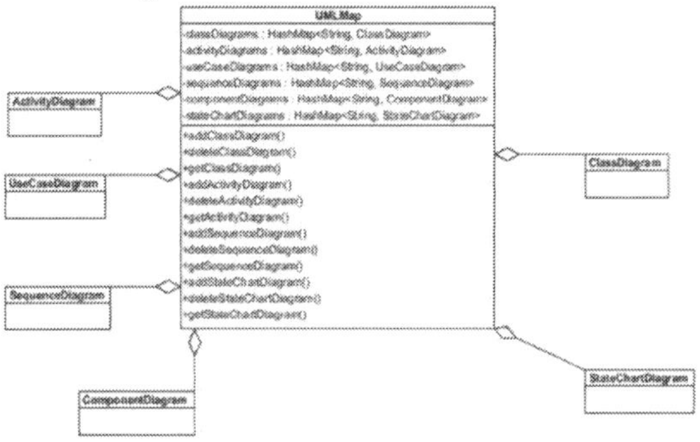

Fig. 2. Reduced class diagram of the UML Map abstract data structure

The detailed UML class diagram of the classes, providing analysis and transformation of UML class diagrams is shown in Fig. 3.

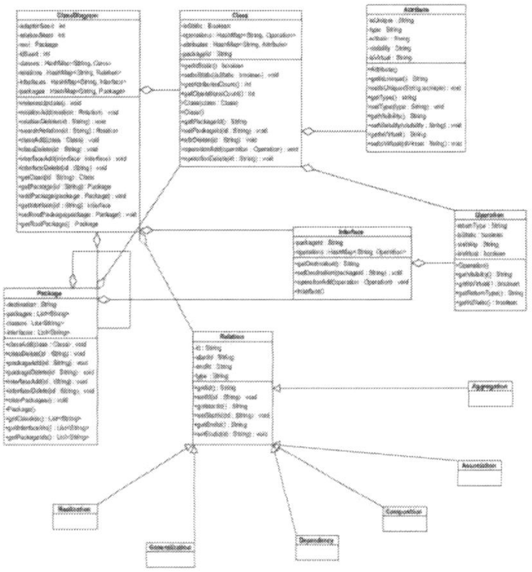

Fig. 3. UML class diagram of the UML Map classes providing UML class diagram storage, analysis and transformation

For example, the complexity of searching a class with the xmi:id = "X" in an XMI text document is evaluated as $O(n)$, while the complexity of searching in a hash map storing pairs of keys and values {xmi:id, Class} is evaluated as $O(1)$.

Special Translator has been developed to translate an XMI file to the UML Map and from the UML Map to an XMI file.

With the UML Map, it is possible to calculate metrics, search elements where transformation application is convenient, automatically transform diagrams, etc.

3 Algorithms of the object-oriented UML class diagram metrics calculation

The Average CBO metric can be calculated as follows:

```
public double calculate(ClassDiagram classDiagram) {
  double result = getAverageCBO(classDiagram);
  this.value = new SimpleDoubleProperty(result);
  return result;
}
public double getAverageCBO( ClassDiagram classDiagram) {
  int classCount = classDiagram.getClasses().size();
  double sumCBO = 0;
  for (Entry<String,Class> entry :
classDiagram.getClasses().entrySet()) {
     sumCBO += getClassCBO(entry.getKey(),classDiagram);
  }
  return  roundUp(sumCBO/classCount,3);
}
//Coupling Between Objects for a class
public Integer getClassCBO(String classID, ClassDiagram
classDiagram) {
  Integer classCBO=0;
  for (Entry<String, Relation> entry :
(classDiagram.getRelations()).entrySet()) {
     Relation relation = entry.getValue();
     if (!relation.getType().equals("generalization")) {
        if (relation.getEndId().equals(classID) ||
relation.getStartId().equals(classID) ) {
           classCBO++;
        }
     }
  }
  return classCBO;
}
```

A graph depicting the execution time of the algorithm depending on the UML class diagram size is shown in Fig. 4. The value of the execution time was calculated as the average execution time measured during 10000 runs for each UML class diagram size.

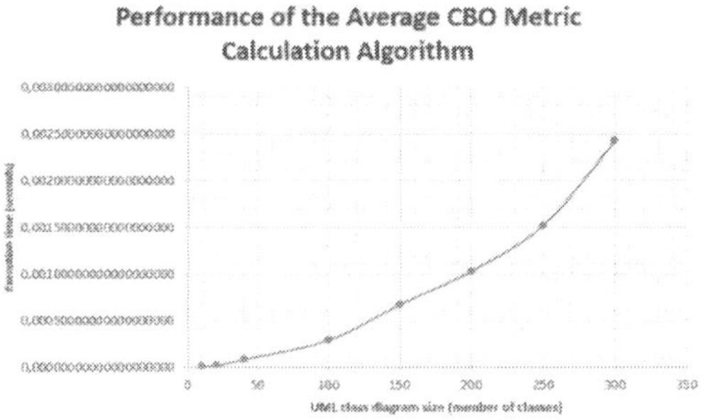

Fig. 4. Performance of the Average CBO Metric Calculation Algorithm

The Average DIT metric can be calculated as follows:

```
public double getAverageDIT( ClassDiagram classDiagram ) {
  int classCount = classDiagram.getClasses().size();
  double sumDIT = 0;
  for (Entry<String,Class> entry :
classDiagram.getClasses().entrySet()) {
    sumDIT += getClassDIT(entry.getKey(),classDiagram);
  }
  return  roundUp(sumDIT/classCount,3);
}
//Depth of Inheritance Tree
public Integer getClassDIT (String classID, ClassDiagram
classDiagram ){
  int classDIT = 0;
  List<String> classParentIds = new ArrayList<String>();
```

```
for (Entry<String, Relation> entry :
(classDiagram.getRelations()).entrySet()) {
    Relation relation = entry.getValue();
    if (relation.getType().equals("generalization")) {
      if (relation.getStartId().equals(classID)) {
        classParentIds.add(relation.getEndId());
      }
    }
  }
  for (int i=0; i<classParentIds.size();i++) {
    int classDITTemp =
getClassDIT(classParentIds.get(i),classDiagram);
    if (classDIT < classDITTemp+1) {
      classDIT = classDITTemp+1;
    }
  }
  return classDIT;
}
```

A graph depicting the execution time of the algorithm depending on the UML class diagram size is shown in Fig. 5. The value of the execution time was calculated as the average execution time measured during 10000 runs for each UML class diagram size.

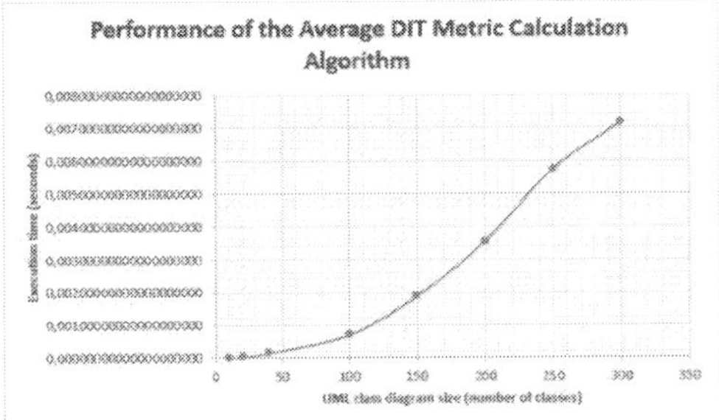

Fig. 5. Performance of the Average DIT Metric Calculation Algorithm

The Average NOC metric can be calculated as follows:

```
public double getAverageNOC(ClassDiagram classDiagram) {
  int classCount = classDiagram.getClasses().size();
  double sumNOC = 0;
  for (Entry<String,Class> entry :
classDiagram.getClasses().entrySet()) {
    sumNOC += getClassNOC(entry.getKey(),classDiagram);
  }
  double averageNOC = roundUp(sumNOC/classCount,3);
  return  averageNOC;
}
//Number of Children  - number of immediate classes
public  Integer getClassNOC (String classId,ClassDiagram
classDiagram){
  int classNOC = 0;
  for (Entry<String, Relation> entry :
(classDiagram.getRelations().entrySet())) {
    Relation relationTemp = entry.getValue();
    if (relationTemp.getType().equals("generalization"))
{
      if (relationTemp.getEndId().equals(classId)) {
        classNOC++;
      }
    }
  }
  return classNOC;
}
```

A graph depicting the execution time of the algorithm depending on the UML class diagram size is shown in Fig. 6. The value of the execution time was calculated as the average execution time measured during 10000 runs for each UML class diagram size.

The Average DAC metric can be calculated as follows:

```
public double getAverageDAC(ClassDiagram classDiagram) {
  double averageDAC = 0;
  int sumDAC = 0;
  for (Entry<String,Class> entry :
classDiagram.getClasses().entrySet()) {
    Class classTemp = entry.getValue();
    sumDAC += getDAC(classTemp,classDiagram);
  }
  int classCount = classDiagram.getClasses().size();
  averageDAC = roundUp(sumDAC/classCount,3);
  return  averageDAC;
}
public int getDAC(Class classTemp, ClassDiagram
classDiagram) {
  int DAC = 0;
  for (Entry<String,Attribute> entry:
classTemp.getAttributes().entrySet()) {
    Attribute attributeTemp = entry.getValue();
    if ( searchClassByName(attributeTemp.getType(),
classDiagram)) {
      DAC++;
    }
  }
  return DAC;
}
```

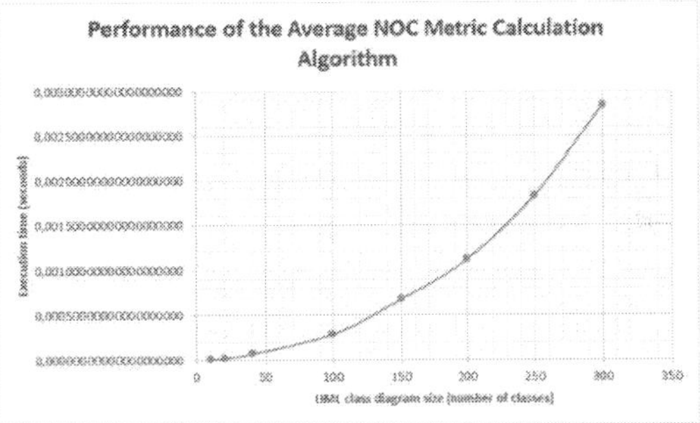

Fig. 6. Performance of the Average NOC Metric Calculation Algorithm

A graph depicting the execution time of the algorithm depending on the UML class diagram size is shown in Fig. 7. The value of the execution time was calculated as the average execution time measured during 10000 runs for each UML class diagram size.

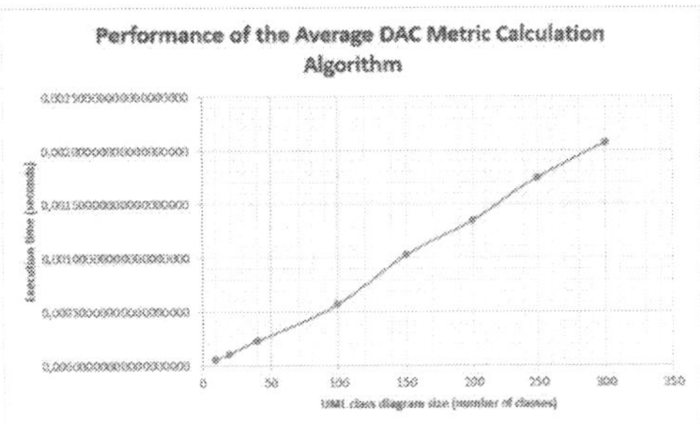

Fig. 7. Performance of the Average DAC Metric Calculation Algorithm

The Average NLM metric can be calculated as follows:

```
public double getAverageNLM(ClassDiagram classDiagram) {
  int classCount = classDiagram.getClasses().size();
  double sumNLM = 0;
  for (Entry<String,Class> entry :
classDiagram.getClasses().entrySet()) {
    sumNLM += getNLM(entry.getKey(),classDiagram);
  }
  double averageNLM = roundUp(sumNLM/classCount,3);
  return  averageNLM;
}
```

```
public int getNLM(String classId, ClassDiagram
classDiagram) {
  int NLM = 0;
  Class classTemp = classDiagram.getClass(classId);
  for (Entry<String,Operation> entry :
classTemp.getOperations().entrySet()) {
    Operation operationTemp = entry.getValue();
    if (!operationTemp.getVisibilty().equals("public")) {
      NLM++;
    }
  }
  return NLM;
}
```

A graph depicting the execution time of the algorithm depending on the UML class diagram size is shown in Fig. 8. The value of the execution time was calculated as the average execution time measured during 10000 runs for each UML class diagram size.

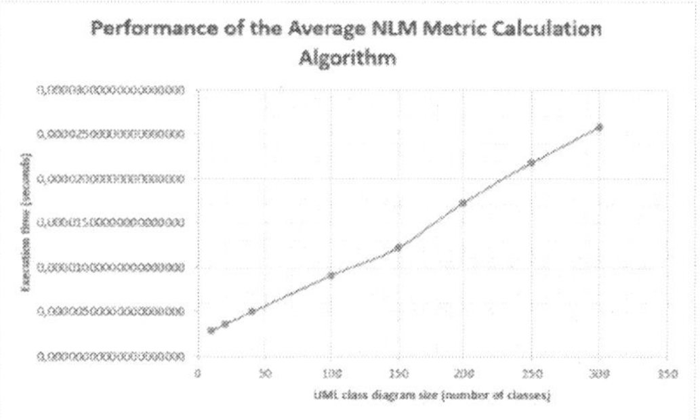

Fig. 8. Performance of the Average NLM Metric Calculation Algorithm

The Average NOM metric can be calculated as follows:

```
public double getAverageNOM(ClassDiagram classDiagram) {
  int classCount = classDiagram.getClasses().size();
  double sumNOM = 0;
  for (Entry<String,Class> entry :
classDiagram.getClasses().entrySet()) {
    Class classTemp = entry.getValue();
    sumNOM += getNOM(classTemp);
  }
  double averageNOM = roundUp(sumNOM/classCount,3);
  return  averageNOM;
}
public int getNOM(Class classTemp) {
  return classTemp.getOperations().size();
}
```

A graph depicting the execution time of the algorithm depending on the UML class diagram size is shown in Fig. 9. The value of the execution time was calculated as the average execution time measured during 10000 runs for each UML class diagram size.

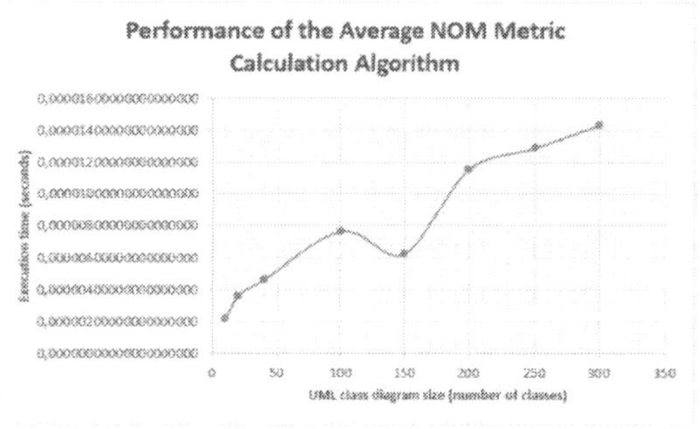

Fig. 9. Performance of the Average NOM Metric Calculation Algorithm

The Average DAC2 metric can be calculated as follows:

```
public int getDAC2(ClassDiagram classDiagram) {
  int DAC2 = 0;
  for (Entry<String,Class> entry :
classDiagram.getClasses().entrySet()) {
    Class classTemp = entry.getValue();
    if (getDAC2(classTemp,classDiagram)) {
    DAC2++;
    }
  }
  return  DAC2;
}
public boolean getDAC2(Class classTemp, ClassDiagram
classDiagram) {
  for (Entry<String,Attribute> entry:
classTemp.getAttributes().entrySet()) {
    Attribute attributeTemp = entry.getValue();
    if ( searchClassByName(attributeTemp.getType(),
classDiagram)) {
      return true;
    }
  }
  return false;
}
```

A graph depicting the execution time of the algorithm depending on the UML class diagram size is shown in Fig. 10. The value of the execution time was calculated as the average execution time measured during 10000 runs for each UML class diagram size.

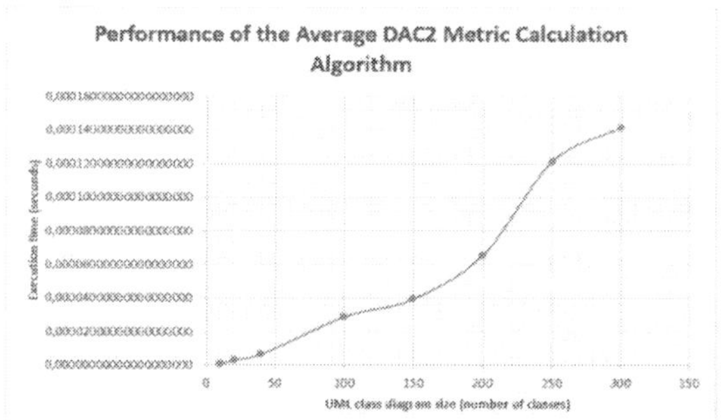

Fig. 10. Performance of the Average DAC2 Metric Calculation Algorithm

The Average SIZE2 metric can be calculated as follows:

```
public double getAverageSIZE2(ClassDiagram classDiagram) {
  int classCount = classDiagram.getClasses().size();
  int sumSIZE2 = 0;
  for (Entry<String,Class> entry :
classDiagram.getClasses().entrySet()) {
    sumSIZE2 += getSIZE2(entry.getKey(),classDiagram);
  }
  double averageSIZE2 = roundUp(sumSIZE2/classCount,3);
  return  averageSIZE2;
}
public double getSIZE2(String classId, ClassDiagram
classDiagram) {
  Class classTemp = classDiagram.getClass(classId);
  DACMetric dac = new DACMetric();
  double SIZE2 = classTemp.getAttributes().size() +
dac.calculate(classId, classDiagram);
  return SIZE2;
}
```

A graph depicting the execution time of the algorithm depending on the UML class diagram size is shown in Fig. 11. The value of the execution time was calculated as the average execution time measured during 10000 runs for each UML class diagram size.

https://doi.org/10.1051/itmconf/20181803001

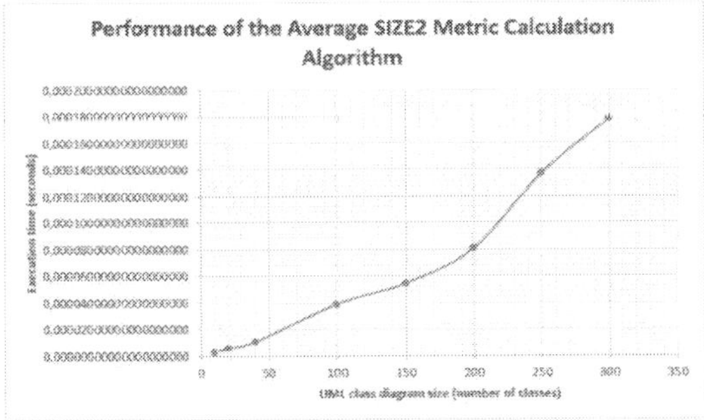

Fig. 11. Performance of the Average SIZE2 Metric Calculation Algorithm

The DSC metric can be calculated as follows:

```
public double getComplexity(ClassDiagram classDiagram) {
  int c = classDiagram.getClasses().size(); //classes count
  int i = classDiagram.getInterfaces().size(); // interfaces count
  int r = classDiagram.getRelations().size(); // relations count
  //count attributes
  int a = 0; // attributes count
  for (Entry<String, Class> entry : classDiagram.getClasses().entrySet()) {
     Class c0 = entry.getValue();
     a += c0.getAttributes().size();
  }
  //count class methods
  int m1 = 0;
  for (Entry<String, Class> entry : classDiagram.getClasses().entrySet()) {
     Class c0 = entry.getValue();
     int m0 = c0.getOperations().size();
     int m00 = 0;
     //search interfaces, realized by this class
     for (Entry<String, Relation> relEntry : (classDiagram.getRelations()).entrySet()) {

        Relation rel = relEntry.getValue();
        if (rel.getStartId().equals(c0.getId())) {
          if (rel.getType().equals("realization")) {
            Interface interTemp = classDiagram.getInterfaces().get(rel.getEndId());
            m00 += interTemp.getOperations().size();
          }
        }
     }
     m1 += m0 - m00;
  }
  //count interface methods
  int m2 = 0;
  for (Entry<String, Interface> entry : classDiagram.getInterfaces().entrySet()) {
     Interface i0 = entry.getValue();
     m2 += i0.getOperations().size();
  }
  double complexity = k1*c + k2*i + k3*r + k4*a + k5*m1+k6*m2;
  complexity = roundUp(complexity,3);
  return complexity;
}
```

A graph depicting the execution time of the algorithm depending on the UML class diagram size is shown in Fig. 12. The value of the execution time was calculated as the average execution time measured during 10000 runs for each UML class diagram size.

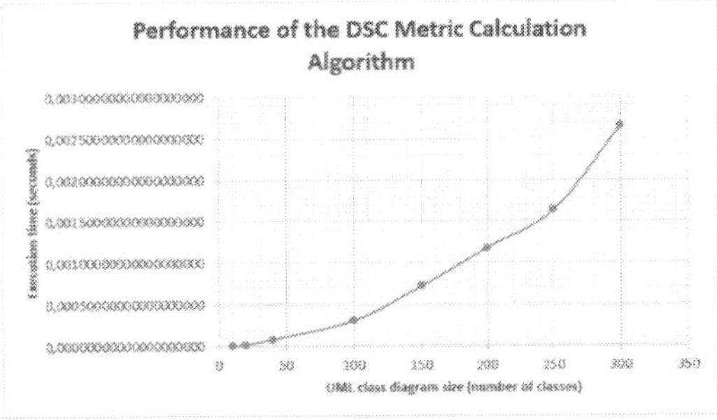

Fig. 12. Performance of the DSC Metric Calculation Algorithm

6 UML Refactoring tool

The introduced algorithms have become a part of the automated UML class diagram refactoring framework UML Refactoring [9], which can be downloaded from the official site of the project: www.uml-refactoring.ru.

This tool calculates various object-oriented metrics (such as Avg. DIT, Avg. CBO, DAC, SIZE2, etc.) and proposes a list of transformations (Interface Insertion, Façade, Strategy), which minimize a fitness function value. In addition, the tool applies the chosen transformation to the diagram. Framework can import/export projects from/to the XMI format.

The main window of the UML Refactoring tool is shown in Fig. 13.

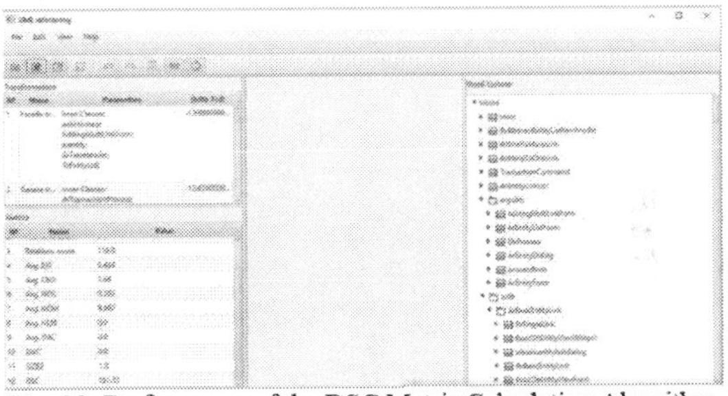

Fig. 13. Performance of the DSC Metric Calculation Algorithm

The fitness function selection window is shown in Fig. 14.

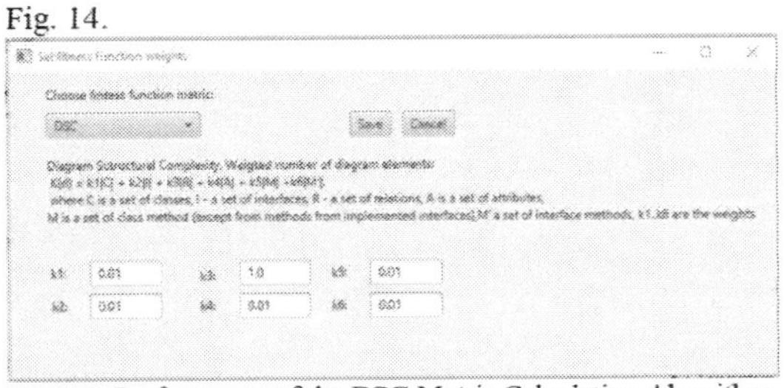

Fig. 14. Performance of the DSC Metric Calculation Algorithm

7 Conclusions

The proposed UML Map abstract data structure provides convenient UML class diagram analysis and transformation.

The proposed algorithms of the object oriented UML class diagram metrics calculation (including Average CBO, Average DIT, Average NOC, Average DAC, Average NLM, Average NOM, DAC2, SIZE2, and DSC are proposed) have become a part of the UML Refactoring software tool.

References

[1] OMG Model Driven Architecture (http://www.omg.org/mda)

[2] OMG Meta Object Facility Core Specification. Version 2.5.1. (http://www.omg.org/spec/MOF/2.5.1)

[3] OMG Unified Modelling Language UML. Version 2.5 (http://www.omg.org/spec/UML/2.5)

[4] XML Metadata Interchange (XMI) Specification. Version 2.4.2 (http://www.omg.org/spec/XMI/2.4.2)

[5] M. O'Keeffe and M. Ó Cinnéide, *Towards automated design improvements through combinatorial optimization* (W2S, 2004)

[6] S. Hadaytullah, Vathsavayi, O. Räihä, and K. Koskimies, *Tool support for software architecture design with genetic algorithms* (IEEE CS Press, 2010)

[7] M. O'Keeffe and M. Ó Cinnéide, *Search-based software maintenance* (CSMR, 2006)

[8] S. Mancoridis, B.S. Mitchell, C. Rorres, Y.F. Chen, and E.R. Gansner, *Using automatic clustering to produce high-level system organizations of source code* (IWPC, 1998)

[9] E. Nikulchev, O. Deryugina, International Journal of Advanced Computer Science and Applications, **7**, 76 (2016)

[10] S. R. Chidamber and C. F. Kemerer, IEEE Transaction on Software Engineering, **20**, 476 (1994)

[11] M. Lorenz and J. Kidd, *Object-Oriented Software Metrics: A Practical Guide*, Prentice Hall, Englewood Cliffs, New Jersey, (1994)

[12] F. Brito e Abreu, L. Ochoa and M. Goulao, *The MOOD metrics set* (INESC/ISEG, 1998)

[13] L. Briand, W. Devanbu and W. Melo, *An investigation into coupling measures for C++* (ICSE, 1997)

[14] M. Marchesi, *OOA Metrics for the Unified Modeling Language* (Euromicro Conference on Software Maintenance and Reengineering, 1998)

[15] M. Genero, M. Piattini and C. Calero, L´Objet, **6**, 4, 489 (2001)

Creating the mobile apps independence rating

Anton Kukanov [1, 2, *] and *Elena* Andrianova [1]

[1]Moscow Technological University (MIREA), 119454 Moscow, Russia
[2]ANO "Russian System of Quality" (RusQuality), 115184 Moscow, Russia

Abstract. Nowadays the mobile apps market is experiencing unprecedented growth. The quantity of mobile applications, which is proposed for installation, has exceeded 6 million. It causes, that it's difficult for common consumers to choose a safety and high-quality product from this amount. The proposed independent rating called up for helping ordinary consumers. It is based on the special standard of mobile apps quality requirements and group of test procedures, that allow to evaluate the quality of mobile software.

1 Introduction

Nowadays the market of mobile applications has an unprecedented growth. Users often buy smartphones instead of classical computers. Mobile app is the software, which is intended for working on smartphones, tablets and other mobile gadgets. On average, the usual consumer uses mobile applications for 3 hours every day. The most active users of mobile devices spend on interaction with smartphones up to 5 hours daily. In this case, the number of smartphone apps in the two largest application stores – App Store and Google Play – totaled more than 6 million units. And the total number of downloaded applications in both stores (not including reinstallations and updates) in January 2018 reached 27 billion. The main reason for such rapid growth of the mobile market is a great growth in sales of tablets, smartphones and other mobile devices. Considering a huge number of applications, it may be quite difficult for an ordinary consumer to choose a software product which corresponds to his needs and the proper level of safety and quality. Independent surveys of mobile applications with subsequent assessment and rating creation are needed to help in sort outing in such an abundance of applications and help to make the right choice.

2 Standard of quality requirements

For organization, independent research and creating mobile apps ratings first of all, it is necessary to have standardized requirements to the quality and safety of mobile software products [1]. Up to this point, there were no Russian and international standards that would give an exhaustive answer to the question of what a quality of mobile application should be. The questions should be taken into account in order to develop a high-quality software product for smartphones. In this regard, it was decided to develop the standard of special requirements for the quality of mobile applications. During developing the standard about 60 existing standards, methodologies and manuals from leading companies in the sphere of mobile software & IT were learned. As a result, 16 State standards, 5 international standards, guidelines and methodologies of corporations (Apple, Google, AQuA and OWASP) were used and the Standard of Autonomous Non-profit Organization "RusQuality" STO 46429990-065-2017 "Mobile applications for smartphones"[2]. Special requirements for quality" was developed. It includes 87 requirements for the quality of mobile apps for smartphones. The Standard was discussed by the working group of the Project Technical Committee PTC 702 "Russian System of Quality", which includes IT and app's experts and was repeatedly refined [3–8].

The Standard STO 46429990-065-2017 is suitable for conducting of comparative tests of mobile software products. It includes the requirements of seven categories: Functionality, Usability, Performance and Reliability, Security, Portability, Accompaniment and Mobile App Description.

Criteria of functionality, usability and safety are the most important because ordinary consumers are primarily interested in the possibilities, their simplicity of use and safety. "Functionality" includes 9 requirements of the quality of mobile applications. Among which:

– The mobile application must have all the functionality specified in the description and title of the software product, shown in the screenshots and demonstrated in the demo video.

– The paid version of mobile application should be able to free trial acquaintance, regardless of the business model of its distribution.

– The mobile application must support the services and platform extensions corresponding to the target functionality of the application: Health Kit and Google Fit (for Fitness and Health applications), Siri voice

* Corresponding author: kukanov@roskachestvo.gov.ru

assistant, Wallet (for applications that allow buying tickets), iMessage and others.

– A mobile application that has built-in purchases must have a restore tool that allows you to return an additional (enhanced) functionality purchased earlier after reinstalling or updating an application.

As for "Usability" the requirements of this category are devoted to the simplicity and quality of navigation, russification, design, advertising, etc. (total 29 requirements):

– The navigation process should be designed in such a way that the user can determine where he was, where he is and where he can move in the future. During the using of the application, the user should not be in a situation in which it is not clear what is happening and what to do.

– The quantity of navigation steps, which are necessary for access to a certain part of the information should be minimal.

– The mobile application must use the Standard navigation components of the platform such as navigation panels, page controls, tab panels, and do not change the system navigation functions. If the platform supports the "Back" button, clicking on it should always lead to the previous screen. If the platform supports the "Home" button, pressing on it should always lead to the home screen of the device.

– The mobile application must comply with the guidelines (recommendations) for the design and usability of the platform for which it was created. The mobile application for the iOS operating system must comply with the Apple guidelines, and the mobile application for the Android operating system must comply with Google guidelines.

– Users should easily distinguish the basic information of the mobile application from the advertising materials.

– The mobile application should be adapted for using by disabled people: full support for dynamic font is provided (or the application has its own font size settings, allowing it to be increased 2 or more times) and voice input control is implemented. If there is video content or audio recording, you can display subtitles.

– The mobile application should demonstrate large amounts of information (organized in the form of dimensionless lists) according to the principle of "information environmental friendliness": to show first of all the desired and most relevant information to a particular user and then the rest, if it is possible and expedient. For example, using advanced search options.

– The mobile application must be protected against user errors. A mobile application designed to work with text, graphics and other editable documents should allow you to undo at least the last action associated with manual input or editing of data, committed by the user. The mobile application should warn the user about the consequences of its actions, if any of them are serious and irreversible, and ask for confirmation before performing such actions (for example, when deleting data).

As mentioned earlier, in addition to functionality and usability, the security of mobile applications is extremely important. This category has 21 requirements. The main of them are the following:

– The processes of using and storing data by a mobile application must correspond to the requirements of Federal Law No.152 of 27.07.2006 "About Personal Data".

– When collecting personal data, developers of mobile applications are required to provide recording, systematization, accumulation, storage, updating (modification), extracting personal data of Russian citizens using databases located in the territory of the Russian Federation. This is according to the Federal Law of July 21, 2014 No. 242 "About Amendments to Certain Legislative Acts of the Russian Federation Regarding Specification of the Procedure for the Processing of Personal Data in Information and Telecommunications Networks".

– A mobile application must require an absolute minimum of permissions for the core functionality (and do not require unambiguously redundant permissions).

– The mobile application must have an unequivocally interpreted privacy policy, which must be placed in the application or given a direct link to it.

– The mobile application must successfully withstand the 10 main current threats to mobile application security according to OWASP and not have critical vulnerabilities.

– If the application collects, stores, or transmits personal data, it must ensure the security of these operations using up-to-date reliable encryption methods and ensure data transfer over a secure channel (for example, the HTTPS protocol) using interception techniques of the communication channel (for example, SSL Pinning).

Also, the Standard sets requirements for the performance and reliability of mobile software products (12 requirements):

– The amount of memory occupied by the mobile application should be minimally possible and justified.

– The mobile application must notify the user about the long time starting. If the application starts longer than a reasonable time, it should show a download or message indicator informing the user about the time remaining before the application will open or about the progress of opening the application.

– The mobile application should work correctly on all supported versions of the mobile OS without unexpected falls and damages to the main functionality.

In addition, the requirements for Accompaniment and Portability are standardized (there are 5 requirements in these categories):

– The mobile application must be updated by the developer at least once a year, otherwise this application is qualified as "abandoned".

– A mobile application must be able to synchronize user data between different devices on different mobile platforms (if there are versions of the mobile application for different OS).

Separate attention deserves the last category of requirements – "Mobile App Description". Any user should be able to learn about the functions and purpose of the mobile application even before it is downloaded and installed. Therefore, the information posted by the developer in the application stores should be as complete, competent and, most importantly, relevant reality. Among the 11 requirements for Mobile App Description are listed below:

- The name of the mobile application displayed in the application store should be brief and capacious, reflect the essence of the service offered to the user and its name, also be translated into Russian.
- The description of the mobile application should contain detailed information about the key functions of the application and the main tasks solved with it. The description should be translated into Russian, not contain grammatical, syntactic and lexical errors. The description should include a list of functionality that is not available for free use or provided only for money (for applications with built-in purchases). The description of the mobile application should be correctly written in Russian (translated into Russian) with the observance of grammatical, syntactic, lexical and other norms.
- The description of the mobile application should contain information only about the implemented functionality.
- The page of the mobile application in the store should contain actual screenshots corresponding to the current version of the application, and the current video demonstrating the work of the software product. Screenshots and video should only show the existing (already implemented) functionality of the mobile application.
- The mobile app page in the application store should contain a link to the developer's site and Privacy policy.

Apart from quality requirements, the Standard contains a description of test methods and technical requirements. They are directly verified in comparative tests.

The fact is that not all requirements of the mobile applications quality described in the Standard can and should be checked in the framework of testing and rating. Some of them are designed to inform developers about what a quality and safe mobile application should be, but it is superfluous for consumer testing. So, there are 3 testing methods described in the Standard: Manual testing, Instrumental testing and Visual assessment.

1. **Manual testing** is an operational method for apps' testing by an expert on a mobile device without the use of special tools or software. Within this type of testing, the expert uses the mobile application as an ordinary user, assessing the degree of correspondence app's feature to criteria set in quality standard.
2. **Instrumental testing** is an app testing method by an expert using special tools and software, followed by analysis and evaluation of the results obtained with the help of tools based on an expert understanding of the subject matter of the research and converting them into a final rating.
   Types of tools:
   - Software for malware detection;
   - Software for analyzing network traffic;
   - Stopwatch.
3. **Visual assessment** is an expert's assessment of the degree to which the properties of the mobile application or its information characteristics correspond to criteria without manual or instrumental testing. The visual assessment can be used to obtain general information about an app (such as the size of the downloadable application package, the date of the last update, the user rating, etc.) from public sources (application store and developer site).

3 Test procedures

To create an independent rating of mobile applications unambiguously interpreted test procedures in addition to the Standard are also required. Testing software products using them will allow obtaining final ratings of mobile applications, which will make it possible to compose the rating.

Test procedures are developed on the basis of the Standard of mobile apps quality requirements. The list of test parameters may vary depending on the category of mobile applications under investigation and the mobile operating system for which the researched applications are developed. The test procedure, the test plan and the weights of the criteria and their groups are determined separately for each researched category.

The universal category map was developed and socially significant topics for research were identified in order to determine the most priority for the researches groups of applications (see the Figure 1). Socially significant categories are groups of apps that concern the majority of citizens and affect their quality of life. These include Work, Realty, Personal Finance and Productivity, Health and Fitness, Social, Travel, Education and others.

Any developed test procedure contains general paragraphs that include test principles and methods, testing tools, conditions, plan, criteria and weights which experts will use while testing mobile applications.

Criteria of the test procedure can be conditionally divided into two groups:

1. Applicable and current requirements for this apps' category from the relevant chapter of the Standard.
2. Functional criteria not contained in the Standard and separately discussed with the expert community.

The necessary functionality is determined by studying the most popular software products from the application stores and discussing them with profile experts on the working group's meetings of the Project Technical Committee PTC 702 "Russian System of Quality".

An assessment must be made for each individual criterion to obtain an app's final rating. The testing method specifies the uniquely determined attribute or the value of the application and its corresponding rating.

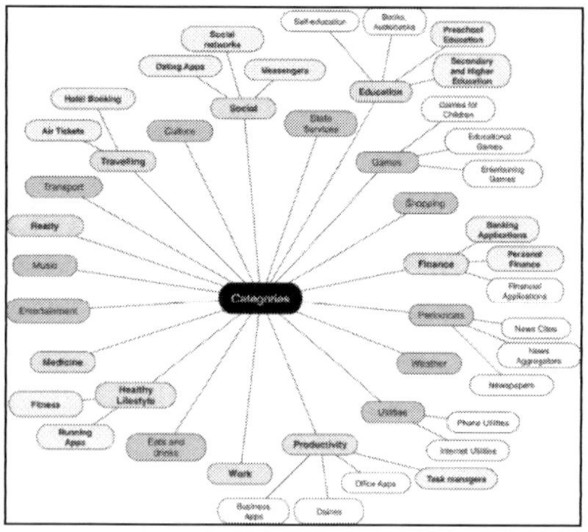

Fig. 1. Apps categories

Example:

Privacy policy*. The mobile application has a privacy policy with the digest of the main paragraphs formulated in a comprehensible language. They are located in the application or there are direct links on them in the mobile app.*

Valuation options*:*

5.5 – There are full version of the privacy policy and the digest of the main provisions of the confidentiality policy formulated in a comprehensible language;

5.5 – Privacy Policy is a short document (no more than 15 paragraphs) formulated in a comprehensible language;

4.0 – There is no digest of the main paragraphs formulated in a comprehensible language; the privacy policy is a long document (more than 15 paragraphs);

0.5 – No reference to the Privacy policy.

Additionally, subtract from the rating*:*

1.0 – Privacy Policy (or a link to it) is shown in the application only while registration.

Each group of criteria and each separate criterion mentioned in current test method has a different weight because of it's different significance. The criteria have a different effect on the final evaluation of the application. Weights are assigned to each parameter in such a way that their sum in each criteria groups is equal to one (100%). The more important the parameter, the greater its weight. In the same way, weights are assigned to the groups of criteria, in this case, not only the importance of the group of criteria plays a role, but also the number of parameters contained in it. If the parameter is not applicable to this application, a dash is placed in the corresponding field, and a rating equal to the arithmetic mean of the values of all applications for this parameter is used for calculating the final rating for the entire research. The calculation of the final evaluation of the application is carried out as follows: the value of each parameter (rating from 0.5 to 5.5) is multiplied by the corresponding weight. All resulting weighted values are summed up within each group of criteria, thus assessing the criteria groups themselves (Mobile App Description, Functionality, Usability, Performance and Reliability, Security, Portability). Then the obtained estimates of the criteria groups are multiplied by the corresponding group weights, and the multiplication results are summed. As a result of the calculation, the final rating of the application is obtained. See the formula:

$$I = \sum_{m=1}^{M} \left(z_m \sum_{n=1}^{N} (x_n y_n) \right).$$

Here: I – the final rating of the application; x_n – the value of the criterion; y_n – the weight of the corresponding criterion; N – the number of criteria; z_m – the weight of the corresponding group of criteria; M – the number of groups of criteria.

The following test principles should be observed while evaluating the quality of mobile applications:

1. Tests of mobile applications should be conducted by an expert group of at least two experts.
2. Tests must be conducted on at least two mobile devices. All mobile devices used for testing are released not earlier than two years from the date of testing and belonged to different price categories.
3. Experts should strictly follow the test plan and perform all operations on several mobile devices.
4. As a result of the discussion, the expert group comes to an agreement on each of the criteria and presents a final rating on it.

4 Discussions

In one article it is impossible to describe all process of making the mobile apps independence rating and the way people use it after creation. However, analysis shows that consumers handle researches results to make a choice what application to download if they don't know the apps market enough. First of all they pay attention to the final rating of apps and then look at the security and functionality ratings to make more informed decisions. This proves the relevance and importance of creation the mobile apps independence rating. Of course, there are a lot of different sites in the Internet where different apps reviews and compilations are published but they don't provide exhaustive independent and transparent information. Sometimes developers pay for these reviews, so people increasingly do not believe them. Taking this into consideration making the consumer applications navigator is needed by ordinary people. But it's worth considering that developers update their apps very quickly (sometimes every week). So the rating may become obsolete after a few months, and it will be needed to test applications again. In turn, this requires large human and time resources.

5 Conclusions

As a result of testing and assessment of applications, it becomes possible to compile an independent rating of mobile software products of a certain category. All mobile applications have specific final ratings and are sorted in descending order.

Moreover the Standard of mobile apps quality requirements is not only a normative base for creating test procedures, but also a guide for developers to develop high-quality software products. From this, first of all, ordinary users win. And thanks to the proposed independent rating of mobile applications, consumers can now easily select the mobile software products that suit their needs and correspond to the proper level of security, functionality and usability.

References

1. Analytical report "App Annie 2017 Retrospective", App Annie, 2018, www.appannie.com/ru/insights/market-data/app-annie-2017-retrospective/ (accessing 05.03.2018)
2. RQ Standard 46429990-065-2017 "Mobile applications for smartphones. Special requirements for quality", ANO "RusQuality", 2017
3. Mobile Applications Test Methodology "Work", ANO "RusQuality", 2017
4. Mobile Applications Test Methodology "Personal Finance", ANO "RusQuality", 2017
5. Mobile Applications Test Methodology "Realty", ANO "RusQuality", 2017
6. Mobile Applications Test Methodology "Fitness", ANO "RusQuality", 2017
7. Mobile Applications Test Methodology "Dating", ANO "RusQuality", 2017
8. Mobile Applications Test Methodology "Task managers", ANO "RusQuality", 2018

Optimizing UML Class Diagrams

Maxim Sergievskiy[1] and *Ksenia* Kirpichnikova[1]

[1] Department of System Analysis, National Research Nuclear University MEPhI, Moscow, Russia

Abstract. Most of object-oriented development technologies rely on the use of the universal modeling language UML; class diagrams play a very important role in the design process play, used to build a software system model. Modern CASE tools, which are the basic tools for object-oriented development, can't be used to optimize UML diagrams. In this manuscript we will explain how, based on the use of design patterns and anti-patterns, class diagrams could be verified and optimized. Certain transformations can be carried out automatically; in other cases, potential inefficiencies will be indicated and recommendations given. This study also discusses additional CASE tools for validating and optimizing of UML class diagrams. For this purpose, a plugin has been developed that analyzes an XMI file containing a description of class diagrams.

1 Introduction

Most recently, UML has become the most commonly used tool for modeling object-oriented software systems [1]. At the design stage, the most widely used UML tool is class diagram (CD). It is known, that any mistakes at the design stage, then affect the implementation phase and either require an additional fine-tuning, or, in more serious cases, could eve require an additional prototype. Complexity and wide applications of different UML patterns could potentially restrict the ability of automatic verification: screening for structural errors, incompatible or redundant components. It is also important to be able to assess the efficiency of CD from the point of view of subsequent implementation.

Since the knowledge of developers in the design of software system are not always sufficient, it not unusual to see CDs which require adjustments. This process can be organized in such a way, that changes are made to the diagram manually in a graphical format. However, certain changes can be carried out automatically with the help of a specialized CASE tool, which contains additional validation functions. To do this, the developer need to be able to analyze the description of the CD and identify structural errors in the diagrams. In addition, it is desirable to have a set of CD transformation rules in accordance, for example, with design patterns that allow you to optimize the model.

2 Representation of class diagrams

Let us focus on the approaches that exist for the representation of the CD. The two main ones are a standard description in the form of a graph with different types of vertices and edges, and a representation in the form of a formal system. There are several ways to formally describe a CD; the most commonly used of them are those that are based on the use of OCL, Z + language and descriptive logics. A real verification is feasible for the two latter options [3, 8].

Consistency check of a CD. It is known that semantics of UML does not allow the use of certain combinations of structures. For example, classes do not allow any direct or indirect inheritance from itself, also class associations should not have the same attributes as classes associated with them, etc. A formal description of all available limitations (of which are many) could turn into a complex and time-consuming process. Any attempts to do this lead to excessive complexity of formal models [10]. Instead, additional analysis can be used that will allow to detect errors of this kind.

Optimization of a CD is the development of rules for replacing certain constructions with more optimal ones. Which CD should be considered more optimal is often not a straightforward question [7]. For example, the use of many standard design patterns [2] leads to an increase in the number of CD elements, but improves its quality in terms of subsequent code generation and modifiability. For example, the inclusion of interfaces to the CD often increases the versatility and reusability of the future code, but this could reduce clarity. Optimization if often associated with identification of inefficient parts of a CD, from the point of view of the subsequent realization. For example, certain fragments of a diagram could have a more efficient form of representation. An approach based on the concept of a design anti-pattern – unpromising to implement a CD fragment [9] – can also be applied. The essence of this approach is that if an anti-pattern is identified in a CD, the designer is given information on the nature of the

* Corresponding author: sermax@yandex.ru

problem and proposes to make changes to the CD. Here is a list of typical fragments of the CD [2, 5], which either contain errors, or can be optimized.

In some cases, these fragments can be described in the form of design patterns or anti-patterns (see Table 1).

Table 1. Typical fragments of a class diagram

№	Name of a fragment	Importance	Reaction
1	Inheritance of classes	High	Error
2	Inheritance of interfaces	High	Error
3	Aggregation	High	Error
4	Class, not associated with other elements	Medium	Error
5	Interface, not associated with classes	High	Error
6	Multiple inheritance of classes	High	Warning
7	Multiple aggregation	Low	Warning
8	Circular association relations	Low	Warning
9	Circular association relations and associated classes	Low	Warning
10	Ternary association relations	Low	Warning
11	Pattern, lowering the arity of the association relation	Low	Recommendations for correction
12	Anti-pattern "Blot"	Medium	Warning
13	Pattern "Chain of duties"	Low	Recommendations for correction
14	The same attributes of the class and association class	High	Error
15	Pair dependency relations between classes: A -- B and B -- A	Low	Warning
16	Big number of methods in the class	Low	Recommendations for correction
17	Big number of parameters of the method	Low	Warning

3 Examples of optimization

Below are examples of several design patterns and anti-patterns the paragraph are straight.

3.1 The same attribute for class and class association associated with them

In general, the same attributes in different classes are permissible, although, in order to avoid ambiguity, one should strive to minimize their number. But duplicating attributes of a class and class association linked to it indicates an error, because directly or indirectly, class association attribute also applies to all classes that are members of the association. In this example (Figure 1), the NAME attribute in the TIMETABLE class is superfluous.

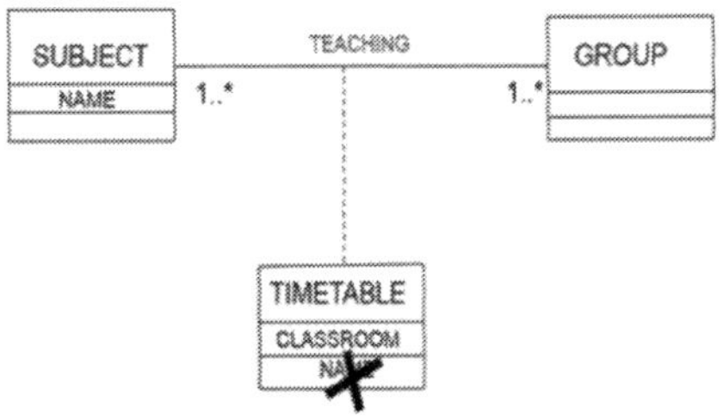

Fig. 1. The same attributes.

3.2 Anti-pattern "blot"

This situation arises when a given class monopolizes both the data itself and the methods of working with this data. That means that this anti-pattern is characterized by the presence of one complex class ("blot"), which includes many fields and methods, while the associated classes contain fields and possibly a small number of methods. The essence of the blot anti-pattern is that, most likely, the methods of the blot-class can and should be included in other classes containing information related to the work of these methods.

3.3 A cycle of association relations, which includes an association class

The meaning of this anti-template is the following: if semantically linked relations form a cycle that passes through a class association, then it is likely that one of them is redundant (Figure 2). A removal of the redundant association can be made only by the designer.

In this case, it is logical to select the TEACHING association relation for deletion. This choice is determined by the fact that you can find out which disciplines the lecturer teaches by navigating through the TIMETABLE association class to objects of the SUBJECT class.

https://doi.org/10.1051/itmconf/20181803003

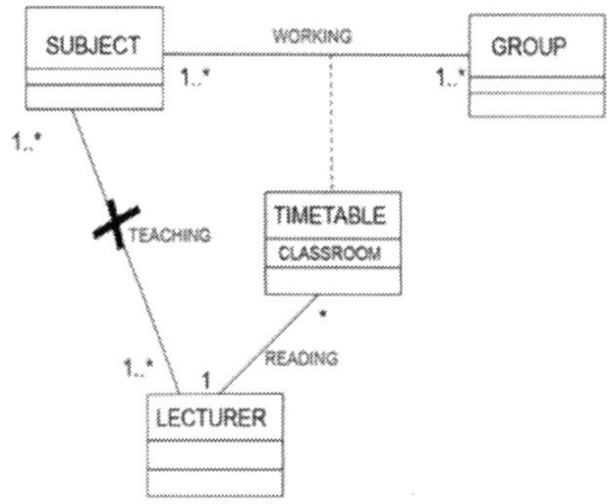

Fig. 2. Example of the anti-pattern "Cycle of association relations, including the class-association".

3.4 A pattern that allows you to switch from a ternary association to a binary association

If the ternary association has a class with multiplicity (1), then the ternary association can be replaced by a combination of a binary association and a class association [6]. Class diagram, illustrating this case, is shown in Figure 3.

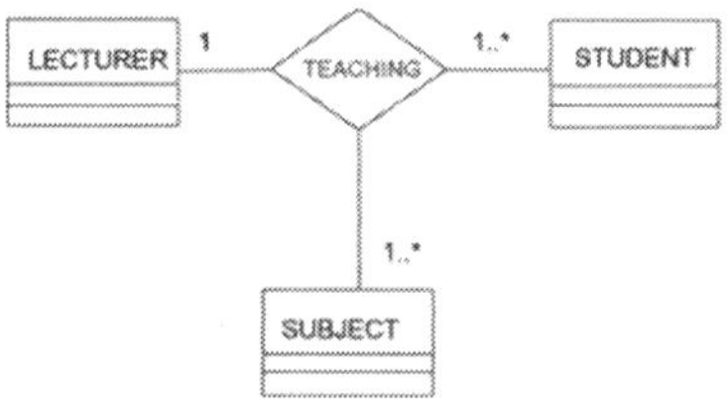

Fig. 3. Example of the ternary association.

The optimized diagram is shown in the Figure 4.

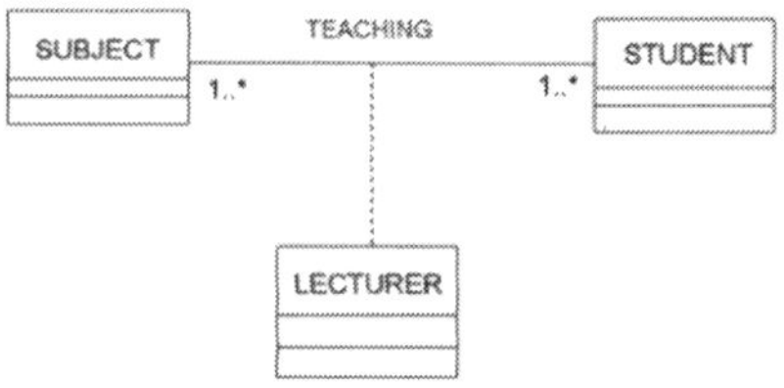

Fig. 4. Replacing ternary association on binary and class-association.

4 The tool for optimizing the class diagram

Modern CASE tools usually contain simplified means of validating CD, which identify only gross errors connected solely with the rules of charting, and do not contain optimization tools. Although the latter is fully understandable, since generally accepted rules for optimizing the CD do not exist, this does not prevent us from using existing methods of describing a CD on the one hand, and a set of optimization rules on the other. To expand CASE-tools with validation and optimization mechanisms for a CD is necessary to implement the following: (1) to develop a method of screening for non-optimal fragments of the CD, using available patterns and anti-patterns. (2) to introduce a method allowing for automatic optimization of certain fragments of CD.

As a basic CASE tool, let us consider IBM's Rational Software Architect package based on the Eclipse platform. It supports all basic elements of the CD, including interfaces, class associations, scopes, etc. Rational Software Architect is written on Java and easily extendable with plugins. To search for erroneous and non-optimal fragments, it is necessary to know the internal representation of a CD for the CASE tool. To store the UML CD in Rational Software Architect the XML Metadata Interchange (XML) format is used, being standard for exchanging metadata using the XML language [11]. Files, created in XMI format, are most often used to exchange UML diagrams between different applications. They store information about diagrams in XML format.

Let us briefly consider the structure of the XMI file. After root tag followed by <packagedElement> tags, corresponding to various elements of the diagram. Each chart element must have the attributes xmi: type and xmi: id.

For the class (xmi: type = "uml: Class") and the interface (xmi: type = "uml: Interface") the name attribute is the class name. The class fields are marked with the child tag <ownedAttribute>, whose attributes are xmi: type = "uml: Property", xmi: id, name and visibility. The methods of the class are marked with the child tag <ownedOperation>, whose attributes are xmi: type = "uml: Operation", xmi: id, name, the method parameters are represented as the child elements <ownedParameter> with the attributes xmi: type = "uml: Parameter", xmi: id and name. A template for the fragment of the XMI code, describing the class, is shown below:

```
<packagedElement
    xmi:type="uml:Class"
      xmi:id="class ident"
    name="class name">
  <ownedAttribute
    xmi:type="uml:Property"
    xmi:id=" attribute ident"
      name="attribute name"
    visibility="access modificator"/>
    <ownedOperation
      xmi:type="uml:Operation"
      xmi:id="operation ident"
      name="operation name">
    <ownedParameter
        xmi:type="uml:Parameter"
        xmi:id=" parameter ident"
        name="parameter name"/>
    </ownedOperation>
 </packagedElement>
```

The generalization relation is represented by a child element in the class-successor with the <generalization> tag whose attributes are xmi: type = "uml: Generalization", xmi: id and general - identifier xmi: id of the ancestor class.

The implementation relationship is represented by a separate element with tag <packagedElement>, whose attributes are xmi: type = "uml: Realization", xmi: id, supplier - xmi: id of the provider interface, client - xmi: id of the consumer class. Also the clientDependency attribute appears in the client class, in which the xmi: id of the implementation relationship is stored.

The dependency relationship is represented as a separate element with the <packagedElement> tag whose attributes are xmi: type = "uml: Dependency", xmi: id, name name, supplier - xmi: id of the provider class, client - xmi: id of the consumer class. Also the clientDependency attribute appears in the client class, in which the dependency relation identifier is stored.

The association relation is represented by a separate element with the <packagedElement> tag, whose attributes are xmi: type = "uml: Association", xmi: id, name of the dependency name, memberEnd - space-separated xmi: id of the child elements of the member classes of the association. These elements are represented by the <ownedAttribute> tag and have the attributes xmi: type = "uml: Property", xmi: id, name, visibility, xmi: id of another association member type, association identifier. The children of the children represent the association rates with the <upperValue> and <lowerValue> tags.

The aggregation and composition relationships are represented in the same way as the binary association relation, but for them additional attributes of the class-integer marked with the <ownedAttribute> tag are added to the aggregation attribute, which takes the value "shared" for aggregation and "composite" for the composition. The child element appears in the association element itself, which contains similar information for the part class.

The class association is represented as a separate element with the <packagedElement> tag and the attributes xmi: type = "uml: AssociationClass", xmi: id, name, memberEnd - space separated xmi: id of additional child elements of the association class. The child elements of the association class are similar to the elements of the class. Additional children are elements with the tag <ownedEnd>, they are similar to the same elements of the aggregation and composition relations. Below is the fragment of the XMI code, describing the association relation:

```
<packagedElement
    xmi:type="uml:Association"
    xmi:id="relation ident"
    name="association name"
    memberEnd="class1 ident" "class2 ident"/>
```

5 Description of the presentation of the class diagrams

To implement algorithms allowing to search for various fragments of a diagram (see Table 1), the excessive standardized XML form is ineffective. Hence, it is more efficient to use a different form of storage, focused on a faster search for elements of a CD. Let us describe it. A CD can be described with a set of classes (each class contains a name, attributes and methods) and a set of directed unweighted graphs for all types of relations. Such a representation is possible, since the relations between classes and interfaces - generalization, association, aggregation, composition, implementation and dependence do not contain circular references. Thus, CD can be presented as a set of graphs, with peaks being classes (interfaces), and arcs - relations. In each graph the set of peaks will be the same; all the graphs will be oriented. As the data structure for the presentation of relationship graphs in CD, lists should be preferred to arrays, since in most cases graphs of relations arches. Base element and the list of adjacent to it should not be presented in the form of a mapping, with a base class identifier playing the key role and the value is a list of identifiers of adjacent classes.

What is stored in contiguity lists? For the relationship graph, the generalizations are the ancestor classes for the descendant, for the implementation relationship graph, the interfaces implemented by the class, for the dependence relationship graph, the source classes for the client class, for the aggregation and composition graph, the class-integer for the part class. Since the attitude of the association is not oriented, it will be represented by two relations, hence the association relation in the graph is duplicated. A class-association is represented as a standard class, associated with classes that generate it. In relation to identifying structural errors in UML class diagrams, duplications of association relationships are not critical and can be omitted. To avoid multiple copying, information about the fields and methods of the class is
placed in a separate list, objects of which will be objects-concepts (classes and interfaces) with mandatory fields and methods.

This presentation form is particularly useful to detect errors such as circular reference, multiple inheritance, or aggregation and incoherence of fragments. Note that transformation from the XMI format to the form of multi-level linked lists is usually a straightforward exercise, which could be performed by an existing algorithm, based on the standard capabilities of parsers. Since the total number of elements in the class diagrams is relatively manageable (usually within several thousand), the problem of finding erroneous and non-optimal fragments with this form of representation could be solved with a standard search algorithms.

The structural scheme, describing the result of adding the validation and optimization plugin to the CASE tool of Rational Software Architect, is shown in Figure 5. The scheme demonstrates additional functionality and data used.

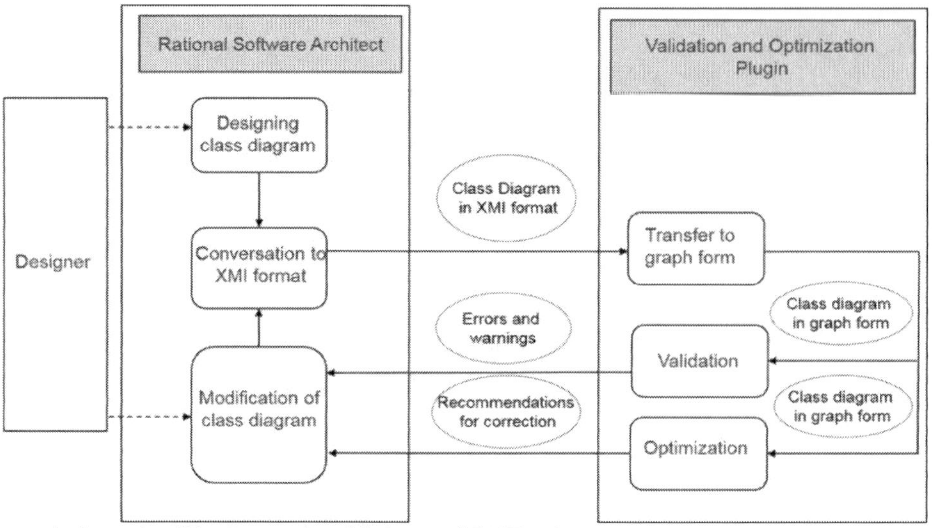

Fig. 5. Structural scheme, describing the operation of the improved CASE tool.

6 Conclusion

The manuscript describes an approach to optimizing models of software systems at their design stage. The described approach is based on an automated search for erroneous and inefficient fragments, using both design patterns and anti-patterns. The report with detected inefficient fragments is being made available to a designer, who makes final modifications to the model. In addition, the system can recommend certain transformations, and in some cases carry out the required transformation automatically. The relative advantage of the approach is that verification and optimization of the model are carried out at the design stage, which allows to minimize the time processes of debugging and refactoring code. This work describes the implementation of optimization of a CD for IBM's Rational Software Architect package. Since the description of CD in Rational Software Architect is presented in the XMI format, widely used for transferring UML diagrams, the developed optimization tool can be used for other CASE tools that support this format. To implement the algorithms of searching fragments of a CD, it appears to be more efficient to use another form of storage (not XMI) - a multilevel system of linked lists.

References

1. J. Rumbaugh, I. Jacobson, G. Booch, *The Unified Modeling Language. Reference Manual* (Addison-Wesley, Reading, MA 1998)
2. E. Gamma, R. Johnson, Helm R., J. Vlissides. *Design Patterns. Elements of Reusable Object-Oriented Software* (Addison-Wesley, 2001)
3. D. Berardi, D. Calvanese, G. D. Giacomo, Artificial Intelligence, **168**, 70 (2005)
4. M. Sergievskiy, A. Konkin6 Cloud of Science, **4**, 465 (2017)
5. M. Sergievskiy, International Journal of Advanced Computer Science and Applications, **8**, 268 (2017)
6. M. Sergievskiy, International Journal of Advanced Computer Science and Applications, **7**, 265 (2016)
7. E. Niculchev, O. Deryugina, International Journal of Advanced Computer Science and Applications, **7**, 76 (2016)
8. A. Cali, D. Clavanese, G. D. Giacomo, M. Lenzerini, A Formal framework for reasoning on UML class diagram. *In Proc. of the 13th Int. Sym. on Methodologies for Intelligent Systems* (2002)
9. W. Brown, R. Malveau, H. McCormick III, T. Mowbray. *AntiPatterns. Refactoring software, architectures, and projects in crisis* (John Wiley & Sons, Inc. 1998)
10. A. Grigoriev, A. Kropotin, E. Ovsyannikova. The problem of detecting consistencies on UML class diagrams. *In Proc. of International scientific-practical conference on modern problems and ways of their solution in science, transport, production and education'2012* (2012).
11. Materials of OMG (2005) http://www.omg.org/spec/XMI/2.1/

ITM Web of Conferences **18**, 03004 (2018) https://doi.org/10.1051/itmconf/20181803004
ICS 2018

Soft clustering method for text mining, with an opportunity to attribute them to different semantic groups

Dmitriy Zhukov[1], *Elena* Andrianova[1] ,*Konstantin* Otradnov[1],and *Leonid* Istratov[1,*]

[1]Moscow Technological University (MIREA), 119454 Moscow, Russia

Abstract. The work describes new soft clustering method for text mining, developed by the authors, with an opportunity to attribute them to different semantic groups. The work of this algorithm is based on usage of definition parameter, when deterimining clustering accuracy, which can be defined for texts of various subject areas either on basis of percolation properties of text clusters, or estimated theoretically based on the redundancy model for text messages. By the author's assumption , proposed algorithm must have speed and accuracy for clustering of texts , depending on value of clustering accuracy parameter. The advantage of this algorithm is that no need to set an initial value of clusters.

1 Introduction

Analysis of unstructured or semi-structured natural language text date, is the very important task to search for hidden patterns in large volumes of data and for creating of predictive models of different processes (including social and economic ones) and extraction of knowledge. A significant number of existing models of analysis is associated with computer linguistics, based on the presentation of texts in vector form and their further clustering by semantic groups.

The construction of models for the clustering of textual documents is based on the methodology for selecting the essential features for the solution of the problem of information retrieval. It should be noted that the set of attributes required for analysis of hidden patterns in large amounts of data is a priori unknown, so when constructing such models it is necessary to use the minimum number of assumptions, with the maximum preservation of the various features used for clustering. However, it should be borne in mind that the run time of the model should remain acceptable, and the implementation of the computation does not require significant computing resources.

You can list the following requirements, which, if possible, the clustering algorithm should meet:

1. At operation of algorithm there should be a minimum possible quantity of passes on a database.
2. Work should be carried out in a limited amount of computer RAM.
3. The work of the algorithm can be interrupted with the preservation of intermediate results, in order to continue the calculations later.
4. The algorithm should work when objects from the database can be retrieved only in the mode of the unidirectional cursor (ie, in the navigation mode by records).

Thus, it is desirable that the algorithm should be scalable (if the capacity of the RAM is unchanged, with an increase in the number of records in the database, its operating time increases linearly).

2 Overview of some modern clustering methods

There are a large number of studies devoted to the development of methods and algorithms for clustering, the description of which can only be presented in a separate paper. It should be noted that a significant part of them is devoted to the improvement of existing algorithms that have already become classical.

Modern technologies provide a huge number of ways in which you can implement document clustering [1]: Custom Search Folders method; LSA/LSI – Latent Semantic Analysis/Indexing;

The methods of complex or single communication of the middle group; method of specific dispersion; method of recursive bisection, etc. It is worth highlighting several methods to which many articles are devoted.

The method of Custom Search Folders [2], which consists in the formation of folders for the separation of textual information by categories. This technology is no longer a new one and is implemented within the search system, with the choice of categories [2].

LSA / LSI - Latent Semantic Analysis / Indexing uses factor analysis techniques to search for hidden factors, on the basis of which cluster analysis groups are formed. The application of LSA is reflected in [3].

The methods of complex or single communication, called Single Link [4], Complete Link [4], involve

* Corresponding author: kuyahshtibov@gmail.com

splitting the entire set of processed documents into clusters using dendrograms and agglomerative clustering (constructing a dendrogram with such a special functionality that defines merging clusters).

At the same time, it should be noted that the issue of effective and qualitative clustering is not yet fully resolved and it is necessary to search for new models and algorithms.

Recently, the Expectation-maximization algorithm or the EM-algorithm [5, 6] is becoming very popular, which, like K-means, is also iterative. In it, first, some initial approximation for the existing clusters is set, and then a refinement is carried out. Vectors are redistributed and cluster centers are calculated, the positions of which are considered in this model as a parameter of the distribution function. Then a new redistribution is carried out until the specified clustering accuracy is reached.

In order to solve the problem of clustering with the help of this algorithm, it is necessary to estimate the probability of belonging of each vector to the cluster, in addition, it is necessary to know that there are a priori probabilities of clusters - w_1, ..., w_k, of cluster distribution density p_1 (x), ..., p_k (x), and of the distribution density of the feature vector x.

In work [7], to solve the problem of analyzing a billion pages of natural language texts in the internet, we propose a scalable parallel stream EM algorithm for clustering a sample of web scales that can be used on inexpensive hardware.

The authors of [7] present an algorithm for a parallel streaming EM tree for clustering a sample of web scales on inexpensive hardware. The quality of clustering solutions and the efficiency of processing depend on the representation of objects.

Therefore, when presenting the data model in [7], random projections are used to represent a collection of documents in the form of binary signatures. The authors of [7] apply the algorithm of the parallel streaming EM-tree, which is specialized for binary signatures for segmenting the sample into clusters. The proposed method is evaluated using Web data sets ClueWeb09 and ClueWeb12, containing respectively 500 and 733 million documents in English. This experiment was carried out by the authors on the basis of the two-element system Xeon E5-2665.

Each processor has an 8 × 2.4 GHz core frequency, connected in a ring network, for a total of 16 processor cores. The program used 64 GB of memory to store a tree in memory, where The data set takes from 240 GB to 350 GB on the disk. Data streams were transferred from the SATA disk at 7200 rpm to 3 TB, providing 150 MB per second of serial read performance.

The ClueWeb 09 and 12 sets took about two and three days to index and resulted in indices at 240GB and 350GB. This is a brief representation of the sets, which are measured in dozens of terabytes when uncompressed. The EM tree processes these documents to create clusters. ClueWeb 09 and 12 clustering took approximately 15 and 20 hours. Both worked in five iterations, and produced 700,000 and 600,000 clusters, respectively.

In [8], the authors presented, using the EM-tree algorithm, solutions for two basic problems of clustering on web pages-scalability and efficiency. The EM tree algorithm can assemble hundreds of millions of documents in hundreds of thousands of clusters on a single 16-core processor in less than 24 hours. Disadvantages of this work is that the approach does not cluster documents that are sparse and high-dimensional. Also, the approach requires significant computing resources, which is far from available for most organizations.

A new hierarchical clustering algorithm based on the principle of the minimum description length (MDL) is presented in [9].

The authors demonstrate that the proposed solution is much better than k-means or EM. In this paper, we propose to refine the algorithm, called EXDBSCAN, to cover data sets with multiple densities (multi-density), where the classical algorithm is inefficient, since it is not able to identify clusters of different density in the data set. This method only receives one parameter from the user, and besides, it correctly detects clusters with different density.

In the Internet there is a very important task of analyzing and optimizing the requests of visitors to sites or users of search engines.

In [10], to solve this problem, it is proposed to use Suffix Tree Clustering (STC) method based on the construction of a suffix clustering tree (Su-x). The tree is formed based on the selected keywords and word combinations from the documents.

In this paper, the authors solve the problem of mass clustering of short texts, whose vectors are by definition very sparse, and clustering methods based on vector space face difficulties in processing matrixes of high dimensionality. The authors distinguished two different characteristics, in the tree document model and the STC algorithm.

First, the document model proposes a new approach to identify all overlapping nodes (phrases) Second, one or more phrases are selected in such a way as to generate a summary of the topic to indicate the corresponding cluster when they are created.

The authors of [10] found that the algorithm of the STC method can show good results when clustering short texts, as well as fragments of the document. However, the STC algorithm sometimes generates some poor quality large-scale clusters when clustering standard documents.

These results reduce the overall effectiveness of the STC algorithm. In the opinion of the authors of [10], this problem can be solved by conducting a measure of the similarity of the Su-x tree.

A brief literature review shows that at the present time there is no clustering model that at the same time would have short execution time, would have absolute accuracy and would process large amounts of unstructured or semi-structured data.

Therefore, the development of new clustering algorithms is very urgent.

3 The proposed method for clustering text documents

3.1 Description of the proposed clustering algorithm

We propose the following clustering algorithm, which at the stage of creating the matrix: the term – document, match with the existing algorithms.

1. From the collection of N-text documents, using the dictionary containing M terms (words and n-grams), using the TF-IDF technique, we create the matrix L: term-document, which have N-columns and M-rows.

$$L_i = \begin{vmatrix} l_{1,i} \\ l_{2,i} \\ \cdot \\ l_{k,i} \\ \cdot \\ l_{M,i} \end{vmatrix}, \quad (1)$$

where $l_{j,i}$ —is the characteristic of the occurance of the j-th term in the i-th document.
For each document i of the collection N will have corresponding vector L_i:
The creation of vectors can be carried out in parallel taking into account the number of processors and cores of the computer system.

2. Find the position of the center (centroid) of the vector space of the document collection (the center of the information space), as the average arithmetic vector of all vectors:

$$L_C = \begin{vmatrix} \frac{\sum_{i=1}^{N} l_{1,i}}{N} \\ \frac{\sum_{i=1}^{N} l_{2,i}}{N} \\ \cdot \\ \frac{\sum_{i=1}^{N} l_{k,i}}{N} \\ \cdot \\ \frac{\sum_{i=1}^{N} l_{M,i}}{N} \end{vmatrix}. \quad (2)$$

3. For each collection vector in a multidimensional space (RM), calculate the Euclidean distance (geometric distance) between the given vector and the vector that determines the position of the centroid:

$$d_i(l_{j,i}, L_C) = \sqrt{\sum_{j=1}^{M}\left\{l_{j,i} - \frac{\sum_{i=1}^{N} l_{j,i}}{N}\right\}^2}. \quad (3)$$

4. We sort all the $d_i(l_{j,i}, L_C)$ from 0 to $max\{d_i(l_{j,i}, L_C)\}$ and divide the numerical sequences obtained for $d_i(l_{j,i}, L_C)$into subgroups of the size rξ:

$$0 \le r_1 < \xi \cdot d_i(l_{j,i}, L_C)$$
$$\xi \cdot d_i(l_{j,i}, L_C) \le r_2 < 2\xi \cdot d_i(l_{j,i}, L_C)$$
$$2\xi \cdot d_i(l_{j,i}, L_C) \le r_3 < 3\xi \cdot d_i(l_{j,i}, L_C)$$
....
$$(m-1)\xi \cdot d_i(l_{j,i}, L_C) \le r_m \le max\{d_i(l_{j,i}, L_C)\} \quad (4)$$

We denote the number of subgroups as m. The definition of the quantity ξ (we call it the clarity parameter of clustering) will be discussed later. In each of the m subgroups we place the vectors $L_{i,p}$ that have entered it (let their number in each of the subgroups equal to some value of Sm):

$$L_{i,p} = \begin{vmatrix} l_{1,(i,p)} \\ l_{2,(i,p)} \\ \cdot \\ l_{k,(i,p)} \\ \cdot \\ l_{M,(i,p)} \end{vmatrix} \quad (5)$$

where p is the index (number) of the subgroup (p takes values from 1 to m), i is the number of the vector (document) in the collection N.
The algorithm for vector clustering within each of the subgroups m will be the same, and will not depend on the vectors available in other subgroups, so clustering can be carried out in all m subgroups in parallel, taking into account the number of processors and cores of the computer system.

5. Consider, for example, the first subgroup (m = 1). We choose any vector in it (for example, the first $L_{i,1}^{(1)}$) and find the Euclidean distance between this vector and each of the other vectors of the given subgroup:

$$d_{m=1}^{(1)}(L_{i,1}^{(1)}, L_{i,1}^{(q)}) = \sqrt{\sum_{q=2}^{Sm}\left\{L_{i,1}^{(1)} - L_{i,1}^{(q)}\right\}^2} \quad (6)$$

From the whole set of vectors of a subgroup we choose vectors for which the following condition is satisfied:

$$d_{m=1}^{(1)}(L_{i,1}^{(1)}, L_{i,1}^{(q)}) \le \xi \cdot |L_{i,1}^{(1)}|, \quad (7)$$

where $|L_{i,1}^{(1)}|$ – is the length of a vector $L_{i,1}^{(1)}$
All vectors which satisfying this condition are placed in one cluster. If there is not a single vector for which the given condition was fulfilled, then the cluster consists of only one first vector ($L_{i,1}^{(1)}$).

6. We choose the second vector ($L_{i,1}^{(2)}$) from the vectors not included in the first cluster of the given subgroup, and find the Euclidean distance between this vector and each of the other vectors of the given subgroup (including those that could already be in the first cluster of this subgroup), with the exception of the first vector (they were already considered in pairs):

$$d_{m=1}^{(2)}(L_{i,1}^{(2)}, L_{i,1}^{(q)}) = \sqrt{\sum_{q=3}^{Sm}\left\{L_{i,1}^{(2)} - L_{i,1}^{(q)}\right\}^2} \quad (8)$$

From the whole set of vectors of a subgroup we choose vectors for which the following condition is satisfied:

$$d_{m=1}^{(2)}(L_{i,1}^{(2)}, L_{i,1}^{(q)}) \le \xi \cdot |L_{i,1}^{(2)}|, \quad (9)$$

where $|L_{i,1}^{(2)}|$ – is the length of vector $L_{i,1}^{(2)}$
All vectors satisfying this condition are placed in one cluster. If there is not a single vector for which this condition was fulfilled, then the cluster consists of only one second vector ($L_{i,1}^{(2)}$).

7. Next, we repeat step № 6 for all vectors that have not been considered. When performing this stage of clustering, it may turn out that some vectors turn out to belong to different clusters.

8. We find centroid for each of the clusters obtained in the steps 5–6 (its coordinates are calculated in the standard way, as the average arithmetic vector of all the vectors of the cluster).
9. For each of the clusters subgroups, we find Euclidean distances (we denote each of them for brevity as d, without considering the membership indices, to any cluster) between its centroid and each of the vectors of the given cluster. The value of the centroid, for brevity, we denote as R, without considering the membership indices, to any cluster. Next, in each of the clusters, we check that each of its vectors satisfies the condition: $d \leq \xi R$. We remove vectors that do not satisfy this condition from clusters. If the removed vector was included in several clusters, then we leave it in those of them for which this condition was fulfilled, and remove from further consideration.
10. We calculate new centroids for the clusters obtained at step 9. Then, we find the Euclidean distances between each of the centroids and unit vectors which have not entered any clusters. The vectors for which the condition is satisfied: $d \leq \xi R$, is added to this cluster.
11. We calculate new centroids for the clusters obtained at step 10. Further, we find Euclidean distances between each of the centroids, and unit vectors which have not entered any clusters. The vectors for which the condition is satisfied: $d \leq \xi R$, is added to this cluster. Repeat this step until the vectors belong to the clusters is changing. Note that there may exist clusters containing only one vector. Steps 5–11 can be performed in parallel for each of the m subgroups, taking into account the number of processors and cores of the computer system.
12. Further, it is necessary to check whether clusters located near the boundaries of each of the m subgroups enter into one common boundary cluster. For example, a common cluster can form clusters located on the boundary of the first (m = 1) and second (m = 2) subgroups, or the second and third, etc. Note that this operation can also be performed in parallel taking into account the number of processors and cores of the computer system.
13. We take the centroids of the first (m = 1) and the second (m = 2) subgroups. We select any of the centroids in the first subgroup and find the Euclidean distance between this vector and each of the vectors of the centroids of the second subgroup (we denote each of these Euclidean distances for brevity as d, without considering the membership indices, to any cluster). We check in each pair the fulfillment of the condition: $d \leq \xi R$ (where R is the length of the centroid vector selected from the first subgroup). For a pair of centroids, for which this condition is fulfilled, conditionally combine their clusters into a single new cluster.
14. We calculate the centroid for the conditional cluster obtained at step 13. We find Euclidean distances (we denote each of them for brevity as d, without considering the membership indices, to any cluster) between its centroid and each of the vectors of the given cluster. For brevity, we denote the centroid value as R (without considering the membership indices, to any cluster). We check for each of its vectors the following condition: $d \leq \xi R$. If this condition is fulfilled for all vectors, then we join the clusters into one common one. If this condition is not filfilled, then we consider the belonging of each of the vectors of one of the clusters of the given pair to the second participant of the pair. Any of the vectors can simultaneously enter into different clusters, i.e. we have two different intersecting clusters. For this, we find the Euclidean distances between the vectors of one cluster and the centroid of the second, we check them for the condition $d \leq \xi R$ (R is the length of the centroid). The vectors for which this condition is fulfilled are added to another cluster. Next, after the addition of vectors, we calculate the position of the new centroids and check the condition that some vectors do not drop out of the new cluster. If the vectors do not drop out, then we accept the addition condition. If any vectors drop out, then we do not accept the addition condition, and the vector remains only in its cluster.
15. In step 13 it may turn out that there are several pairs of the same centroid from the first subgroup, for which the condition: $d \leq \xi R$ (where R is the length of the centroid chosen from the first subgroup) is satisfied. Then we consider each pair separately using step No. 14, and after merging the two pairs, if there are still pairs that satisfy the merger condition for the same centroid from the first subgroup, then repeat steps 13–15 to merge the clusters until the membership of the vectors to the cluster will not cease to change.
16. We select the second centroid in the first subgroup and repeat steps 13 to 15 until the vectors belong to the clusters will not cease to change.
17. Repeat steps 13–16 for all the remaining centroids of the first subgroup.
18. We now turn to the consideration of the centroids of the second (m = 2) and third (m = 3) subgroups, and repeat steps 13 to 17. Next, we turn to the centroid of the third (m = 4) and fourth (m = 4) subgroups, and furher until all the subgroups are considered.

3.2. The clarity parameter of clustering (ξ)

The clarity parameter of clusterization (ξ) characterizes the semantic difference (or similarity) of textual information. To determine the value of the clarity parameter of clusterization (ξ), we use the notion of redundancy, which is used in information theory.

Redundancy – is exceeding the amount of information used to transmit or store a message over its information entropy. According to one of the definitions, redundancy is a measure of uselessly performed alternative choices when reading the text.

It shows how much extra information is contained in the texts of the given language, and can be restored without an explicit indication in alphabetic form. For example, in telegraphic texts the abbreviations "ZPT" and "TCHK" can be used instead of full words without a loss of meaning, conjunctions and prepositions are excluded from the texts of the proposals. Human easily perceives the meaning of words with missed letters etc. The presence of redundancy allows the reduction of texts without loss of their semantic content.

Redundancy determined by the structure of the language used, and its numerical value can be used to determine the boundary of loss of meaning contained in textual information. Text information can be represented by a message consisting of some sequence of characters that are the alphabet of the given language.

In the simplest case, redundancy can be defined as follows. Let's consider messages consisting of one sign of the alphabet. We first find the information, which is an average of one sign of the alphabet. To do this, you can imagine the appearance of any sign of the alphabet as an event, the probability of which outcomes (the probability of occurrence of a particular letter in the text) are the same.

According to the theory of information entropy, the uncertainty introduced by each of the K equiprobable outcomes is:

$$H = -\sum_{n=1}^{K} p_n \, log_2 p_n,$$

where p_n is the probability of any of the K equiprobable outcomes. With this approach, one sign of the Russian alphabet on average should be:

$$H_0 = -\sum_{n=1}^{K} p_n \, log_2 p_n = -\frac{34}{34} log_2 \frac{1}{34} = 5{,}087$$

bits of information. The value of 34 is used because the Russian alphabet contains 33 letters and, in addition, it is necessary to take into account the gaps between words, which will also be a symbol of the alphabet. However, in reality, the probability of the appearance of letters in the text is different. For the Russian alphabet, these probabilities are presented in Table 1.

Using the probability of occurrence of letters in a message (see Table 1), we can find information obtained from a message source with one sign:

$$H_1 = -\sum_{n=1}^{K} p_n \, log_2 p_n = 4{,}350 \text{ bits.}$$

According to the definition of redundancy, for messages consisting of one character of the alphabet, redundancy can be calculated by the following formula: $D_1 = (H_0 - H_1)/H_0 = (5.0876\text{-}4.350)/5.087 = 0.13$.

In this case, the clustering clarity parameter (ξ) can be specified as follows. If $\xi \leq 0{,}13$ text documents should have the same semantic value, with $\xi > 0{,}13$ - the text documents will have different meanings.

In reality, it is necessary to take into account that messages have longer length than one character, i.e. it is necessary to talk about the average length of messages (words) for the Russian language. For two characters, $H_2 = 3.52$ bits; for three, $H_3 = 3.01$ bits; for an infinitely long word $H_\infty \rightarrow 1$ bit.

According to Leonid Delitsyn's statistical research, the average word length in Russian is about 6 characters, but depends on the body (set) of texts. For the body of Russian colloquial speech, the average word length will usually be from 3.9 to 4.9 letters. For the body of Russian fiction – from 4.9 to 5.9. For the news-news corps – from 5.9 to 6.9. For the body of scientific and business literature – from 6.9 to 7.9 letters. If the body is made so that each of the four specified types (functional styles) entered equally (for example, for a million words), then the average word will be 6 letters (5.9). Given that scientific and business speech is less common, you can reduce their share. For example, if you reduce to zero, the average word length will be reduced to 5.5 letters.

Table 1. The probability of the appearance of symbols for texts in Russian

Letter	Space	О	Е, Ё	А
Relative frequency	0.175	0.090	0.072	0.062
Letter	И	Т	Н	С
Relative frequency	0.062	0.053	0.053	0.045
Letter	Р	В	Л	К
Relative frequency	0.040	0.038	0.035	0.028
Letter	М	Д	П	У
Relative frequency	0.026	0.025	0.023	0.021
Letter	Я	Ы	З	Ь, Ъ
Relative frequency	0.018	0.016	0.016	0.014
Letter	Б	Г	Ч	Й
Relative frequency	0.014	0.013	0.012	0.010
Letter	Х	Ж	Ю	Ш
Relative frequency	0.009	0.007	0.006	0.006
Letter	Ц	Щ	Э	Ф
Relative frequency	0.004	0.003	0.003	0.002

An experimental study of the effect of the clarity parameter on the clustering of texts can be carried out using the following algorithm:

1. Take a statistically significant (for example, N = 100000) sample of text documents (for example, news reports for any year).
2. Then we vectorize text documents.
3. Set the value ξ = 0.01, and clusterize the vectors according to the algorithm described earlier. Determine the number of resulting clusters (C) and calculate the value F = C / N.
4. Change ξ by $\Delta\xi$ = 0.01 and repeat step 3 until ξ is equal to 1.
5. We plot the dependence of F on the value of ξ.

4 Discussion

In one article, it is impossible to compare developed model of text clustering with all existing approaches and algorithms

However, analysis shows that all existing algorithms have both advantages and disadvantages. In particular, for example, the algorithm can be fast and scalable, but you must specify the initial number of clusters for which you need to divide a set of texts, and the result of clustering will depend on the initialization phase of the algorithm and be poorly reproducible in the structure of the resulting clusters. Or, on the contrary, to have a high quality of clustering, but to have a long execution time and poor scalability, to be sensitive to the initial data, to work badly with sparse or dense vector spaces, etc.

Unfortunately, the disadvantages and advantages of existing algorithms do not intersect, this leads to the need to find ways to combine several algorithms in one text clustering method . However, in our opinion, it is more promising to continue searching for an algorithm which could combine advantages and would be deprived of the listed disadvantages. Proposed algorithm does not need to specify in advance the number of clusters and the position of their centers, so the result of clustering will not depend on the initialization stage. The algorithm does not depend on the density of the location of objects, does not have a high complexity, which should affect.

5 Conclusion

According to our assumptions, the proposed algorithm should have good speed and accuracy of text clustering, depending on the value of the clarity parameter of clustering. This parameter can be determined for texts of different thematic groups experimentally or given by selection. The advantage of this algorithm is that its operation does not require the initial set of clusters.

This work was supported by the Ministry of Education and Science of the Russian Federation [grant number 28.2635.2017/ПЧ, under project title "Development of stochastic dynamics models with memory and self-organization for weakly structured information, to forecast news events based on natural language textual arrays"].

References

1. M. Śmieja, Ł Struski., J. Tabor, Expert Systems with Applications, 85, 146 (2017)
2. E.N.C. Wai, P.-W. Tsai, J.-S. Pan, Advances in Intelligent Systems and Computing, **536**, 36 (2017)
3. Y. Zhang, J. Mańdziuk, C.H. Quek, B.W. Goh Information Sciences, **415/416**, 414 (2017)
4. Y. Zhang, G. Geng, X. Wei, C. Shi, S. Zhang, Xi'an Dianzi Keji Daxue Xuebao/Journal of Xidian University, **44**, 114 (2017)
5. L. Yaohui, M. Zhengming, Y. Fang, Knowledge-Based Systems, **133**, 208 (2017)
6. D. Agnihotri, K. Verma, P. Tripathi, Expert Systems with Applications, **81**, 268 (2017)
7. V. Radhakrishna, C. Srinivas, C.V. Gururao, A modified Gaussian similarity measure for clustering software components and documents, *In Proceedings of the International Conference on Information Systems and Design of Communication* pp. 99-104 (2014)
8. C.M. De Vries, L. De Vine, S. Geva, , R. Nayak Parallel streaming signature EM-Tree: A clustering algorithm for web scale applications, *In WWW 2015 Proceedings of the 24th International Conference on World Wide Web*, pp. 216-226 (2015)
9. A. Ghanbarpour, B. Minaei, EXDBSCAN: An extension of DBSCAN to detect clusters in multi-density datasets, *In 2014 Iranian Conference on Intelligent Systems, ICIS 2014*, article number 6802561 (2014)
10. M. Peng, J. Huang, J. Zhu, J. Huang, J. Liu, Jisuanji Yanjiu yu Fazhan/Computer Research and Development, **52**, 1941 (2015)

Data classification based on the hybrid intellectual technology

Liliya Demidova [1, *], *Maksim* Egin [1]

[1]Ryazan State Radio Engineering University, 390005 Ryazan, Russia

Abstract. In this paper the data classification technique, implying the consistent application of the SVM and Parzen classifiers, has been suggested. The Parser classifier applies to data which can be both correctly and erroneously classified using the SVM classifier, and are located in the experimentally defined subareas near the hyperplane which separates the classes. A herewith, the SVM classifier is used with the default parameters values, and the optimal parameters values of the Parser classifier are determined using the genetic algorithm. The experimental results confirming the effectiveness of the proposed hybrid intellectual data classification technology have been presented.

1 Introduction

Nowadays, the different methods and algorithms of data mining applied to development of the data classifiers are known. The most famous data mining algorithms, such as the SVM algorithm (Support Vector Machine Algorithm) [1 – 5] and the *k*NN algorithm (*k* Nearest Neighbors Algorithm) show the high data classification quality [6]. The Parzen window algorithm is less famous in the solving the data classification problems, but it also shows the high data classification quality, and possesses by some advantages over the *k*NN algorithm. A herewith, the *k*NN classifier and the Parzen classifiers use the essentially similar approaches to the data classification.

However, as the experimental results show, currently there is no data classifier which is the best for all classification problems, as it doesn't allow providing the high classification quality for any datasets because of specifics of the tools applied in case of its development and, respectively, limitation of its opportunities. Therefore, the decision on hybridization of the SVM and Parzen classifiers for classification of the elaborate multidimensional data was accepted.

Nowadays, a small number of approaches to hybridization of the mentioned above classifiers is known. The approach, suggested in [7], uses in the *k*NN classifier the support vectors of the developed SVM classifier as the representative objects to classify the data within the separating strip. It is claimed that in this case the most useful information is utilized. The basic idea of the hybrid SVM-*k*NN classifier in the approach, offered in [8], is to find the nearest neighbors to a query sample and train a local support vector machine that preserves the distance function on the collection of neighbors. The novel SVM-*k*NN technique for data classification was suggested by one of authors of this paper in [9]. It showed the improving the accuracy of the SVM classification for the different datasets.

In this paper we describe the data classification technique, implying the consistent application of the SVM and Parzen classifiers in the found experimentally subareas of the characteristics space. This data classification technique uses some ideas of the SVM-*k*NN technique. We develop the Parzen classifier for data within the separating strip, in particular, within the Ω area containing all objects which are mistakenly classified by the SVM classifier. Also, the Ω area can contain a some number of objects classified correctly. We use data outside the Ω area as the representative objects of the corresponding classes.

We suggest to use the SVM classifier with the default parameters values, and to define the optimal parameters values of the Parser classifier using the genetic algorithm. The use of such approach to determining the parameters values of the used classifiers will allow to reduce the time costs for obtaining the hybrid classifier which ensures the high data classification accuracy.

2 SVM classification

To find the separating hyperplane in the SVM algorithm it is necessary to solve the dual problem of searching a saddle point of the Lagrange function, which can be reduced to the problem of quadratic programming [1, 2]:

$$\begin{cases} -L(\lambda) = -\sum_{i=1}^{S}\lambda_i + \\ \quad +\frac{1}{2}\cdot\sum_{i=1}^{S}\sum_{\tau=1}^{S}\lambda_i\cdot\lambda_\tau\cdot y_i\cdot y_\tau\cdot\kappa(z_i,z_\tau)\rightarrow\min_{\lambda}, \\ \sum_{i=1}^{S}\lambda_i\cdot y_i = 0, 0\le\lambda_i\le C,\ i=\overline{1,S}, \end{cases} \quad (1)$$

where λ_i is a dual variable; z_i is the object of the training set; y_i is a number (+1 or −1), which characterize the class of the object z_i from the experimental dataset; $\kappa(z_i, z_\tau)$ is a kernel function; C is a regularization parameter; S is a number of objects in the experimental dataset; $i=\overline{1,S}$.

* Corresponding author: demidova.liliya@gmail.com

Usually, the SVM classifier, even with the default settings, provides a high-quality data classification. To improve the accuracy of the SVM classification, it is necessary to analyse the location of the erroneously classified objects. In most cases, the mistakenly classified objects are located near the separating hyperplane. Therefore, it is necessary to use the additional tools to improve the classification accuracy for the objects within the separating strip.

3 Parzen Classification

The Parzen window method is a special case of the generalized metric classifier, defined by the following classification rule:

$$a(u, Z^{train}) = \arg\max_{y \in Y} \sum_{i=1}^{\gamma} w_i [y_z^{(i)} = y] \quad (2)$$

where z is the object, whose class affiliation should be established; Z^{train} is the training set of objects, whose class affiliation is known; w_i is the weight of the i-th object of the training set; Y is the set of classes of objects of the training set; $y_z^{(i)}$ is the class affiliation of the i-th neighbor of the object z; $[y_z^{(i)} = y]$ equals to 1, if $y_z^{(i)} = y$, else $[y_z^{(i)} = y]$ equals to 0.

In the case of the Parzen window, the weight w_i of the i-th object is given by the kernel function, which does not grow in $[0, \infty)$ [10]. Depending on the type of the Parzen window, the following ways of the weights' setting can be applied.

1. For the fixed-width Parzen window, the weights of objects are limited by the certain real number h, which defines the maximum distance at which the objects are considered:

$$w_i = K\left(\frac{d(z, z_z^{(i)})}{h}\right) \quad (3)$$

where K is the kernel function; $d(z, z_z^{(i)})$ is the distance from the object z to the i-th neighbor $z_z^{(i)}$, calculated in accordance with a certain metric.

2. For the variable-width Parzen window, the integer number k of the neighbor, whose contribution to the classification of the unknown object is taken into account instead of the window width. The number h is defined according to the distance to the k-th neighbor from the training set:

$$w_i = K\left(\frac{d(z, z_z^{(i)})}{d(z, z_k^{(i)})}\right) \quad (4)$$

Due to advantages of the variable-width Parzen window, it will be used in the future.

For the Parzen classifier development, it is necessary to determine the following parameters: the number k of neighbors, the metric and the kernel function.

To calculate distance between the objects $t = (t_1, t_2, \ldots, t_q)$ and $p = (p_1, p_2, \ldots, p_q)$ in the q-dimensional space, the following metrics can be used:

• the Euclidean distance:

$$d(t, p) = \sqrt{\sum_{i=1}^{q} (t_i - p_i)^2}, \quad (5)$$

• the square of the Euclidean distance:

$$d(t, p) = \sum_{i=1}^{q} (t_i - p_i)^2, \quad (6)$$

• the Manhattan distance:

$$d(t, p) = \sum_{i=1}^{q} |t_i - p_i|, \quad (7)$$

• the Chebyshev distance:

$$d(t, p) = \max_i |t_i - p_i|. \quad (8)$$

The following kernel functions can be used in the Parzen classifier:

• the Epanechnikov kernel function:

$$K(r) = \frac{3}{4} \cdot (1 - r^2); \quad (9)$$

• the quadratic kernel function:

$$K(r) = \frac{15}{16} \cdot (1 - r^2)^2; \quad (10)$$

• the triangular kernel function:

$$K(r) = 1 - |r|; \quad (11)$$

• the Gaussian kernel function:

$$K(r) = (2\pi)^{-\frac{1}{2}} \cdot e^{-\frac{1}{2} \cdot r^2}, \quad (12)$$

where r is the real number; $r \in [0; 1]$.

4 Data Classification Technique

Improving the accuracy of the SVM classification can be achieved using the following data classification technique.

1. To develop the SVM classifier on the basis of the initial dataset. To estimate the data classification quality with application of the various classification quality indicators.

2. To form the dataset, which will contain all objects which are mistakenly classified by the SVM classifier and are located in the Ω area near the separating hyperplane. It is possible to use the symmetric or asymmetric Ω area. The asymmetric Ω area can be defined as $\Omega = \Omega^- \cup \Omega^+$, where Ω^- and Ω^+ are the subareas with the mistakenly classified objects which belong to the classes with the labels "–1" and "+1" in the initial dataset correspondently. The symmetric Ω area can be defined as the area containing the objects located at the distance which isn't exceeding $\Delta = \max\{d_{\Omega^-}, d_{\Omega^+}\}$, where d_{Ω^-} and d_{Ω^+} are the distances from the separating hyperplane to the furthest erroneously classified objects which belong to the classes with the labels "–1" and "+1" in the initial dataset correspondently. Also, some objects which are correctly classified by means of the SVM classifier can be in the Ω area.

3. To form the new dataset that will consist only of those objects of the initial dataset with their corresponding class labels, for which the class affiliation using the SVM classifier was defined correctly.

4. To develop the Parzen classifier based on the dataset obtained at the step 3, using the genetic algorithm applied to find the optimal parameters values of the Parzen classifier such as the number k of the nearest neighbors, the kernel function type and the distance metric type when classifying the objects from the dataset obtained at the step 2.

6. To estimate the final data classification quality with application of the quality indicators mentioned at the step 2.

5 Genetic algorithm

The search for the optimal parameters values of the Parzen classifier can be realized by looking through all possible combinations of the nearest neighbors k, the kernel function type and the distance metric type. However, such search can be accompanied by the tangible time expenditures with an increase in the number of the kernel functions types, the number of the distance metrics and, especially, the number of the possible neighbors. To reduce the time expenditures, it is suggested to use the genetic algorithm that operates with the integer parameters values.

Let the number k of the possible neighbors satisfies the condition: $1 \le k \le N/3$, where k is the integer odd number (that allow to avoid problems with voting); N is the of objects in the training dataset, formed at the step 3 of the hybrid intellectual classification technology; the distance metric types (5)–(8) are coded by the integer number from 1 to 4; the kernel function types (9)–(12) are coded by the integer number from 1 to 4. Then, the m-th chromosome in the genetic algorithm can be coded as:

$$v = (v_1, v_2, v_3), \tag{13}$$

where v_1 is the number of the nearest neighbors; v_2 is the number of the kernel function type; v_3 is the number of the distance metric type.

The classification quality indicator such as the overall accuracy, sensitivity, specificity, F-measure can be used as the fitness function of the genetic algorithm. The fitness function should be maximized.

In this research the standard scheme of realization of the genetic algorithm has been used. It can be described by the following sequence of steps.

1. To initialize the chromosome population size P.

2. To calculate the "success" of each chromosome using the fitness function. To check the condition for stopping the genetic algorithm. If the break condition is satisfied, then exit from the genetic algorithm, otherwise go to step 3.

3. To perform the genetic selection operator to choose the most successful chromosomes for the role of parents to create the children generation on the basis of the parents genes.

4. To create the children generation with the use of the genetic operators of crossing and mutation. Depending on the operator used, the children can be produced from one parent by accidentally changing its genes (in the case of the mutation operator) or from two parents by combining their genes (in the case of the crossing operator).

5. To form the resulting generation of chromosomes by size P, using the generation of parents and the generation of children in accordance with the principle of elitism.

The following criteria can be used as the stopping criterion for the genetic algorithm: the criterion of achievement of the maximum number of generations, the criterion of achievement of the maximum execution time of the algorithm, the criterion of achievement of the maximum number of stagnant generations. The generation of chromosomes can be considered as the stagnant generation, if the best value of the fitness function does not differ by some small constant ε ($\varepsilon > 0$) from the best value of the fitness function of the previous generation.

The options for specifying the genetic operators such as selection, crossing and mutation (for example, the options for setting the parameters values of the crossing and mutation operators – the probabilities values of the crossing and mutation) are of essential interest.

Within the scope of the problem being solved, there is no need for excessively complex and self-adjusting crossing and mutation operators in view of the discreteness of the parameters values of the fitness function. In this connection, the standard options of specifying for the genetic operators are used: in the case of the mutation operator, the random numbers from the Gauss distribution are added to the values of the random chromosome genes of the parent, in the case of the crossing operator, the child chromosome randomly inherits the gene of one of the parents.

The considered genetic algorithm can be used after appropriate adaptation for the simultaneous search of the best variant of the auxiliary classifier from the set of the potentially possible classifiers and the parameters values of of the best auxiliary classifier.

For example, the kNN classifier and Parzen classifier can be used as the potential auxiliary classifiers, because the effectiveness of these classifiers has already been proven separately in the implementation of the hybrid intellectual technology. In the future, the set of the potentially auxiliary classifiers can be extended.

6 Experimental studies

Approbation of the offered data classification technique was made on the real datasets taken from the Statlog project and the UCI Machine Learning Repository. Particularly, we used experimental datasets of medical diagnostics [WDBC (http://archive.ics. uci.edu/ml/machine-learning-databases/breast-cancer-wisconsin/); Heart (http:// archive.ics.uci.edu/ml/machine-learning-databases/statlog/ heart/)], credit scoring (German, http://archive.ics.uci.edu/ ml/machine-learning-databases/statlog/german/), the artificially created data MOTP12 (MOTP12; http://machine-learning.ru/ wiki/images/b/b2/MOTP12_svm_ example.rar) (Table 1). The case of binary classification takes place in all experimental datasets.

Table 1. The values of the classifiers parameters and the values of the classification quality indicators.

Dataset	SVM classification			Classification type	Ω		Parzen classification			Number of errors	
	Number of support vectors	Number of erros									
		Er_{train}	Er_{test}		d_{Ω}	N_{Ω}	h	Metric	Kernel	Er_{train}	Er_{test}
1	2	3	4	5	6	7	8	9	10	11	12
WDBC (569 × 30)	455	0 of 456	42 of 113	SVM	—	—	—	—	—	0	42
				+aSim	0.373	42	3	Euclid.	Epanechn.	0	1
				+Sim	0.745	42	3	Euclid.	Epanechn.	0	1
German (1000 × 24)	796	0 of 800	60 of 200	SVM	—	—	—	—	—	0	60
				+aSim	0.784	199	137	Chebyshev	Quadr.	1	48
				+Sim	1.567	434	-	—	—	—	—
Heart (270 × 13)	216	0 of 216	20 of 54	SVM	—	—	—	—	—	0	20
				+aSim	0.138	37	23	Chebyshev	Epanechn.	0	7
				+Sim	0.276	38	33	Chebyshev	Gaussian	0	7
MOTP12 (400 × 2)	132	32 of 360	1 of 40	SVM	—	—	—	—	—	32	1
				+aSim	2.000	97	5	Chebyshev	Epanechn.	26	2
				+Sim	2.000	97	5	Chebyshev	Epanechn.	26	2

Each dataset was repeatedly divided into training and test sets with the subsequent training of the SVM classifier. The SVM classifiers were trained with the default parameters: the regularization parameter C is equal to 1, the kernel function is the radial basis, the kernel function parameter σ is equal to 1. Then, after selecting the partition with the smallest number of errors at the training and test sets, the main classification quality indicators were calculated. Further, the decision on the possibility of using of the Parzen classifier should be adopted: the majority of mistakenly classified objects should be on the separating strip, the number of representatives of each class should be at least 20% of the new reduced training set.

If the use of the Parzen classifier is approved, it is necessary to find the optimal values of the following parameters: the number of neighbors k, the metric and the kernel function. We use the genetic algorithm to solve this problem.

In this research, the size of the genetic algorithm population is equal to 20, the number of the stagnant generations is equal to 20, the minimum value deviation of the objective function for determining the stagnant generation is equal to 1e-10, the maximum generations number is equal to 200, the crossing probability is equal to 0.8, the mutation probability is equal to 0.2.

As the justification for the genetic algorithm's preference for the full search of the parameters values during the Parzen classifier development, the following example can be cited. For the MOTP12 dataset, consisting of 400 objects with two characteristics, the full search of the parameters values of the Parzen classifier requires the development of 864 Parzen classifiers, which demands 12 seconds, if 4 kernel functions, 4 distance metrics, and 67 variants of the number k of nearest neighbors (the number k of the nearest neighbors satisfies the condition: $1 \le k \le [320/3] = 107$, where k is the odd number) are used. A herewith, the training and test sets contained 320 and 80 objects, respectively.

The development of the Parzen classifier implies: the calculating of the distance from the object with the unknown class membership to each object of the training set, sorting of the objects of the training set in accordance with the calculated distance, determining of the class membership of the unknown object, taking into account the weights of the neighbors.

If the genetic algorithm is used to find the optimal parameters values of the Parzen classifier for 50 runs of the genetic algorithm, the average search time is 3 seconds for the population with 20 chromosomes and the number of stagnant generations which is equal to 5. The average number of the developed Parzen classifiers is equal to 185. Thus, the search time for the optimal parameters values of the Parzen classifier decreased by 4 times.

Column 1 of Table I contains the name of the experimental dataset, the number of objects and the number of object's features. Columns 2 – 4 combine information about the results of the SVM classifier developed at the first step: the number of the support vectors and the number of errors for each set. Column 5 indicates the algorithm type SVM classifier (SVM), SVM classifier and Parzen classifier with the asymmetric area (+aSim), SVM classifier and Parzen classifier with the symmetric area (+Sim). Columns 6 and 7 show the width of the Ω area and the number of objects lying in this area. The parameters values found by the genetic algorithm are shown in columns 8 – 10. Number of errors at the training and test sets are shown in columns 11 and 12.

For the WDBC dataset the SVM classifier gives 0 and 42 errors at the training and test sets respectively. The mistakenly classified objects are at the distance of 0.373 from the separating strip on the one side (the supports vectors are at distance of 1 from the separating hyperplane). The symmetric and asymmetric areas contain equal number of objects. Therefore, the Parzen classifier will give the identical results for both areas. The areas with the mistakenly classified objects contain 42 objects. The search of the optimum parameters' values of the Parzen classifier with application of the genetic algorithm has defined the number of neighbors equal to 3 at the Euclidean metrics and the Epanechnikov kernel function. The number of errors at the use of the offered classification technology equal to 0 and 1 at the training and test sets respectively.

For the German data the SVM classifier gives 0 and 60 errors at the training and test sets respectively. The use of the symmetric area is inexpedient as the number of the excluded objects makes the most part of initial dataset and owing to the removal of objects the classes become considerably unbalanced. At the removal of objects of the symmetric area, the number of errors at the training and test sets equal to 1 and 48 respectively. Increase in the number of errors at the training set can be explained by a possible removal of the support vectors. The search of the optimum parameters' values of the Parzen classifier with application of the genetic algorithm has defined the number of neighbors equal to 137 at the Chebyshev's metrics and the Epanechnikov kernel function.

For the Heart dataset the SVM classifier gives 0 and 20 errors at the training and test sets respectively. The asymmetric and symmetric areas contain 37 and 38 objects respectively. The removal of objects for both variants of areas and the subsequent use of the Parzen classifier has lowered the number of errors at test set to 7. The search of the optimum parameters' values of the Parzen classifier with application of the genetic algorithm has defined the number of neighbors equal to 33 at the Chebyshev's metrics and the Gaussian kernel function.

For the MOTP12 dataset the SVM classifier gives 32 and 1 errors at the training and test sets respectively. As this dataset has the difficult division into classes, the large number of the mistakenly classified objects lies out of the separating strip. In the case, when the mistakenly classified objects lie out of the dividing strip, the distance from the dividing strip to these objects is big than 1. In order to avoid the excess removal of objects, the decision on the exception only of objects in the strip is made. Therefore, the width of the symmetric and asymmetric area is equal to 2. In both cases the area includes 97 objects. The search of the optimum parameters' values of the Parzen classifier with application of the genetic algorithm has defined the number of neighbors equal to 5 at the Chebyshev's metrics and the Epanechnikov kernel function. The number of errors at the use of the offered classification technology equal to 26 and 2 at the training and test sets respectively.

7 Conclusions

By results of the conducted experimental researches, it is possible to draw a conclusion that the use of the offered technique increases the classification quality, as the application of the Parzen classifier to the objects located near the hyperplane dividing the classes and determined by the SVM classifier reduces the number of the mistakenly classified objects. The offered classification technique allows making the high-precision decisions on classification of the elaborate multidimensional data.

The use of the Parzen classifier as the auxiliary classifier instead of the *k*NN classifier can be justified by the fact that the *k*NN classifier uses the distance to the object to determine the nearest neighbors, but does not use this distance for making decisions on the class affiliation of the object. The definition of the weights functions as the dependence of the quantitative nearest neighbor number in some modifications of the *k*NN classifier is impractical, since it is not possible to evaluate the actual location of objects in the feature space. The Parzen classifier makes the decision on the class affiliation of object on the basis of the distance to the neighbor by means of the kernel function.

The purpose of further research is the adaptation of the genetic algorithm to realization of the simultaneous search for the best variant of the auxiliary classifier from the set of the potentially possible classifiers and the parameters values of the best auxiliary classifier.

The reported study was funded by RFBR according to the research project № 17-29-02198.

References

1. V. Vapnik, *Statistical Learning Theory* (New York: John Wiley & Sons, 1998)
2. O. Chapelle, V. Vapnik, O. Bousquet, S. Mukherjee, Machine Learning, **46**, 131 (2002)
3. L. Yu, S. Wang, K. K. Lai, L. Zhou, *Bio-Inspired Credit Risk Analysis. Computational Intelligence with Support Vector Machines* (Springer, 2008)
4. L. Demidova, Yu. Sokolova, *International Conference "Stability and Control Processes" in Memory of V.I. Zubov* (2015)
5. L. Demidova, E. Nikulchev, Y. Sokolova, International Journal of Advanced Computer Science and Applications, 7, 294 (2016)
6. H. Wang, D. Bell, The Computer Journal, **47**, 11 (2004)
7. R. Li, H.-N. Wang, H. He, Y.-M. Cui, Zh.-L. Du, Chinese Journal of Astronomy and Astrophysics, **7**, 7 (2007)
8. H. Zhang, A.C. Berg, M. Maire, J. Malik, *Computer Society Conference on Computer Vision and Pattern Recognition*, **2**, 11 (2006)
9. L. Demidova, Yu. Sokolova, *6-th Mediterranean Conference on Embedded Computing*, 4 (2017)
10. E. Parzen, *The Annals of Mathematical Statistics*, **33**, 12 (1962)

SVM prediction of the attestation success on the base of the poll results

Liliya Demidova [1, *], *Maksim* Egin [1] and *Yulia* Sokolova [1]

[1]Ryazan State Radio Engineering University, 390005 Ryazan, Russia

Abstract. The problem of the data analysis in the educational sphere in the context of prediction of the passing's success of the final state attestation by the graduates of the secondary school has been considered. Such data can be imbalanced substantially. To solve this problem it is offered to use the SVM classifiers on the base of the modified PSO algorithm, which allows choosing the kernel function type, the values of the kernel function parameters and the value of the regularization parameter simultaneously. In advance, the different rebalancing strategies, based on the basic SMOTE algorithm, can be applied for rebalance the classes in the experimental datasets. The prediction results with the use of the SVM classifiers on the base of the modified PSO algorithm and the different rebalancing strategies have been presented and compared with the prediction results received on the base of the most known software packages, such as Statistica StatSoft and IBM SPSS Modeler.

1 Introduction

In the data mining problems list, there is a special place for the classification problem, the solution of which is necessary, for example, in the credit scoring area, in the field of medical diagnostics, in the area of text categorization, for the face identification etc. A good solution to this problem is also in demand in the educational sphere. In recent years, high school students and pupils (graduates) of the secondary school are actively involved in various polls and tests, including the use of the widely approved methods to review their intellectual level, individual psychological characteristics, specialization profiling, etc.

For example, to estimate the first-year students, the motivational component diagnostics can be performed [1, 2]. The cognitive component can be inspected by R. Amthauer's intelligence test [3], which allows evaluating the verbal, mathematical and spatial intelligence. Besides, the personality component diagnostics can be performed by means of the five-factor personal questionnaire, which allows evaluating the expression degrees of personal qualities on the base of five factors (introversion – extroversion, emotion stability – neuroticism, non-perception of new information – perception, non-concentration – consciousness, hostility – goodwill) [4]. Also, the problem of diagnostics of the graduates' readiness to pass the final state attestation is very relevant. To solve this problem, in particular, it is necessary to analyze the data which consolidates information on individual self-reviewing, as well as information on immediate environment and the habitat comfort. This problem can be solved as the prediction problem whether the result of the final state attestation will be high-scoring. Obviously, the results of polls and tests accumulated in large amount can be used to extract the additional hidden information, in particular, to identify the certain cause-effect relationships and interrelations in the context of the graduates' personal diagnostics and to develop the classifiers.

Nowadays, the various algorithmic tools are used to solve the problems which require to make the data analysis. The most famous algorithmic tools are the following: linear and logistic regressions, Bayesian classifier, decision trees, decision rules, neural networks, the nearest *k*-neighbors algorithm (*k*-Nearest Neighbors Algorithm), support vector machine algorithm (SVM algorithm), and so on. A herewith, from the point of view of the presented possibilities and the undeniable advantages declared in the works of the scientific community, in the context of solving the data analysis problems in the educational sphere, the most promising is the use of the SVM algorithm. It is suggested to use the SVM classifiers on the base of the modified PSO algorithm, adapted to specifics of the problem of the data analysis in the educational sphere.

The SVM algorithm is successfully used for the SVM classifiers development [5]. The SVM classifier uses the kernel function to construct a hyperplane separating the classes of data. The satisfactory quality of training and testing of the SVM classifier allows using this SVM classifier in the classification of new objects. Choosing the optimal parameters values for the SVM classifier is a relevant problem. A herewith, it is necessary to find the kernel function type, the values of the kernel function parameters and the value of the regularization parameter [5, 6]. It is impossible to provide implementing of high-accuracy data classification with the use of the SVM classifier without adequate solution to this problem. In the simplest case solution to this problem can be found by a search of the kernel function types, the values of the kernel function parameters and the value of the

* Corresponding author: demidova.liliya@gmail.com

regularization parameter that demands significant computational expenses. The gradient methods are not suitable for search of the optimum of this problem, but the stochastic optimization algorithms, such as the genetic algorithm (GA), the artificial bee colony algorithm (ABC algorithm), the particle swarm algorithm (PSO algorithm), etc., have been used.

The PSO algorithm is the simplest stochastic optimization algorithm. The traditional approach to application of the PSO algorithm for the SVM classifier development consists of the repeated applications of this algorithm for the fixed type of the kernel function to choose the optimal values of the kernel function parameters and the value of the regularization parameter with the subsequent choice of their best combination for the best kernel function type. It is suggested to use the modified PSO algorithm to find the kernel function type, the values of the kernel function parameters and the value of the regularization parameter of the SVM classifier simultaneously.

The poll results, which are applied to form the datasets for training and testing of the SVM classifier can be imbalanced substantially. It can significantly worsen the quality of the developed SVM classifier and lower the values of its quality indicators.

Currently, the different rebalancing strategies are applied to solve the problem of the imbalance datasets. It is suggested to use the synthetic sampling algorithm called as the SMOTE (Synthetic Minority Oversampling Technique) to restore the balance between the classes. In particular, it is planned to investigate the opportunities of such variations of this algorithm, as "regular", "borderline1", "borderline2" and "SVM".

It should be noted the existence of implementations of the SVM algorithm in various software packages, for example, in Statistica StatSoft and IBM SPSS Modeler. A herewith, IBM SPSS Modeler has some implementations of the SMOTE algorithm. However, all these implementations are not sufficiently flexible and do not allow changing all of their parameters as it is necessary for the developer.

Therefore, the problem of the SVM classifiers development on the base of the modified PSO algorithm and the different rebalancing strategies in the context of prediction of the passing's success of the final state attestation by the graduates of the secondary school is very relevant.

2 Theoretical part

Let the experimental data set be a set in the form of $\{(z_1,y_1),\ldots,(z_S,y_S)\}$, in which each object $z_i \in Z$ ($i=\overline{1,s}$; s is the number of objects) is assigned to a number $y_i \in Y=\{+1;\,-1\}$ having a value of $+1$ or -1 depending on the class of the object z_i. It is assumed that every object z_i is mapped to q-dimensional vector of numerical values of features $z_i=(z_i^1,z_i^2,\ldots,z_i^q)$, where z_i^l is the numeric value of the l-th feature for the i-th object ($i=\overline{1,s}$, $l=\overline{1,q}$) [5 – 7]. In training of the SVM classifier it is necessary to determine the kernel function type $\kappa(z_i,z_\tau)$, the values of the kernel parameters and the value of the regularization parameter C [5 – 7]. One of the following functions is used as the kernel function $\kappa(z_i,z_\tau)$: linear function; polynomial function; radial basis function; sigmoid function [5 – 7].

To build "the best" SVM classifier it is necessary to implement the numerous repeated training (for the training data set with S elements) and testing (for the test data set $s-S$ elements, $S<s$) on the different randomly generated training and test sets with following determination of the best SVM classifier in terms of the highest possible classification quality provision [6 – 8]. The quality of the SVM classifier can be measured, for example, by the overall accuracy indicator [9 – 11].

The classification function is determined in the form:

$$f(z)=\sum_{i=1}^{S}\lambda_i\cdot y_i\cdot\kappa(z_i,z)+b\,. \qquad (1)$$

The classification decision is adopted in accordance with the rule [5]:

$$F(z)=sign(f(z))=sign(\sum_{i=1}^{S}\lambda_i\cdot y_i\cdot\kappa(z_i,z)+b)\,. \qquad (2)$$

The training of the SVM classifier results in determining the support vectors [5].

2.1 The modified PSO algorithm

Using the modified PSO algorithm provides the better classification accuracy by choosing the kernel function type, the values of the kernel function parameters and the value of the regularization parameter. Also, the modified PSO algorithm allows reducing the time expenditures for development of the SVM classifier [7].

In the traditional PSO algorithm the n-dimensional search space is inhabited by a swarm of a particles. The position of the i-th particle is determined by vector $x_i=(x_i^1,x_i^2,\ldots,x_i^n)$. Each i-th particle ($i=\overline{1,a}$) has its own vector of speed $v_i \in R^n$ which influence i-th particle coordinates' values. The coordinates of the i-th particle in the n-dimensional search space uniquely determine the value of the objective function $u(x)$ which is a certain solution of the optimization problem. For each position of the n-dimensional search space where the i-th particle was placed, the calculation of value of the objective function $u(x_i)$ is performed. Each i-th particle remembers the best value of the objective function found personally as well as the coordinates of the position in the n-dimensional space corresponding to the value of the objective function. Each i-th particle "knows" the best position among all positions that had been "explored" by particles. After a number of iterations particles must come close to the best position.

In the classical version of the PSO algorithm correction of each j-th coordinate of the velocity vector

($j=\overline{1,n}$) of the i-th particle is made in accordance with formula [9, 10]:

$$v_i^j = v_i^j + \hat{\varphi}\cdot\hat{r}\cdot(\hat{x}_i^j - x_i^j) + \tilde{\varphi}\cdot\tilde{r}\cdot(\tilde{x}^j - x_i^j), \quad (3)$$

where v_i^j is the j-th coordinate of the velocity vector of the i-th particle; x_i^j is the j-th coordinate of vector x_i, defining the position of the i-th particle; $\hat{x}_i^j$ is the j-th coordinate of the best position vector found by the i-th particle; $\tilde{x}^j$ is the j-th coordinate of the globally best position within the swarm in which the objective function has the optimal value; $\hat{r}$ and $\tilde{r}$ are random numbers in (0, 1); $\hat{\varphi}$ and $\tilde{\varphi}$ are personal and global coefficients for particle acceleration.

The correction of each j-th coordinate of the velocity vector of the i-th particle is performed in accordance with formula [9]:

$$v_i^j = \chi\cdot[v_i^j + \hat{\varphi}\cdot\hat{r}\cdot(\hat{x}_i^j - x_i^j) + \tilde{\varphi}\cdot\tilde{r}\cdot(\tilde{x}^j - x_i^j)], \quad (4)$$

where χ is a compression ratio;

$$\chi = 2\cdot K / \left|2-\varphi-\sqrt{\varphi^2-4\cdot\varphi}\right|; \quad (5)$$

$$\varphi = \hat{\varphi}+\tilde{\varphi} \ (\varphi > 4); \quad (6)$$

K is some scaling coefficient ($K\in(0, 1)$).

The correction of the j-th coordinate of the i-th particle can be executed in accordance with the formula:

$$x_i^j = x_i^j + v_i^j. \quad (7)$$

For each i-th particle the new value of the objective function $u(x_i)$ can be calculated and the following check must be performed: whether a new position with coordinates vector x_i became the best among all positions in which the i-th particle has previously been placed. If new position of the i-th particle is recognized to be the best at the current moment the information about it must be stored in a vector $\hat{x}_i$. The value of the objective function $u(x_i)$ for this position must be remembered. Then among all new positions of the swarm particles the check of the globally best position must be carried out. If some new position is recognized as the best globally at the current moment, the information about it must be stored in vector $\tilde{x}$. Value of the objective function $u(x_i)$ for this position must be remembered.

There is a new approach to the use of the PSO algorithm that implements a simultaneous search for the best kernel function type $\tilde{T}$, the parameters' values $\tilde{x}^1$ and $\tilde{x}^2$ of the kernel function and the value of the regularization parameter $\tilde{C}$. In this case each i-th particle defined by a vector which describes particle's position in the space: (T_i, x_i^1, x_i^2, C_i), where T_i is the number of the kernel function type; the parameters x_i^1, x_i^2, C_i are the parameters of the kernel function and the regularization parameter [10]. It is possible to "regenerate" particle through changing its coordinate T_i on number of that kernel function type, for which particles show the highest quality of classification. In the case of particles' "regeneration" the parameters' values change so that they corresponded to the new type of the kernel function. Particles which didn't undergo "regeneration", carry out the movement in own space of search of some dimension. The number of particles taking part in "regeneration" must be determined before start of algorithm. The modified PSO algorithm can be presented by the following consequence of steps.

Step 1. To determine parameters of the PSO algorithm: number m of particles in a swamp, velocity coefficient K, personal and global velocity coefficients $\hat{\varphi}$ and $\tilde{\varphi}$, maximum iterations number N_{max} of the PSO algorithm. To determine types T of the kernel functions, which take part in the search and ranges boundaries of the kernel function parameters and the regularization parameter C for the chosen kernel functions' types T: x_{min}^{1T}, x_{max}^{1T}, x_{min}^{2T}, x_{max}^{2T}, C_{min}^{T}, C_{max}^{T} ($x_{min}^{2T}=0$ and $x_{max}^{2T}=0$ for $T=1$ and $T=2$). To determine the particles' "regeneration" percentage p.

Step 2. To define equal number of particles for each kernel type function T, included in search, to initialize coordinate T_i for each i-th particle, other coordinates of the i-th particle must be generated randomly from the corresponding ranges: $x_i^1\in[x_{min}^{1T}, x_{max}^{1T}]$, $x_i^2\in[x_{min}^{2T}, x_{max}^{2T}]$ ($x_i^2=0$ under $T=1$ and $T=2$), $C_i\in[C_{min}^{T}, C_{max}^{T}]$. To initialize random velocity vector $v_i(v_i^1, v_i^2, v_i^3)$ of the i-th particle ($v_i^2=0$ under $T=1$ and $T=2$). To establish initial position of the i-th particle as its best known position $(\hat{T}_i, \hat{x}_i^1, \hat{x}_i^2, \hat{C}_i)$, to determine the best particle with coordinates' vector $(\tilde{T}, \tilde{x}^1, \tilde{x}^2, \tilde{C})$ from all the a particles, and to determine the best particle for each kernel function type T, including in a search, with coordinates' vector $(\tilde{T}, \tilde{x}^{1T}, \tilde{x}^{2T}, \tilde{C}^{T})$. Number of executed iterations must be considered as 1.

Step 3. To execute while the number of iterations is less than the fixed number N_{max}: "regeneration" of particles: to choose $p\%$ of particles which represent the lowest quality of classification from particles with coordinate $T_i \neq \tilde{T}$; to change coordinate on $\tilde{T}$; to change values of the parameters x_i^1, x_i^2, C_i of "regenerated" particles to let them correspond to a new kernel function type $\tilde{T}$; correction of the velocity vector v_i and position (x_i^1, x_i^2, C_i) of the i-th particle using formulas:

$$v_i^j = \begin{cases} \chi\cdot[v_i^j + \hat{\varphi}\cdot\hat{r}\cdot(\hat{x}_i^j - x_i^j) + \tilde{\varphi}\cdot\tilde{r}\cdot(\tilde{x}^{jT} - x_i^j)], & j=1,\ 2, \\ \chi\cdot[v_i^j + \hat{\varphi}\cdot\hat{r}\cdot(\hat{C}_i - C_i) + \tilde{\varphi}\cdot\tilde{r}\cdot(\tilde{C}^T - C_i)], & j=3, \end{cases} \quad (8)$$

$$x_i^j = x_i^j + v_i^j \text{ for } j=1,\ 2;\ C_i = C_i + v_i^3,$$

where $\hat{r}$ and $\tilde{r}$ are random numbers in (0, 1), χ is a compression ratio; accuracy calculation of the SVM classifier with parameters' values (T_i, x_i^1, x_i^2, C_i) with aim to find the optimal combination $(\tilde{T}, \tilde{x}^1, \tilde{x}^2, \tilde{C})$, which will provide high quality of classification; increase the number of iterations on 1.

The particle with the optimal combination of the parameters' values $(\widetilde{T},\widetilde{x}^1,\widetilde{x}^2,\widetilde{C})$ will be defined after execution of the offered algorithm.

2.2 The SMOTE algorithm and its variations

The dataset is imbalanced if the classes are not approximately equally represented. The SMOTE technique is an important approach by oversampling the minority class. The SMOTE algorithm [12] creates the artificial objects of the minority class based on the similarities in the feature space between the existing objects using the *k*-nearest neighbor algorithm (*k*NN algorithm). The artificial objects which are "similar" to the objects of the existing minority class, do not duplicate them. Nowadays, the following variations of the SMOTE algorithm are most known: "regular" [12], "borderline1" [13], "borderline2" [13] and "SVM" [14].

The "regular" SMOTE algorithm is the basic [12]. The "borderline1", "borderline2" and "SVM" variations of the SMOTE algorithm look for objects that could be considered noise and objects that live near the boundary between the classes. Therefore, before creating synthetic objects using the *k* neighbors in the kNN algorithm, they look for *m* nearest neighbors to decide whether or not an object is noise or near the boundary.

The "borderline1" and "borderline2" variations of the SMOTE algorithm generate synthetic objects, but only to objects that are near the border between different classes. These variations look for objects "in danger" [13]. In the "borderline1" variation initially *m* nearest neighbours for every object in the minority class are found. Minority objects that are completely surrounded by majority objects, i.e.: all *m* nearest neighbours belong to the majority class, are considered to be noise and left out of the process. Objects with at most *m*/2 NNs from the majority class are considered to be safe, and also left out of the process. Objects for which the number of NNs from the majority class is greater than *m*/2 are considered in danger (near the borderline) and used to generate synthetic objects. New minority objects are generated along the lines connecting minority objects only to their nearest minority neighbours. The "borderline2" variation is similar to the "borderline1" one. What differs the "borderline2" variation from the "borderline1" one is that synthetic objects are created both from nearest minority neighbours as well as nearest majority neighbours. However, synthetic objects created from majority neighbours are created closer to the minority objects then when created from minority neighbours. "SVM" variation of the SMOTE algorithm fits a support vector machine classifier to the data and uses the support vector to provide a notion of boundary [14]. In the "regular" variation of the SMOTE algorithm such notion relies on proportion of nearest neighbours belonging to each class. The "regular" variation of the SMOTE algorithm does not look for objects in danger, instead it creates synthetic objects directly from the k-th nearest neighbours with not filtering.

3 Experimental studies

The synthesized poll results of 546 graduates of the secondary school before passing the unified state examination (USE) and their test marks in USE on "Russian language" and "Mathematics" disciplines were used to develop the SVM classifiers on the base of software packages, such as Statistica StatSoft [15] and IBM SPSS Modeler [16], and the author's program "Intellectual Classification" (IC).

The sections of the questionnaire can be divided into 3 groups: the general questions (the questions concerning the pupil's plans after passing the exam; questions about what the pupil considers important for admission; the questions allowing to estimate the pupil's relation to the to the subjects being passed; the questions allowing to estimate the relationship of the pupil with the surrounding people, financial position of family); the questions connected with "Russian language" discipline; the questions connected with "Mathematics" discipline.

The USE system means the translation of the primary scores of exam into the test ones which are exposed according to the hundred-score scale as a result of the scaling procedure considering all statistical materials received within the USE of this year. Scaling allows to compare and estimate the level of the pupils' readiness. The results for admission to educational institutions of the secondary vocational and higher education are provided in the test scores. "Russian language" and "Mathematics" disciplines are obligatory to delivery for obtaining the certificate about the secondary education. A herewith, the minimum thresholds specified in the scores and determined in advance must be overcome. Taking into account the mentioned above, the data preparation for the training dataset on the base of the poll results of the pupils consists in performance of the following steps: the choice of discipline and installation of the threshold of division into classes in the form of test score of the USE; the formation of the characteristics' vector for each object (pupil) on the base of his poll's results in the context of the chosen discipline.

For "Russian language" and "Mathematics" disciplines two training datasets of the identical power (with 546 objects) have been created. But these datasets have the different number of characteristics: 133 characteristics for "Russian" discipline and 141 characteristics for "Mathematics" discipline that is explained by the different number of questions having direct or indirect relation to the corresponding discipline. The synthesized poll results of 546 graduates of the secondary school before passing the unified state examination (USE) and their test marks in USE on "Russian language" and "Mathematics" disciplines were used to develop the SVM classifiers on the base of software packages, such as Statistica StatSoft [15] and IBM SPSS Modeler [16], and the author's program "Intellectual Classification" (IC).

Table 1. The results of the SVM classifiers development.

Dataset $s \times q$	Building environment otf the SVM classifier	Number of objects in the Train and Test sets (Train/Test)	Kernel function parameters		Number of support vectors	Accuracy			1-st class (class with label "+")			2-nd class (class with label "–")		
			C	σ		Train	Test	Overall	Real number of objects in the class	Number of errors	Percent from the number of objects in the class	Real number of objects in the class	Number of errors	Percent from the number of objects in the class
Rus_80 546×133	*STATISTICA*	436/110	1	0.008	102	94.954	93.636	94.689	29	29	100	517	0	0
	SPSS Modeler	436/110	10	0.1	–	100	94.55	98.90		6	20.69		0	0
	IC	437/109	9.88	7.03	217	100	99.08	99.82		1	3.45		0	0
Rus_SVM 814×133	*STATISTICA*	651/163	5	0.008	211	98.310	93.252	97.297	297	4	1.35	517	18	3.48
	SPSS Modeler	649/165	10	0.1	–	100	100	100		0	0		0	0
	IC	652/162	8.86	8.16	166	100	100	100		0	0		0	0
RUS_ regular 1034×133	*STATISTICA*	827/207	8	0.008	215	98.791	96.618	98.356	517	0	0	517	17	3.29
	SPSS Modeler	826/208	10	0.1	–	100	100	100		0	0		0	0
	IC	828/206	3.49	5.75	269	100	100	100		0	0		0	0
Rus_ borderline1 1034×133	*STATISTICA*	827/207	9	0.008	183	98.670	96.135	98.162	517	4	0.77	517	15	2.901
	SPSS Modeler	826/208	10	0.1	–	100	100	100		0	0		0	0
	IC	828/206	7.35	9.11	152	100	99.51	99.9		1	0.19		0	0
Rus_ borderline2 1033×133	*STATISTICA*	826/207	10	0.008	225	98.668	96.135	98.161	516	4	0.78	517	15	2.90
	SPSS Modeler	825/208	10	0.1	–	100	100	100		0	0		0	0
	IC	827/206	9.59	8.68	185	100	99.51	99.90		1	0.19		0	0
Math_70 546×141	*STATISTICA*	436/110	7	0.007	91	95.560	92.727	95.788	38	22	57.89	508	1	0.20
	SPSS Modeler	436/110	10	0.1	–	99.77	100	99.82		1	2.63		0	0
	IC	437/109	5.38	8.20	176	100	97.25	99.45		1	2.63		2	0.39
Math_SVM 1016×141	*STATISTICA*	812/204	5	0.007	182	98.030	95.098	97.441	508	4	0.79	508	22	4.33
	SPSS Modeler	812/204	10	0.1	–	99.88	99.51	99.8		1	0.20		1	0.20
	IC	813/203	7.22	7.90	202	100	99.51	99.9		1	0.20		0	0
Math_ regular 1016×141	*STATISTICA*	812/204	5	0.007	178	98.645	96.078	98.13	508	3	0.59	508	16	3.15
	SPSS Modeler	812/204	10	0.1	–	99.88	100	99.9		0	0		1	0.20
	IC	813/203	6.73	7.96	174	100	100	100		0	0		0	0
Math_ borderline1 1016×141	*STATISTICA*	812/204	7	0.007	149	99.138	96.078	98.524	508	2	0.39	508	13	2.56
	SPSS Modeler	812/204	10	0.1	–	99.88	100	99.9		0	0		1	0.20
	IC	813/203	9.28	9.95	144	100	99.51	99.9		1	0.20		0	0
Math_ borderline2 1016×141	*STATISTICA*	812/204	10	0.007	182	99.138	96.078	98.524	508	4	0.79	508	11	2.17
	SPSS Modeler	812/204	10	0.1	–	99.88	99.51	99.8		1	0.20		1	0.20
	IC	813/203	8.85	6.52	279	100	100	100		0	0		0	0

The sections of the questionnaire can be divided into 3 groups: the general questions (the questions concerning the pupil's plans after passing the exam; questions about what the pupil considers important for admission; the questions allowing to estimate the pupil's relation to the to the subjects being passed; the questions allowing to estimate the relationship of the pupil with the surrounding people, financial position of family); the questions connected with "Russian language" discipline; the questions connected with "Mathematics" discipline.

The USE system means the translation of the primary scores of exam into the test ones which are exposed according to the hundred-score scale as a result of the scaling procedure considering all statistical materials received within the USE of this year. Scaling allows to compare and estimate the level of the pupils' readiness. The results for admission to educational institutions of the secondary vocational and higher education are provided in the test scores. "Russian language" and "Mathematics" disciplines are obligatory to delivery for obtaining the certificate about the secondary education. A herewith, the minimum thresholds specified in the scores and determined in advance must be overcome. Taking into account the mentioned above, the data preparation for the training dataset on the base of the poll results of the pupils consists in performance of the following steps: the choice of discipline and installation of the threshold of division into classes in the form of test score of the USE; the formation of the characteristics' vector for each object (pupil) on the base of his poll's results in the context of the chosen discipline.

For "Russian language" and "Mathematics" disciplines two training datasets of the identical power (with 546 objects) have been created. But these datasets have the different number of characteristics: 133 characteristics for "Russian" discipline and 141 characteristics for "Mathematics" discipline that is explained by the different number of questions having direct or indirect relation to the corresponding discipline.

It was experimentally established that it is expedient to establish the threshold division of classes equals to 80 scores for "Russian language" discipline and 70 scores for "Mathematics" discipline (although it is considered that the work is high-scoring, if it had more than 80 scores). The establishment of such threshold values in the made experiments can be explained with the limited size of the polls' results and the traditionally lower scores on "Mathematics" discipline (and, as a result, lack of the sufficient number of the high-scoring works).

However, at the chosen variants of the objects (pupils) division into the classes with labels "+1" and "–1" the classes are imbalanced, that is the number of objects of one class (the majority class with label "–1") considerably exceeds the number of objects of the second class (the minority class with label "+1") ("Rus_80" and "Math_70" datasets in Table 1). For example, the minority class with label "+1" in "Rus_80" dataset describe pupils with the scores equal or greater than 80. In this regard, the decision on the use of the SMOTE algorithm variations for the purpose of the imbalance decrease has been made [13]. For example, "Rus_SVM", "RUS_regular", "Rus_borderline1" and "Rus_borderline2" datasets were obtained from the "Rus_80" dataset with the use of the "SVM", "regular", "borderline1" and "borderline2" (with k=5 and m=10) variations of the SMOTE algorithm respectively. As a result, the imbalance of classes was reduced (Table 1).

Then, the experiments on the SVM classifier development were fulfilled with the use of the software packages, such as Statistica StatSoft and IBM SPSS Modeler, and the author's program IC. For all datasets the size of the test set was equal to 20% of the size of the experimental dataset. Table 1 shows the accuracy for the train and test sets, the number of objects in the train and test sets, and the overall accuracy. A herewith, the polynomial kernel function and the radial basis one were used. In all cases the radial basis kernel function showed the best result in the context of ensuring high-quality classification. These results are shown in Tabl. 1. It can be seen that, in the absence of rebalancing, in Statistica StatSoft all objects (i.e. 29 objects) of the minority class of the "Rus_80" dataset and the significant part of the objects (22 objects from 38) of the minority class of the "Math_70" dataset was classified erroneously. For the "Rus_80" dataset we received 100% and 0% of errors in the classes with labels "+1" and "–1" respectively, for the "Math_70" dataset we received 57.89% and 0.20% of errors in the classes with labels "+1" and "–1" respectively, though the overall accuracy of classification is high (94.689 % and 95.788 % respectively). Application of IBM SPSS Modeler to these datasets allow improving the overall accuracy. The program "Intellectual Classification" has a little better fulfilled. But in all cases almost all errors were in the minority class, therefore, the SVM classifier developed on the base of imbalanced dataset, will give incorrect forecasts for new objects of this class (with high-scores' works).

In Statistica StatSoft package the parameters of the kernel function (the radial basis kernel function and the polynomial one) were selected in accordance with the default settings and the value of the regularization parameter was determined using the sliding control procedure. The σ parameter of the radial basis kernel function by default is chosen according to the size of the dataset (the larger the dataset, the smaller the σ). The best results of the SVM classifier development were obtained for the "Rus_regular" dataset for "Russian language" discipline (0.78% and 3.29% errors in the classes) and for the "Math_borderline1" dataset for "Mathematics" discipline (0.39% and 2.56% error in the classes) using the radial basis kernel function. In the IBM SPSS Modeler package there are no means for selecting the parameters of the SVM classifier, which provides the maximum classification accuracy, so the development of the SVM classifier with the radial basic kernel function and the polynomial one was performed using the parameters defined by default. For example, for the radial basic kernel function these default settings are the following: C=10 and σ=0.1. Also, it is impossible to estimate the number of support vectors. The best results of the SVM classifier development were obtained with the use of the radial basic kernel function. For all synthesized datasets for "Russian language" discipline the classification accuracy was equal to 100%. For "Mathematics" discipline the best results were obtained for "Math_regular" and "Math_borderline1" datasets (0 % and 0.20% errors in the classes).

The author's program IC contains the module of the search of the optimal parameters of the SVM classifier using the modified PSO algorithm. This program allows developing the SVM classifiers with the minimum number of errors for the initial imbalanced experimental datasets (1 error for the "Rus_80" dataset and 3 errors for "Math_70" dataset), and reducing to zero the number of errors for "Rus_SVM", "Rus_regular", "Math_regular" and "Math_borderline2" datasets.

4 Conclusions

The use of the SVM classifiers on the base of the modified PSO algorithm and the different rebalancing strategies in the context of prediction of the passing's success of the final state attestation by the graduates of the secondary school allows providing the high classification accuracy. The results of experimental studies confirm the expediency of further development of the offered approach to the SVM classifier development. A herewith, it is planned to use the SVM algorithm for the regression model development, that will allow forecasting the attestation's results in scores.

The reported study was funded by RFBR according to the research project № 17-29-02198.

References

1. J.W. Atkinson, American Psychologist, 36, 117-128
2. P.R. ZelickNova (eds) *Issues in the Psychology of Motivation*. (Science Publishers, Inc., 2007)
3. B. Weiss, V.C. Laties (eds) *Behavioral Toxicology*. (Springer, 1975)
4. Hege H. Bye, Gro M. Sandal, Journal of Business and Psychology, **31**, 569-582 (2016)

5. O. Chapelle, V. Vapnik, O. Bousquet, S. Mukherjee, Machine Learning, **46**, 131 (2002)
6. L. Yu, S. Wang, K. K. Lai, L. Zhou, *Bio-Inspired Credit Risk Analysis. Computational Intelligence with Support Vector Machines* (Springer, 2008)
7. L. Demidova, Yu. Sokolova, E. Nikulchev, International Review on Modelling and Simulations, **8**, 446 (2015)
8. L. Demidova, Y. Sokolova, Modification of particle swarm algorithm for the problem of the SVM classifier development, In *International Conference "Stability and Control Processes" in Memory of V.I. Zubov*, pp. 623-627 (2015)
9. L. Demidova, E. Nikulchev, Y. Sokolova, International Journal of Advanced Computer Science and Applications, **7**, 294 (2016)
10. L. Demidova, Y. Sokolova, ITM Web of Conferences, **6** 02003 (2016)
11. L. Demidova, I. Klyueva, Y.Sokolova, N. Stepanov, N. Tyart, Procedia Computer Science, **103**, 222 (2017)
12. N. Chawla, K. Bowyer, L. Hall, W. Kegelmeyer, JAIR, **16**, 341 (2002)
13. H. Han, W. Wen-Yuan, M. Bing-Huan, Advances in intelligent computing, 878-887, (2005)
14. H.M. Nguyen, E.W. Cooper, K. Kamei, Int. J. of Knowledge Engineering and Soft Data Paradigms, **3**, 4 (2001)
15. http://documentation.statsoft.com/STATISTICAHelp.aspx?path=MachineLearning/MachineLearning/SupportVectorMachine/SupportVectorMachineExample1Classification
16. https://www.ibm.com/support/knowledgecenter/SS3RA7_18.1.0/modeler_tutorial_ddita/clementine/example_svm_intro.html

Data traffic filtration of automated non-destructive testing based on an artificial neural network

Alisa Kosach[1,*], and *Evgeny* Kovshov[1]

[1]JSC «NIKIMT-Atomstroy», Moscow, Russian Federation

Abstract. The principle of constructing a universal software and hardware platform for the collection, processing and storage of data obtained as a result of non-destructive testing of products is considered. The platform also includes a neural network module for filtering data traffic, which has a wide potential for application: from image and multidimensional signal processing to data classification. The system of remote leakage control, built on the basis of a universal digital platform with artificial neural network, is described.

1 Introduction

Modern industrial enterprises are striving for a full-scale transition to digital production with the ubiquitous use of the industrial Internet of things and the management of the life cycle of products. Creation of flexible production systems, in particular, systems of non-destructive testing allows to significantly reducing the influence of the human factor on the results of control, to increase the reliability of the system and to ensure the accuracy of analysis of large unstructured data.

According to [1] all the problems solved by man from the standpoint of neuroinformation technologies can be conditionally classified into two large groups. The first group contains problems that have a known and definite set of conditions, on the basis of which it is necessary to obtain a clear, accurate, unambiguous answer on the known and definite algorithm. The second group includes tasks where it is not possible to take into account all the actual conditions on which the answer depends, but only an approximate set of the most important conditions can be identified. Since some of the conditions are not taken into account, the answer is inaccurate, approximate, and the algorithm for finding the answer can not be written accurately.

In solving the problems of the first group, you can use traditional application software based on an algorithm with a limited set of parameters that allows you to solve the problem.

To solve the problems of the second group, the use of neurotechnologies justifies itself in all respects, under the following conditions: first, the presence of a universal type of architecture and a single universal learning algorithm (no need to develop them for each type of tasks) and secondly, the presence of examples (training samples), on the basis of which neural networks are trained.

Currently, there is a wide range of the most popular among mathematicians and programmers of neural networks such as: multilayer perceptron, Kohonen self-organizing maps, recurrent neural networks, convolutional neural network. All of them have their own distinctive features in topology, activation functions and methods of training, and of course in the mechanisms of software implementation. However, the limitation of the development of neural network algorithms is the high computational cost of their computer implementation. For the successful solution of this problem is used the organization of parallel (e.g. CUDA - Compute Unified Device Architecture) and distributed computing (e.g. SOA - Service-Oriented Architecture), in particular, on specialized hardware.

This article discusses a hardware and software platform consisting of a set of web services and hardware solutions for managing devices, collecting, processing and storing data. Software and hardware solutions based on artificial neural networks of various architectures and topologies are an important and universal part of the above mentioned platform, which can be used in the development of various automated industrial systems for most types of non-destructive testing, in particular, control, where the data is used in digital form: ultrasonic, radiographic and leakage testing.

2 Firmware

2.1. Architecture

The proposed intellectual platform is based on the service-oriented architecture of software solutions [2]. Due to its philosophy, SOA - is a modular approach to the development of application software, based on the use of distributed, loosely coupled standardized services. Services implement various application solutions and can be reused and combined.

When developing any information systems, modularity facilitates the software scaling and enables

* Corresponding author: KosachAA@atomrus.ru

the best use of the information system functions, while some services are still in development. With the growth of volumes of data and calculations, the construction of information systems based on SOA becomes the most preferable. In addition, SOA allows the use of external services and web services (for example, located in a private or public cloud).

2.2 Practical application

A model of an intelligent platform for an automated leakage control system was developed and tested with a mass-spectrometric method. The model included the collection and processing of data from technological devices of the lower level, the analysis of product validity and the automatic formation of technological documentation [3].

The intelligent platform is built on the basis of a service-oriented architecture, which makes it flexible and easily scalable, allows you to use virtual resources for calculations and storage of various information. To store the data received in the process of monitoring, DBMS with open source code PostgreSQL was used. The use of predefined software technologies [4] allows analysing and filtering data in the main software tools of e.g. Microsoft Office or its open source analogue. The automated control system for leakage control was developed in the open integrated programming environment NetBeans with using a pair of Java/C++ programming languages.

The application of the above solutions, based on automation of control and evaluation of the product's usefulness, allows shortening the time of the control. Due to the data storage in the DBMS, it is possible at any time to visualize the obtained dependencies and re-evaluate. The automation of the leakage control procedure excludes the influence of the human factor and increases the safety of the personnel involved.

3 Neural network

Tasks related to non-destructive testing almost always have several solutions and very often the so called "fuzzy" nature of the answer coincides with the way the result is issued by neural networks. In this regard, neural networks are used for classification in the field of computer diagnostics under non-destructive testing. Generation of optimal (adequate to solve the problem) neural network includes a sequence of main steps: the choice of the topology of the network, the choice of the activation function of the neurons of the hidden layer, the choice of the method of training and, in fact, network training.

To treat the data obtained in the process of leak testing, a neural network module was developed that performs the functions of normalization and data purification. The neuronet has the following topology (fig. 1): input neurons (the number varies depending on the data type), two hidden layers of two neurons and one bias neuron, output neuron that outputs the result of data classification (1 – "true" data, 0 – "false" data). The neural network is trained on the basis of a test sample using the algorithm for back propagation of the error [5]. Try to ensure that lines are no thinner than 0.25 point.

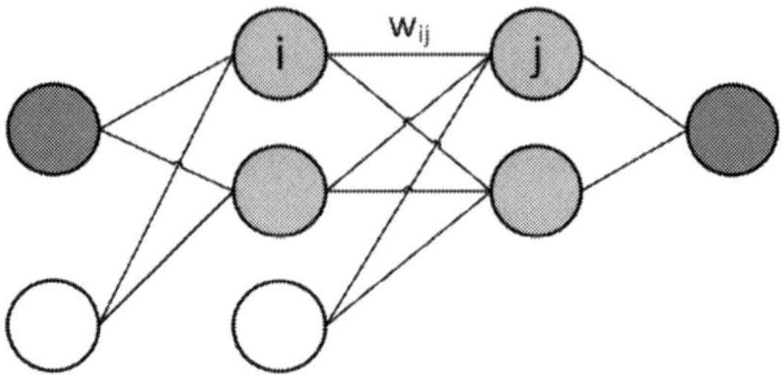

Fig. 1. Topology of the neuronet.

The bias neurons were placed in the neural network to shift the activation function of the neuron and, accordingly, to reduce the number of epochs required for its training. It should be noted that with an increase in the number of neurons in the hidden layers of the network, their weight connections in the learning process tend to zero, and additional neurons are redundant. Thus, to solve this problem of data traffic filtering, the topology of a neural network of this kind is the most appropriate.

When it teaching, the task is to minimize the error function:

$$E = \frac{1}{2}\sum_{j=1}^{k}(y_j - t_j)^2 \quad (1)$$

where y_j is the real value j of the network output; t_j is the desired value j of the network output; k is the number of outputs of the network. The minimum of the error function is determined by the stochastic gradient descent method. The activation function is:

$$f(x_j) = \frac{1}{1+e^{-x_j}} \quad (2)$$

where x is the weighted sum at the input of the neuron:

$$x_j = \sum_{i=1}^{k} w_{ij} y_i \quad (3)$$

where w_{ij} are the weights of the connection between and neurons; y_i is the output of the previous layer neuron i.

At the beginning of training, the weights of the neuronal connections are initiated randomly in the interval [-0.1; 0,1]. Next, a training sample with known values at the outputs arrives at the neural network. For each sampling vector, the error value is calculated and an adjustment is made to the weights of the neuron connections according to the formulas:

$$w_{ij} = w_{ij-1} + \Delta w_{ij} \quad (4)$$

where w_{ij-1} is the weight of the connection between i and j neurons.

$$\Delta w_{ij} = -\eta \delta_j y_i + \mu \Delta w_{ij-1} \quad (5)$$

where δ_j is the error of the neuron in the layer j; Δw_{ij-1} is the correction to the weight of the neuron connections made for the previous operation.

$$\delta_j = f'(x_j)\sum_{n=1}^{k}\delta_n w_{jn} \quad (6)$$

$$\delta_{out} = f'(x_{out})(t_{out} - y_{out}) \quad (7)$$

where δ_n is the error of the neuron in layer n; n is the layer of neurons that stands after layer j; out is the layer of output neurons.

The coefficients η and μ are introduced to control the training speed and the successful passage of the local minimum of the error function, respectively.

The main idea of this method is to spread the error signals from the outputs of the network to its inputs, that is, in the direction opposite to the direct propagation of signals in the normal mode of operation. After the repeated passage of the training sample (about 5000 epochs), the neural network is ready to process and clean incoming data.

Neural networks can be effectively applied in digital platform not only for data classification, but also for multidimensional digital signal recognition and image processing.

With the increase in the number of neurons, the size of the training sample and the complexity of the NDT tasks (for example, for image and sound recognition and processing etc.), when implementing a pilot industrial project of a digital platform for non-destructive testing of products and materials discusses to use specialized software libraries allow to effectively solve and implement applied software solutions as well as the Java Neural Network Framework [6].

For a full-scale implementation of the possibility of a parallel system for computing using a graphics card, the algorithm of configuration and direct operation with the neural network should be appropriately converted. Obviously, in this case, in addition to the computing resources of the central processor unit (CPU), CUDA – compatible graphics processor is used, for example, NVIDIA [7], implementing the architecture of parallel computing CUDA [8, 9], which provides a specialized programming interface for calculations that are not directly related to raster and/or vector graphics.

Currently, the NVIDIA GPU Cloud (NGC) provides an easy access to the full catalogue of software for deep learning and high performance computing, optimized for the GPU [10]. The NGC repository includes containers with leading deep learning frameworks for neural networks, which are configured, tested, certified, and serviced by NVIDIA.

References

1. V.V. Parubets, O.G. Berestneva, D.V. Devyatykh, Bulletin of the Tomsk Polytechnic University, **320** (2012)
2. N. Bieberstein, S. Bose, M. Fiammante, *Service-Oriented Architecture (SOA) Compass: Business Value, Planning, and Enterprise Roadmap* (IBM Press, 2005)
3. A. Kosach, E. Kovshov, Contemporary Engineering Sciences, **10**, 367 (2017)
4. Microsoft Download Center. URL: www.microsoft.com
5. S. Osovskiy, *Neural networks for information processing* (Finance and Statistics, 2002)
6. Java Neural Network Framework. URL: http://neuroph.sourceforge.net/index.html
7. NVIDIA Developer. https://developer.nvidia.com/
8. CUDA Toolkit Documentation v. 9.1.85. URL: https://docs.nvidia.com/cuda/
9. NVIDIA Accelerated Computing. Deep learning. https://developer.nvidia.com/deep-learning
10. NVIDIA GPU Cloud. https://www.nvidia.ru/gpu-cloud/

ITM Web of Conferences **18**, 04004 (2018) https://doi.org/10.1051/itmconf/20181804004
ICS 2018

Development of a Common Format of Questionnaire Tests for a Web-based Platform of Population and Experimental Psychological Research

Evgeny Nikulchev[1,2], *Dmitry* Ilin[1,2,*], *Pavel* Kolyasnikov[1], *Victoria* Ismatullina[3] and *Ilya* Zakharov[3]

[1]Russian Academy of Education, 119121 Moscow, Russia
[2]Moscow Technological University MIREA, 119454 Moscow, Russia
[3]Psychological Institute of Russian Academy of Education, 125009 Moscow, Russia

Abstract. A web platform for psychological research needs a single format of questionnaire tests to ensure interaction between its components. The study proposes a general test structure, variant questions, variations in response types, and an embedded domain-specific language for computations. The use of JSON is proposed and justified to store the hierarchical structure of the questionnaire test, and JSON Schema is defined as a technology suitable for the formation of the standard. From the considered validation instruments for compliance with the standard described in JSON Schema, ajv was defined as the most applicable to the task. To build the documentation, Doca is relevant, but this tool needs to be modified to meet the requirements of the task.

1 Introduction

Today, online tools are increasingly used for research [1]. In addition to universal solutions, which are equally applied in different disciplines, there are also used developments that are specific for a given area of research. For research in the field of psychology, survey facilities [2] are used, which are a substitute for the traditional pen and paper approach. Such a tool reduces the work of the researcher [1, 3], allowing to work with large samples [4]. There are also projects [5, 6] that transfer the tools for conducting cognitive research online.

The RAE Psychological Institute is developing a web platform [2] for conducting psychological research both online and offline in order to take into account a wide range of requirements for setting up experiments. The platform consists of many components, the integration of which requires the creation of unified standards for data exchange. For a simple interaction between components, the REST API is sufficient [7], whereas to establish reproducible experiments a more formalized approach is needed. Previous analogues have been analyzed [2]. The results showed that there is no single standard for the development of psychological questionnaire tests, and therefore the developed of psychological platform requires selection of appropriate software instruments and identification of approaches that would allow to solve the task.

2 Analysis of requirements and the formation of the structure of the psychological test

2.1 The overall structure of the questionnaire tests

Based on the needs of researchers, each questionnaire test can contain:

1. **Questions** as a basis for data collection.
2. **Scales** for computation based on answers to questions.
3. **Feedback**, which the subject will receive as a result of passing the test.
4. **Reports**, namely the description of how to provide summary information to the researcher.

Variants of representation of questions can differ, therefore it is expedient to group questions into blocks within which there will be specific for it settings. One of the requirements is to interrupt the passage of a block of questions on the fulfillment of a certain condition (for example, exceeding the number of incorrect answers). In addition to the questions, two more kinds of elements should be included in these blocks:

1. **Text areas** that allow writing instructions to the test.
2. **Page breaks** that may be needed if the test involves exceptions to the rule that determines the number of questions/text areas displayed on a single page.

* Corresponding author: i@dmitryilin.com

2.2 The structure of questions in the questionnaire tests

By analyzing the requirements for the content of psychological questionnaire tests, existing systems and examples of tests, key types of questions for the functioning of the platform were obtained. Each type has a characteristic set of properties. Types of questions can be divided into simple and composite. Simple questions will be answered by one single key regardless of whether it is a scalar or a vector value. Compound questions imply that there may be more than one key in their composition, for each of which a response can be saved. They can also mean different types of data stored in the platform. For clarity, the types of questions are presented in Table 1, indicating the main characteristics.

Table 1. Characteristics of types of questions.

Type	Composite	Valid values	Comment on the answer	Restrictions
Single choice	No	Preset values	Available	No
Multiple choice	No	Preset values	Available	No
Input field	No	Any input values	Not available	Input mask, answer length, number bounds
Complete the gaps	Yes	Any input values	Not available	Input mask, answer length, number bounds
Slider	No	Values in the specified range	Not available	Bounds of number
Date input	No	Values in the specified range	Not available	Date boundaries
Sequence	No	Preset values	Not available	No
Map	No	Preset values	Not available	No
File upload	No	File	Not available	File size, file type
Single choice matrix	Yes	Preset values	Available	No
Multiple choice matrix	Yes	Preset values	Available	No
Input field matrix	No	Any input values	No	Input mask, answer length, number bounds

In turn, the values of answers can also differ in types. Table 2 provides a list of questions, their corresponding data structures for information on responses, and lists of possible value types.

Table 2. Characteristics of the stored response data.

Type	Data on the response	Possible value data types
Single choice	Value, response number and comment	Text, Number, Boolean, Index Number
Multiple choice	Vector of values, answer and comment numbers	Text, Number, Boolean, Index Number
Input field	Value	Text, Number
Complete the gaps	Value	Text, Number
Slider	Value	Number
Date input	Value	Date
Sequence	Vector of values	Text, Number
Map	Vector of values	Text, Number
File upload	Link to file	Link to the uploaded file
Single choice matrix	Value, response number and comment	Text, Number, Boolean, Index Number
Multiple choice matrix	Vector of values, answer and comment numbers	Text, Number, Boolean, Index Number
Input field matrix	Vector of values, row numbers and column numbers	Text, Number

In addition to the above, the answer to each of the simple questions can contain a note of compliance with the expected value (for example, the correct answer). For compound questions, a similar mark can be specified for each of the sub-questions.

2.3 The domain-specific language for calculating the values of the scales

For carrying out the calculations, it is expedient to develop a domain-specific programming language. It must meet the following criteria:

1. Be applicable for calculations both on the server and in the browser.
2. Use only pure calculations to ensure reproducibility of results.
3. Be easily editable both manually and with software tools.

The language corresponding to them can be obtained using declarative and functional programming paradigms. The main aspect of the functional paradigm that is required in the task is pure functions. For execution of the code, the interpreter is used as it can be used regardless of the environment, and the speed of calculations for the task is not critical, because of their relatively small volume within the limits of one psychological test.

The following groups are the main built-in functions of the language:

- Logical functions (and, or, not).
- Comparison functions (equal, greater than, etc.).
- Higher-order functions (map, reduce, etc.).
- Mathematical functions (add, subtract, etc.).
- Functions for working on vectors (sum, size, etc.).
- Functions for obtaining data (getAnswers, getScale, etc.).

At the current stage, the provision of advanced functionality in a domain-specific language does not seem appropriate. Thus, declaring user-defined functions and declaring variables explicitly is not necessary.

3 Data formats analysis

Based on the analysis of functional requirements and limitations related to psychological tests, questionnaires, it can be said with certainty that their description is possible in the form of a document with hierarchical connections. To describe them, the most suitable are the semi-structured data formats. The most common of these are XML and JSON [8]. For this task, BSON can be considered as a variation of JSON for efficient storage in document-oriented non-relational databases, so it will not be considered as a separate format.

In favor of choosing XML, the following series of arguments exist:

- XML is more common, there are more tools to work with it.

In favor of choosing JSON, there are the following arguments:

- Serializing and deserializing JSON is faster [9, 10] than XML
- Since the main target execution environment is the browser, JSON is preferable, because its usage will imply less overhead costs for resources.
- The selected tools (Node.js, MongoDB) also work with JSON directly [11], whereas for XML, conversion is required.

The effectiveness of the software components is important for the web platform, so JSON is preferable.

4 Selection of tools

The choice of tools for forming a standard for describing psychological questionnaire tests is based on the following criteria:

1. The format description tools should allow the validation of the questionnaire instance against the format.
2. There should be an option to automatically build a document describing the format in a way that is understandable to a person.

For the formation of standardized JSON documents, de facto, there is only one solution, which can be called well-established: JSON Schema [12, 13]. This standard contains several revisions. At the moment, the latest version is Draft-07, however, at the time of the analysis, version Draft-06 was actual. The JSON Schema itself is not a tool for solving the tasks, but it is a standard for describing the structure of JSON documents, to which a whole list of tools that allow automating the construction of documentation has been developed. Also a wide range of libraries was developed for various programming languages that can check JSON-objects for compliance with a specified scheme.

The tools for checking JSON objects for JSON Schema compliance must be integrable into the components of the web platform, and therefore, it is necessary to consider development in the JavaScript language. In addition, it is necessary to limit the list of considered tools to those that support Draft-04 and Draft-06, and work in both the browser and Node.js. A brief description of the selected tools is presented in Table 3.

Table 3. Object validation tools for JSON Schema.

Name	ajv	djv
Supported version of JSON Schema	Draft-04, Draft-06	Draft-04, Draft-06
Number of tests per second based on the json-schema-benchmark	47068	48052
Number of failed tests	1	1
Number of downloads per month	~34000000 [14]	~6500 [15]

Both tools are leaders in the number of tests per second according to the version of the json-schema-benchmark [13, 16]. In addition, they have the least number of failed tests. With equal characteristics, they have a significant difference in the size of the community, which is confirmed by the multiple differences in the number of projects with the integration of these tools. Thus, the choice in favor of ajv is adequate, since the reliability of the tool is tested by a large community.

All the documentation tools [13] are free to use. A more detailed description is given in Table 4.

Each of the tools supports Draft-04, which is a sufficient condition for the application. Nevertheless, considering more in detail each of the tools, one can identify additional characteristics that affect the choice. Because the Web platform is based on technologies that are closely related to the JavaScript language, the use of Prmd may require additional time to master. The Matic and Docson tools provide documentation in the form of nested entities that, in general, correspond to the essence of JSON, but can cause difficulties when reading the documentation. They do not implement the construction of a list of all entities included in the schema, which can be good for small objects, but it will negatively affect the readability of large documentation. Each of the tools is designed to build documentation, primarily for the API, which is redundant for the task. This may require one to rework some of the theme files. From this, it should be concluded that each of the tools does not meet the desired characteristics, but the most adequate to the task is the Doca tool.

Table 4. Documents construction tools.

Name	Matic	Docson	Doca	Prmd
License	MIT	Apache 2.0	BSD	MIT
Implementation language	JavaScript	JavaScript	JavaScript	Ruby
Supported version of JSON Schema	Draft-03, Draft-04	Draft-04	Draft-04, Draft-07 (в планах)	Draft-04
Using themes	Yes	No	Yes	Yes
Building content	No	No	Yes	Yes
Number of downloads per month	~500 [17]	~200 [18]	~1400 [19]	-

During operation, it was revealed that the Doca tool has a drawback: the lack of processing of cyclic references inside the JSON schema. In this connection, it was required to move from using a method that combines a schema divided into components into a single JSON object to a method in which a single file with internal links is formed. This led to a loss of the ability to view the cyclically related objects in depth, but allowed to keep the possibility of using Doca as a whole.

5 Conclusions

The study carried out an analysis of existing services for conducting psychological research in the form of questionnaire tests. Since there are no solutions available on the market that would provide a single standard, it was therefore suggested to develop one. Authors formed the structure of the questionnaire test, consisting of four sections (questions, scales, feedback, and reports). In the paper, the first two were considered in more detail, since they are the basis for research and data collection. Analysis of data formats showed that JSON is relevant for the construction, storage, and playback of questionnaires. The review of existing solutions for the formation of standards of semi-structured data in the JSON format showed that the only applicable is JSON Schema. Among the tools for validating questionnaire tests and for constructing documentation, ajv and Doca were selected, respectively. Their use is justified, since they support the latest versions of the JSON Schema standard, and the Doca user interface is the most suitable for the task. Subsequent studies may be aimed at examining two sections of questionnaire tests that are outside the scope of the article (feedback and reports). An important issue for further consideration is migration to a newer version of the standard of questionnaire tests, which is necessary to ensure backward compatibility of the tools.

This research is supported by the RFBR grant no. 17-29-02198.

References

1. S.D. Gosling, W. Mason, Annual review of psychology, **66**, 877 (2015)
2. I. Zakharov, E. Nikulchev, D. Ilin, V. Ismatullin, A. Fenin, ITM Web of Conferences, **10**, 04006 (2017)
3. G. Andersson, N. Titov, World Psychiatry, **13**, 4 (2014)
4. C. Bartneck, A. Duenser, E. Moltchanova, K. Zawieska, PloS one, **10**, e0121595 (2015)
5. [Online]. Available: https://www.labvanced.com/. [Accessed 20 02 2018].
6. J.R. De Leeuw, Behavior research methods, **47**, 1 (2015)
7. R. Sellami, S. Bhiri and B. Defude, ODBAPI: a unified REST API for relational and NoSQL data stores, In Big Data Congress (2014)
8. A.B.M. Moniruzzaman, S.A. Hossain, International Journal of Database Theory and Application, **6**, 1 (2013)
9. N. Nurseitov, M. Paulson, R. Reynolds, C. Izurieta, Comparison of JSON and XML data interchange formats: a case study, *In Caine*, pp. 157-162 (2009)
10. D. Peng, L. Cao, W. Xu, Journal of Computational Information Systems, **7**, 5883 (2011)
11. C. Győrödi, R. Győrödi, G. Pecherle, A. Olah, A comparative study: MongoDB vs. MySQL, *In 2015 13th International Conference on Engineering of Modern Electric Systems* (2015)
12. F. Pezoa, J. L. Reutter, F. Suarez, M. Ugarte, D. Vrgoč, Foundations of JSON schema, *In Proceedings of the 25th International Conference on World Wide Web* (2016)
13. [Online]. Available: http://json-schema.org/implementations.html
14. [Online]. Available: https://www.npmjs.com/package/ajv
15. [Online]. Available: https://www.npmjs.com/package/djv
16. [Online]. Available: https://github.com/ebdrup/json-schema-benchmark
17. [Online]. Available: https://www.npmjs.com/package/matic
18. [Online]. Available: https://www.npmjs.com/package/docson.
19. [Online]. Available: https://www.npmjs.com/package/doca.

Economic optimization and evolutionary programming when using remote sensing data

Roman Shamin[1,*], *Gabriel Enrike* Alberto [1], *Ayzhana* Uryngaliyeva[1] and *Aleksandr* Semenov[1]

[1] People's Friendship University of Russia, 117198, Moscow, Russia

Abstract. The article considers the issues of optimizing the use of remote sensing data. Built a mathematical model to describe the economic effect of the use of remote sensing data. It is shown that this model is incorrect optimisation task. Given a numerical method of solving this problem. Also discusses how to optimize organizational structure by using genetic algorithm based on remote sensing. The methods considered allow the use of remote sensing data in an optimal way. The proposed mathematical model allows various generalizations for optimization of decision making in the presence of remote sensing data. The approach associated with evolutionary programming is an effective solution when optimizing economic structures in the presence of remote sensing data.

1 Introduction

When using remote sensing data of the Earth there are various the problem of economic optimization of the use of these data [1]. This problem has various causes [2]. First, the use of satellite imagery and thematic processing can be economically costly. In addition, in this case, we find that the economic effect has a certain damping, since the information derived from satellite imagery is quickly becoming obsolete. Second, the use of satellite images in monitoring of projects may lead to structural changes in economic planning. In this case, there occurs a problem of evolutionary programming to assess structural changes when using the data of space images. The close topic is discussed in [3-4].

In the present work we consider two economic goals: optimizing the use of satellite images during the implementation of projects and the method of evolutionary programming to optimize economic structures. The research is based on works [5-8].

2 Optimization of economic efficiency

We consider a mathematical model of space imagery on the enterprise. The purpose of this model is the calculation of the optimal use of satellite images in such a way as to maintain a predetermined level of effectiveness in the use of space services.

We will consider some venture P. The management of these enterprises is to use space images. The aim of business management is a generalized indicator of efficiency of enterprise activity. Under performance, you can understand the different indicators, for example: profit; the level of innovativeness; competitiveness and etc.

We introduce the corresponding notation. We will consider a mathematical model with continuous time, which we will denote by t.

The distribution of the use of space services, we will describe the function $u(t)$, while we assume that this function is a linear combination of generalized functions, because of its economic sense – the intensity of the use of space services is the impulse function.

Performance indicator we will denote by $I(t)$. On the economic meaning of the function $u(t)$ and $I(t)$ are nonnegative. To specify the relationship of the functions $u(t)$ and $I(t)$ must enter the transfer function $K(t)$, which will show the result of the contribution to the impact function $I(t)$ under the pulsed action of the function u at time $t = 0$. Using the transfer function, the relationship between the function of the use of space services and performance possible to record in the form of integral equations.

$$I(t) = \int_0^t K(t-s)u(s)ds. \quad (1)$$

The transfer function has the following properties

1) $K(t) \geq 0$
2) $K(t) = 0$, $t \leq 0$
3) $K(t) \to 0$, $t \to \infty$

The first property shows that the impact of the use of space services for the performance cannot be negative. Of course, in some real situations, this property can be violated, but in our model, we believe that this influence cannot be negative. The second property shows that the past does not depend on the future. This is a natural condition that the use of satellite images only affects the future but not the past. The third property reflects the fact that the effectiveness of the use of space images has a finite duration of the performance, and over time their influence is eroding.

Equation (1) is a linear integral equation of the first kind.

* Corresponding author: roman@shamin.ru

3 The optimization problem

As we have noted, in economic situations, we must consider not a continuous function of space services, and pulse function. We will consider the use of space snapshots at specific points in time

$$0 < t_1 < t_2 < \ldots < t_N.$$

In each of the moments t_k the level of use of satellite services will be denoted using u_k. Using the formalism of δ-functions, the impulse function of the use of space services can be written as follows.

$$u(t) = \sum_{k=1}^{N} u_k \delta(t - t_k).$$

Substituting this function in integral equation (1), we get the following equation.

$$I(t) = \sum_{k=1}^{N} K(t - t_k) u_k \quad (2)$$

Suppose we have a desired level of performance of our company, which is expressed as a function J(t). Then the problem reduces to finding such values

$$u_1^*, u_2^*, \ldots, u_N^*.$$

After the substitution these values in equation (2), we get the identity

$$J(t) = \sum_{k=1}^{N} K(t - t_k) u_k^*.$$

From a mathematical point of view this problem is incorrect because it does not have an exact solution, may not be the only solution, and it can be unstable with respect to perturbations.

4 The method of calculating an optimal plan for use of space services

We introduce the next values

$$u_1, u_2, \ldots, u_N.$$

These values we call the plan of use of space services

To optimize the plan that we are thus to minimize the following value

$$D(t, u_1, \ldots, u_N) = \int_0^T |I(t) - J(t, u_1, \ldots, u_N)|^2 dt \to min.$$

Thus, we have a problem of minimizing functions of N variables.

As we have already noted, this task is incorrect, therefore, for numerical calculations it is necessary to use regularization by Tikhonov. To do this, we modify the original problem by adding to D a new function with a small parameter.

$$D(t, u_1, \ldots, u_N) + \alpha\Omega(u_1, \ldots, u_N) \to min.$$

Here $\alpha > 0$ is a small parameter, and the function Ω is called a stabilizer, which is calculated by the following formula

$$\Omega(u_1, \ldots, u_N) = \sum_{k=1}^{N} u_k^2.$$

The use of the stabilizer allows to regularize the original problem.

For the numerical determination of the optimal plan is to use the method of swarming particles, which is effective for multidimensional optimization for nonsmooth functions.

Consider a model example of optimizing the use of space services. We will consider funding for N = 10. We consider the situation where we need to ensure the performance of

$$I(t) = 10$$

dimensionless quantities.

As of the transition function consider the following function.

$$K(t) = \frac{t}{1+t^2}.$$

It is easy to see that this function satisfies the necessary conditions. In addition, it can be shown that this function reflects the economic effect of the use of space services.

We give the results obtained. Optimal use of space services is shown in Fig. 1.

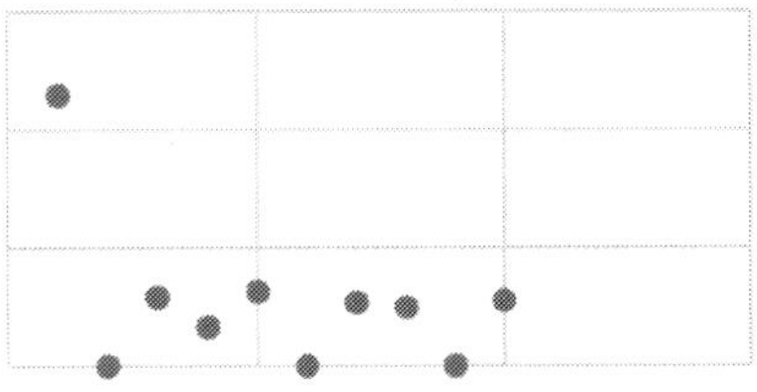

Fig. 1. The optimal plan.

Accordingly, the graph of performance is shown in Fig. 2.

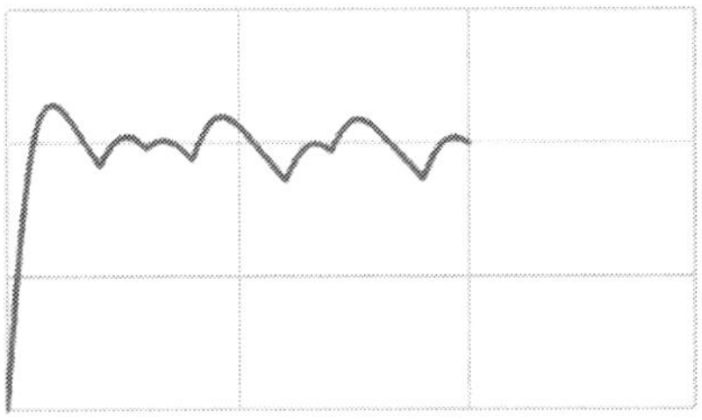

Fig. 2. The performance.

You can see that the proposed plan for the use of space services leads the performance to the desired values, and then supports the desired mode of performance.

5 The use of the evolutionary method in the task of using space services

Consider the task of optimizing the structure of enterprise on the basis of the results of the use of space services. This problem can be solved by using evolutionary methods. Let the considered enterprise has a complex structure, which was considered as a directed graph

$$G = < V, E >,$$

where V is the vertex set of the graph and E is the directed arcs. In the vertexes there may be structural unit of the enterprise, and arcs of the graph Express the subordination of these structural units in the organization.

A fundamental point for the use of economic-mathematical models of optimization is determining the objective function. We consider the following objective function.

$$H = H(G, \xi).$$

The function H accepts numeric values which make sense of economic efficiency of the enterprise. Units of measure this efficiency are irrelevant, because the evolutionary optimization methods do not depend on the actual values of the optimized functions.

Here as the vector ξ, we consider the random parameters that affect efficiency.

We introduced a function depends essentially on the own structure of the organization, i.e., from the selected graph G.

The scheme of using the evolutionary method is the application of genetic algorithms to optimize functions of H. In this case, we vary the graph G. This graph is the structure of your organization.

As an elementary change of the graph we will consider the following operations on directed graphs:

- adding vertices;
- delete vertices;
- adding arcs;
- deletion of arcs.

These operations we will consider as basic changes of the graph. These changes are application to an existing structure (the graph G) one of these operations.

When used in practice, evolutionary methods of optimization of structure of the enterprise, questions arise regarding the calculation function of efficiency relative to the proposed structure (the graph G). To resolve this issue, you can use two fundamental methods

- simulation;
- practical application of the changes.

Simulation is a classical way of evaluating the effectiveness of the organization. An important advantage of this method is the fact that we can carry out this estimate "on the computer" without the involvement of material resources and risks. However, this approach is limited by the quality of the simulation, since many factors influence of organizational structure on efficiency are not continuous parameters, i.e. for a slight change in the structure, the efficiency can change dramatically. Thus, the construction of an adequate simulation model is difficult.

Another approach is more radical because it implies that the changes in the company structure implemented, and then it turns out the change (improvement or worsening) performance of the enterprise. Of course, this approach can be implemented is not always, therefore, requires a certain amount of moderation when you change the structure of the enterprise. At the same time, it should be noted that to calculate the real values of the function H may require lots of time.

Recently, more and more are becoming the methods of artificial intelligence in problems of Economics and management. The use of deep machine learning in conjunction with the construction of expert systems and knowledge bases will allow us to find more accurate methods of evaluating the effectiveness of the structure of the enterprise.

6 Conclusion

The paper presents an original mathematical model for performance evaluation of space imagery data application for enterprises. With this extreme model is formulated an optimization problem to describe the optimal scheme of using satellite images for maintaining a given level of productivity of the enterprise.

It is shown that the obtained extremal problem is incorrect problem, therefore, for the computational procedures necessary to use regularization incorrect extremal problems by Tikhonov.

Given a model example of calculation of optimal use of satellite images, which shows a considered economic-mathematical model.

Considered a model of optimization of structure of the enterprise based on data derived from remote sensing. This model is based on evolutionary programming.

The paper/article was prepared with the financial support of the Ministry of Education of the Russian Federation in the framework of the scientific project No. 14.575.21.0167 connected with the implementation of applied scientific research on the following topic: «Development of applied solutions for processing and integration of large volumes of diverse operational, retrospective and the thematic data of Earth's remote sensing in the unified geospace using smart digital technologies and artificial intelligence».

References

1. A.N. Tikhonov, A. Goncharsky, V.V. Stepanov, A.G. Yagola, *Numerical Methods for the Solution of Ill-Posed Problems* (Springer, 1995)
2. M. Cavazzuti, *Optimization Methods* (Springer-Verlag Berlin Heidelberg, 2013)
3. P.L. Gurevich, R.V. Shamin, S.B. Tikhomirov. SIAM J. Math. Anal, **45**, 1328 (2013)
4. R.V. Shamin, N.V. Bondarchuk, A.V. Fomina, International Journal of Pure and Applied Mathematics, **118**, 691 (2018)
5. R.V. Shamin, A.A. Chursin, L.A. Fedorova. European Research Studies Journal, **20** 39 (2017)
6. C.W. Groetsch, *Inverse problems in the mathematical sciences* (Braunschweig, Vieweg, 1993).
7. H.W. Engl, M. Hanke, A. Neubauer, *Regularization of Inverse Problems* (Dordrecht, Kluwer Acad. Publ., 1996)
8. R.V. Shamin, A. Yudin, K. Kuznetsov, A. Kurkin, D. Tyugin, Methods and algorithms of freak wave detection in the coastal zone, *In Proceedings of the Twelfth International Conference on the Mediterranean Coastal Environment MEDCOAST*, pp. 825-833 (2015)

Does symbolic and non-symbolic estimation ability predict mathematical achievement across primary school years?

Tatiana Tikhomirova[1, 2, *], *Yulia* Kuzmina [1, 2], and *Sergey* Malykh[1, 2]

[1]Lomonosov Moscow State University, Department of Psychology, 119991 Moscow, Russia
[2] Psychological Institute of Russian Academy of Education, 125009 Moscow, Russia

Abstract. The article presents the results of a longitudinal study of the association between number sense and success in learning mathematics in primary school. We analysed the data of 133 schoolchildren on two aspects of number sense related to the symbolic and non-symbolic magnitude estimation abilities and academic success in mathematics in third and fourth grade. The average age of schoolchildren during the first assessment was 9.82 ± 0.30; during the second assessment – 10.82 ± 0.30. For the analysis of interrelations, the cross-lagged method was used. It was shown that the reciprocal model best describes the data suggesting cross-lagged associations between number sense and the success in learning mathematics at primary school age. The results of the longitudinal analysis revealed differences in the relationship between the success in learning mathematics with the two aspects of number sense: academic success in third grade only predicted the indicator of number sense associated with the symbolic magnitude estimation ability in fourth grade. The differences in the age dynamics of the two aspects of number sense in primary school are also revealed: the indicator of number sense associated with the non-symbolic magnitude estimation ability was the most stable over time.

1 Introduction

The social and economical value of individual achievement in mathematics explains the research interest for the search of predictors of mathematical success among a range of cognitive characteristics [1, 2, 3, etc.].

At the same time, number sense might be the most math-oriented and the least studied cognitive trait at least on the Russian sample [4, 5]. Number sense is defined as an ability to estimate quantities wthout counting [4].

A number of studies showed that number sense is closely related to the success in learning mathematics [6, 7, 8, etc.]. In some studies these associations were found only at a certain age (for example, primary school age [9]), whereas others reported none [10, 11]. These observed differences might be explained by the heterogenity of the psychological construct of number sense related to symbolically and non-symbolically expressed quantities [4, 12]. These different aspects of number sense are in turn assessed with various test tasks. The aspects related to operating with symbolically expressed quantities are assessed with number stimuli [13], and the aspects related to operating with non-symbolically expressed quantities are assessed with tests with stimuli consisting of various objects [8].

Despite the similarity of the two principles of quantity operating, the successful performance on the test tasks with symbolically and non-symbolically expressed quantities might vary for the same person which in turn might lead to differences in the association of number sense and mathematical achievememt [6]. This fact requires the assessment of both aspects of number sense – symbolic and non-symbolic – within one research programme.

To understand the mechanisms of the association of the analysed psychological constructs, it is crucial to assess the direction of this association which can only be done in a longitudinal study in which number sense and academic success would be measured in the same individuals across a certain time period [14, 15].

A number of longitudinal studies showed that individual differences in operating with non-sybolically expressed quantities at primary shool predicted success in learning mathematics at high school age [3, 16]. At the same time, for number sense related to operating with symbolically expressed quantities, the results were different suggesting a bigger role of learning the concept of number and arithmetical operations. Individual differences in the ability to estimate the position of a number on the line in children of high school age have lower variance in comparison to children of primary school age [17], and children who got feedback during the test showed more precision in their performance than their peers who did not get any feedback [18].

A number of studies discussed age-related differences in the associations between symbolic and non-symbolic magnitude estimation observed during school mathematics education with development of the concept of the number and experience in operating with

* Corresponding author: tikho@mail.ru

numbers [19]. Thus, a gradual improvement over the school-age period is observed for number sense associated with non-symbolic magnitude estimation [20]. At the same time, improvement in number sense measured with the Number Line test can occur spasmodically under a more significant influence of mathematics education [13].

The purpose of this study is to investigate the causal relationship between number sense and success in mathematics controlling for intelligence throughout the primary school age. In this case, we focused on two aspects of number sense reflecting the ability to operate with both symbolic and non-symbolic quantities. Participation of schoolchildren enrolled in primary school when the most intensive training on the concept of number and related operations occurs offers an opportunity to assess how the learning process mediates the association between number sense and success in mathematics.

2 Methods

2.1 Participants

The sample included schoolchildren from municipal general education institution participating in the Russian longitudinal study of the academic success of schoolchildren.

In the present work, the data of 133 students collected at the end of third and fourth grades were analysed. The average age of participants in third grade was 9.82 years (standard deviation = 0.30, 45.1% boys), in the fourth grade it was 10.82 years (standard deviation = 0.30, 45.1% boys).

The analysis was carried out on the basis of anonimous personal data.

2.2 Measures

2.2.1 Number sense, non-symbolic magnitude estimation ability

In the Number Sense Task, yellow and blue dots different in size are presented on the screen [21]. The children were asked to decide if the array contains more yellow or blue dots, and press the corresponding key on the keyboard (Y or B). The stimuli contained 150 static images with arrays of yellow and blue dots, the number of which varies from 5 to 21 points of each color; the ratio of dots of two colors is either 1:3 or 6:7. The image appears on the screen for 400 ms, maximum response time is 8 seconds. The test consists of three blocks of 50 tasks. The program records the accuracy of responses and response time.

2.2.2 Number sense, symbolic magnitude estimation ability

In the Number Line test, a line with the minimum and maximum values of 0 and 1000, respectively, is displayed on the screen as well as a certain number at the top of the screen [21]. Students were asked to place the number displayed at the top of the screen on the line. Overall, there are 22 numbers in this task which should be placed on the line with the help of a computer mouse. The program registers the average deviation of the position marked by a student on the line from the actual position of each number. Thus, the higher is the value of the indicator for this test, the worse is the individual result.

2.2.3 Intelligence

In the Standard Progressive Matrices test, the tasks are grouped into 5 series, each of which consists of 12 tasks [22]. The number of correctly solved tasks for each series and the total score for the whole test are calculated.

2.2.4 Math achievement

Term grades for mathematics given by a primary school teacher were used as indicators of the success in learning. In the statistical analysis we used the arithmetic mean of the term grades.

2.2.5 Statistical Approach

First, a correlation analysis of the indicators of number sense, nonverbal intelligence and the success in learning mathematics assessed at the end of third and fourth grades was carried out. Spearman correlation coefficients were calculated.

Second, cross-lagged modeling was performed to analyze the longitudinal structure of the cause-effect relationships between the indicators of number sense and success in mathematics measured twice during the primary school age while controlling for intelligence.

Three types of associations were evaluated during the analysis: 1) autoregressive associations reflecting the stability of each trait over time, 2) contemporaneous associations that estimate the total variation of variables within each of the two assessments, and 3) cross-lagged associations showing how the variation of the preceding assessment of one trait explains the variation of the subsequent assessment of another trait.

We consistently compared four competing models of the relationship of the two aspects of number sense and the success in learning mathematics.

Model 1, autoregressive, assumed the connections between number sense and success in learning mathematics only within each time point (M1).

Model 2 assumed that the success in learning mathematics in the fourth grade depended on individual differences in number sense in third grade (M2).

Model 3, on the contrary, assumed that the successful performance on number sense test tasks depended on the successful learning of mathematics in third grade (M3).

Model 4, reciprocal, assumed that the success in mathematics measured in third grade predicted the success in number sense test in fourth grade, and conversely, number sense measured at an earlier age predicted success in mathematics at a later age (M 4).

3 RESULTS

Table 1 presents the descriptive statistics for the indicators of number sense related to operating with arrays of objects (Number Sense) and estimating the position of a number on the line (Number Line), nonverbal intelligence (Standard Progressive Matrices) and success in learning mathematics.

Table 1. Descriptive statistics of the analysed indicators measured in third and fourth grade.

Grade	Indicator	Mean	SD
3rd	Number Sense	95.66	13.33
	Number Line	93.44	68.93
	Success in learning mathematics	4.17	0.61
	Standard Progressive Matrices	40.63	7.86
4th	Number Sense	100.13	14.25
	Number Line	77.80	51.30
	Success in learning mathematics	4.17	0.63

In Table 1, the average number of correct answers is indicated for the Number Sense Task and Standard Progressive Matrices tests, with a maximum of 150 and 60 tasks, respectively. The average deviation of the marked position of the number from the actual position was indicated for the Number line test. In this case, a lower value corresponds to a better, more accurate performance. The success in learning mathematics is estimated as the average value of term grades and varies from 2 to 5.

According to Table 1, throughout primary school, number sense improved with a decrease in the standard deviation. On the contrary, the success in learning mathematics did not change while maintaining its variability.

3.1 Correlation analysis: association between number sense and success in learning mathematics in third and fourth grades

The correlation analysis focused on the structure of the relationship of the two aspects of number sense (Number Sense test – NS, and Number Line test – NL), nonverbal intelligence (Int, Standard Progressive Matrices) and success in learning mathematics (Math) in third and fourth grades. Table 2 presents Spearman correlation coefficients for the analysed indicators ($*p < 0.05$, $**p < 0.01$) measured in third (lower left side) and fourth grades (upper right side).

Table 2. Results of correlation analysis of indicators measured in third and fourth grade.

	NS	NL	Math	Int
NS	1	-0.41**	0.33**	0.30**
NL	-0.45**	1	-0.42**	-0.23*
Math	0.38**	-0.40**	1	0.42**
Int	0.24*	-0.33**	0.45**	1

According to Table 2, moderate significant correlations (from 0.33 to 0.45, $p < 0.01$) are observed between the indicators of cognitive development and the success in learning mathematics.

Comparative analysis of the correlation coefficients obtained in third and fourth grades showed that the association of number sense related to non-symbolic magnitude estimation with the success in learning mathematics in fourth grade becomes less pronounced in comparison with the third grade (0.33 vs. 0.38, $p < 0.01$). The correlation between the two analyzed aspects of number sense is more pronounced in third grade ($r = 0.45$, $p < 0.01$) compared to fourth grade ($r = 0.41$, $p < 0.01$).

In general, according to the correlation analysis, the structure of the interrelationships between the indicators of cognitive development and the success in learning mathematics in third and fourth grade remains unchanged.

3.2 Cross-lagged model: cause-effect relationship of number sense and success in learning mathematics

In the cross-lagged analysis, four competing models of the relationship between the two aspects of number sense and the success in learning mathematics were compared controlling for nonverbal intelligence at primary school age.

Table 3 shows the fit of the four tested models with empirical data: M1 – autoregressive; M2 – number sense in third grade predicts the success in learning mathematics in fourth grade; M3 – success in learning mathematics in third grade predicts number sense in fourth grade; M4 – reciprocal.

According to Table 3, the reciprocal model (M4) best describes the empirical data suggesting that number sense measured in third grade predicts success in learning mathematics in fourth grade, and vice versa, success in mathematics in third grade predicts number sense in fourth grade.

The estimation of cross-lagged associations showed that the relationship between the success in learning mathematics in third grade and number sense in the Number Line task (-0.33, $p < 0.05$) was statistically significant. In other words, none of the aspects of number sense measured in the third grade significantly contributed to the variation in the success in learning mathematics by the end of primary school ($p > 0.05$).

Table 3. Fit indices for models of the relationship between number sense and success in learning mathematics.

Indices		M 1	M 2	M 3	M 4
AIC / BIC	AIC	3663	3666.2	3656.6	3659.9
	BIC	3725.8	3739.4	3728.8	3738.4
	adj. BIC	3650	3650.9	3641.4	3643.6
$\chi 2$	value	16.9	12.09	2.5	1.79
	df	9	5	5	3
	p-value	0.049	0.033	0.78	0.62
RMSEA (CIs)	Est.	0.093	0.118	0.00	0.00
	90% CI	0.002–0.16	0.03–0.21	0.00–0.09	0.00–0.04
CFI / TLI	CFI	0.98	0.98	1.00	1.00
	TLI	0.95	0.92	1.03	1.01

Note: AIC – Akaike Information Criterion; BIC – Bayesian information criterion; adj. BIC – sample-size adjusted BIC; $\chi 2$ (value, df, p) – chi-square test (value, degrees of freedom, pvalue);RMSEA (Est., CIs) – root mean square error of approximation (value, 90% confidence intervals); CFI – comparative fit index; TLI – Tucker-Lewis index

Among the contemporaneous associations, statistically significant connections between all the variables were obtained only at the first assessment while at the second assessment a statistically significant relationship was found only between the two aspects of number sense. At the same time, the correlation analysis performed on the data of fourth grade revealed moderate associations of number sense with the success in learning mathematics ($0.33 < |r| < 0.42$). In addition, a high regression coefficient between two assessments of the success in learning mathematics (0.96, $p < 0.05$) is noteworthy, which might cause distortion of contemporaneous associations [15].

Due to high temporal stability of the success in learning mathematics based on teacher evaluations, two modified theoretical models were examined to estimate cross-lagged associations. In these models, according to the principles of structural modeling, the success in learning is represented by one assessment - only in third or only in fourth grade. This method allowed us to evaluate the cross-lagged relationship between number sense and academic success taking into account the high temporal stability of the success in learning mathematics.

According to the analysis, both modified models have similar indices which confirms their good fit to the empirical data (RMSEA ≤ 0.06, $0.00 \leq 90\%$ CI <0.08; CFI > 0.95; SMRM ≤ 0.06; TLI > 0.90). The estimation of cross-lagged associations showed that the greatest regression weight is the connection, according to which the success in learning mathematics in the third class contributes to individual differences in the feeling of the number measured by the "Number line" test in the fourth class ($\beta = -0.33$).

Thus, even with the high temporal stability of academic success, it was shown that learning mathematics in third grade is the most important factor in shaping individual differences in the aspect of number sense as the ability to pinpoint the position of a number on the number line in fourth grade. The evaluation of the parameters of all theoretical models showed that during primary school the second analyzed aspect of number sense – the non-symbolic magnitude estimation ability – is not related to the causal relationship with the success in learning mathematics.

4 Discussions

In the current article, we focused on the relationship between number sense and success in learning mathematics in a two-year longitudinal study.

According to the results of the correlation analysis, by fourth grade of primary school, the relationship between the success in learning mathematics and number sense as the non-symbolic magnitude estimation ability is weaker than in third grade. A similar trend was detected for nonverbal intelligence. These results are consistent with the studies of Russian schoolchildren reporting a gradual reduction of the role of multiple cognitive characteristics contributing to academic success in school years, from the speed of information processing to nonverbal intelligence [6]. In particular, it was shown that number sense as the non-symbolic magnitude estimation ability and the annual grades in mathematics are closely related in primary school.

On the contrary, number sense measured as the ability to accurately determine the position of a number on the number line is more related to the success in learning mathematics in fourth grade than in third grade. In other words, the longer children study in primary school, the less their success in learning mathematics depends on the non-symbolic magnitude estimation ability and, to a greater extent, on the number sense aspect associated with symbolically expressed quantities. At the same time, the interpretation of the obtained results is also valid in the opposite direction: in fourth grade, in comparison to third grade, the level of development of the number sense aspect associated with non-symbolically expressed quantities to a lesser extent depends on the success in learning mathematics, and to a greater extent on the number sense aspect related to operating with numerical material. Such multidirectional tendencies in the interrelationship of success in mathematics with the perceptions of numbers in non-symbolic and symbolic systems are related to the specifics of the learning process in primary school, in particular with the content of the school mathematics course in Russia [13].

In the cross-lagged modeling, we compared four competing models of the relationship of the two aspects of number sense and success in learning mathematics. According to the analysis, the reciprocal model best described the empirical data suggesting that there are cross-lagged associations between number sense and success in learning mathematics in primary school even after controlling for nonverbal intelligence. The estimation of the cross-lagged associations within the model showed that the only significant association was the one between success in learning mathematics in third grade and number sense measured as the ability to determine the position of a number on the line in fourth grade. In other words, the accuracy of determining the position of a number on a number line depends on the success of mastering the concept of number and arithmetic operations in primary school: the higher were students' marks in third grade, the better they performed in fourth grade on the number sense tasks on symbolic magnitude estimation. On the contrary, for the number sense aspect associated with the non-symbolic magnitude estimation ability by the end of primary school, the success in learning mathematics measured at an earlier age was statistically insignificant.

These differences for the two indicators of number sense indicated a significant effect of training on the accuracy of determining the position of a number on the number line even in the analysis of modified models, which is consistent with previous studies [17]. According to research, number sense is a multidimensional construct in which low- and high-level characteristics can be distinguished [4]. As a rule, low-level characteristics are associated with the ability to estimate and operate with non-symbolically expressed quantities and are cosidered as evolutionarily preserved traits, and high-level characteristics are related to the symbolic representation of objects which is developed in the course of education. The lack of clear boundaries between number sense, especially associated with symbolic magnitude estimation, and mathematical skills leads to the question of what determines success in the Number Line task: the level of mastering the educational program in mathematics or number sense.

However, as described above, non-symbolic and symbolic magnitude estimation is based on the same principles, which makes it possible to analyze both test tasks as diagnostic for number sense but they should be considered as more (in the case of the Number Line) or less related to arithmetic skills [4]. From this point of view, the results obtained in this paper on the role of the success in learning mathematics in third grade in the formation of individual differences in number sense measured as the ability to determine the position of a number on the line look logical: the better the school curriculum is mastered in third grade, including knowledge of the numbers up to 1000, the more precise is the performance on the Number Line task. An additional argument is the tendency of the relationship between academic success and the accuracy of determining the position of a number on the line to strengthen by the end of the primary school, as revealed in the correlation analysis. Thus, as arithmetic knowledge and skills develop, children begin to use more accurate linear representations rather than logarithmic ones [3].

We found no cross-lagged associations between the number sense aspect related to non-symbolic magnitude estimation and the success in learning mathematics. This result is consistent with previous evidence on the lack of prognostic associations between number sense and mathematical success, e.g. at primary school age (see [5]).

In the course of the analysis, differences were also revealed in the dynamics of the two aspects of number sense at primary school: the number sense aspect associated with non-symbolic magnitude estimation was the most stable in time. This result is consistent with the available data on the differences in the temporal stability of the two analyzed aspects of number sense [13, 20]. The observed differences in dynamics can also determine the specific relationship between the various indicators of number sense and the success in learning mathematics.

It should be emphasized that according to the results of this study, none of the number sense aspects measured in third grade significantly contributed to the variation of success in learning mathematics by the end of primary school, which is different from the results obtained on other samples. Thus, in most longitudinal studies, the indicators of number sense associated with the estimation of quantities in symbolic and non-symbolic systems are considered as pre-school predictors of mathematical success at school [7, 16].

The discrepancies in the results might be related to the specifics of the Russian education system, in particular, to the evaluation of the success in learning the school disciplines. As a rule, in the Russian education system, teacher's assessment is the only criterion for assessing the academic success of junior schoolchildren and is based on a subjective vision of the material learned by a child based on a set of tests and individual answers in class throughout the year. In studies involving schoolchildren, for example, from the United States, Great Britain and Western Europe, academic success is also assessed by a teacher but based on the final standardized test assignments, which include not only educational material, but also tasks that require non-standard solutions that are not explained during the school year and the ability to apply the acquired knowledge in real life [5, 8]. For example, in the study on a Russian sample of senior students, only moderate correlations were found (from 0.41 to 0.56, $p < 0.01$) between three different indicators of academic success in mathematics in ninth grade – teacher assessment, the state exam and a computerized test [6]. Such discrepancies in the indicators of academic success might be the reason of changes in the relationship between number sense and the success in learning mathematics observed in the results of previous studies.

At the same time, the obtained data on the cause-effect relationship of number sense and the success in learning mathematics in primary school may reflect the zonal nature of the interaction of psychological and nonpsychological factors, i.e. a variety of cognitive characteristics and indicators of academic success in this study [23]. Such relationship can only be characteristic of the initial stage of schooling when the foundations of mathematical knowledge essential for operating with symbolically expressed quantities are acquired. In a number of studies, it is reported that number sense measured at primary school age is a predictor of later mathematical success measured at the middle or high school age [8, 24]. In this paper, both number sense and the success in learning mathematics were measured in primary school. Perhaps other results would be obtained if number sense measured in primary school was analysed as an earlier predictor of later academic success. However, the verification of this hypothesis lied outside the scope of this paper and will be the subject of a further longitudinal study.

Thus, in this paper it was shown that the learning process can influence the formation of cause-effect relationships between indicators of cognitive functioning and academic success in mathematics. In the context of the relationship between cognitive development and learning, a learning effect was found for the number sense aspect measured as the ability to accurately indicate the position of a number on the line. For the number sense aspect related to non-symbolic magnitude estimation, the success in learning mathematics measured a year earlier did not play an important role. The obtained results highlight the importance of studying the influence of national educational systems on individual psychological development and necessitate a cross-cultural longitudinal analysis of the interaction of cognitive functioning and learning throughout the school age.

This study was supported by the grant from the Russian Science Foundation [grant RSF №17-78-30028].

References

1. T.N. Tikhomirova, Procedia – Social and Behavioral Sciences, **237**, 1260 (2017)
2. M. Rodic, X. Zhou, T. Tikhomirova, W. Wei, S. Malykh, V. Ismatulina, E. Sabirova, Y. Davidova, M. Tosto, J-P. Lemelin, Y. Kovas, Developmental Science, **18**, 165 (2015)
3. D.C. Geary, Developmental psychology, **47**, 1539 (2011)
4. S. Dehaene, *The Number Sense: How the mind creates mathematics* (Oxford University Press USA, Oxford, 2011)
5. T.N. Tikhomirova, S.B. Malykh, M.G. Tosto, Y.V. Kovas, Psychological journal, **35**, 41 (2014)
6. T.N. Tikhomirova, S.B. Malykh, *Cognitive bases of individual differences in academic achievement* (Nestor-History, Moscow, 2017)
7. A. Desoete, A. Ceulemans , F. de Weerdt, S. Pieters, Brit. J. Educ. Psychol, **82**, 64 (2012)
8. J. Halberda, M.M. Mazzocco, L. Feigenson, Nature, **455**, 665 (2008)
9. M. Inglis, S. Batchelor, C. Gilmore, Psychon. Bull. Rev., **18**, 1222 (2011)
10. S.B. Malykh, I.A. Lysenkova, I.M. Zakharov, T.N. Tikhomirova, The European Proceedings of Social & Behavioural Sciences, **33**, 235 (2017)
11. F. Soltész, D. Scőz, L. Scőz, Behav. Brain Funct., **6**, 1 (2010)
12. S.B. Malykh, T.N. Tikhomirova, C. Zhou, W. Wei, M. Rodic, E.B. Misozhnikova, Y.A. Davydova, Y. Kovas, Voprosy psihologii, **5**, 133 (2012)
13. J.E. Opfer, R.S. Siegler, Cogn. Psychol., **55**, 169 (2007)
14. T.N. Tikhomirova, E.B. Misozhnikova, Y.V. Kuzmina, S.B. Malykh, SHS Web of Conferences, **10**, 02007 (2017)
15. T.D. Little, K.J. Preacher, J.P. Selig, N.A. Card, International Journal of Behavioral Development, **31**, 357 (2007)
16. M.M. Mazzocco, L. Feigenson, J. Halberda, PLoS ONE, **6**, 1 (2011)
17. R.S. Siegler, J.L. Booth, Child dev., **75**, 428 (2004)
18. R.S. Siegler, G.B. Ramani, J. Educ. Psychol., **101**, 545 (2009)
19. R.S. Siegler, Y. Mu, Psychological Science, **19**, 759 (2008)
20. J. Halberda, R. Ly, J. Wilmer, D. Naiman, L. Germine, Proc. Natl. Acad. Sci., **109**, 11116, (2012)
21. M.G. Tosto, T. Tikhomirova, E. Galajinsky, K. Akimova, Y. Kovas, Procedia – Social and Behavioral Sciences, **86**, 423 (2013)
22. J. Raven, Cognitive Psychology, **41**, 1 (2000)
23. T.N. Tikhomirova, A.D. Modyaev, N.M. Leonova, S.B. Malykh, Psychological journal, **36**, 43 (2015)
24. J.L. Booth, R.S. Siegler, Child dev., 79, 1016 (2008)

Children's perception of parental attitudes: Russia-Kyrgyzstan cross-cultural study

Tatiana Tikhomirova[1,2*] and *Sergey* Malykh[1,2]

[1]Lomonosov Moscow State University, Department of Psychology, 119991 Moscow, Russia
[2] Psychological Institute of Russian Academy of Education, 125009 Moscow, Russia

Abstract. The article presents the results of a cross-cultural analysis of the perception of parental attitude by children and adolescents. We focused on the indicators of maternal and paternal attitude such as Acceptance, Positive Involvement, Rejection and Hostile Detachment. The Russian sample includes 501 primary school students aged 6.8 to 11.7 years (49.9% boys) and 438 adolescents aged 10.8 to 16.8 years (47.1% boys). The Kyrgyz sample includes 510 primary school students aged from 6.6 to 11.8 years (48.5% boys) and 513 adolescents aged 10.3 to 16.8 years (46.3% boys). Regardless of the macro environment, schoolchildren perceive the attitude of both parents to a greater extent as emotionally accepting and to a lesser extent as rejecting. At the same time, it is shown that cross-cultural differences in the perception of maternal attitude are manifested only in younger schoolchildren: Kyrgyz children assess maternal attitude as more emotionally accepting with positive involvement and less rejecting. Cross-cultural differences in the perception of paternal attitudes are manifested both in younger schoolchildren and in adolescents: Kyrgyz children assess paternal attitude more positively than Russian peers. The results are interpreted in the context of specific socio-economic conditions.

1 Introduction

Research of parental attitudes to a child is, as a rule, considered in the context of its influence on individual differences in the psychological characteristics of children of different ages [1–5]. A parental attitude is understood as a set of situationally nonspecific ways of the emotional attitude and behavior of a parent towards a child. According to the psychological and pedagogical literature, two aspects reflecting the parental attitude to a child might be singled out: (1) the degree of emotional acceptance of a child and (2) the kind of involvement in a child's activity [1, 6].

It should be noted that maternal attitude is analysed more often. At the same time, it is reported that mothers and fathers build a relationship with their child, participate in child's activities and show their feelings in different ways [1, 7, 8, etc.]. In particular, it was shown that the differences in the educational impact of mothers and fathers are related to the degree of involvement in child's activities, satisfaction of needs and desires of the child and stimulation of the information flow [9, 10].

The aspects of parental attitude can be observed both from the parental position and from the position of a child. A number of studies of family environment highlight a low degree of agreement between parents and children responding to the same psychodiagnostic test: correlation coefficients varied from 0.11 to 0.41 for younger adolescents [11] and from 0.31 to 0.41 for young adults [12]. Such differences in results may be explained by unique individual experience through the prism of which the parental attitude is perceived [1, 7, 10].

A number of studies have shown that child-parent relationship were an important link in the relationship between the socio-economic position of the family and the success of the child [13, 14]. Moreover, cross-cultural differences were reported across a range of aspects of child-parent relationships [15]. For example, cross-cultural studies of the perceptions of the relationship between fathers and mothers were studied in the USA and China, as well as on samples of American families of European and Asian origin (for example, [3, 16, 17]). It was shown that the strict father model is characteristic for American families of Chinese origin but not for families of European origin [18].

It is reported that there are parental ethnotheories that unite the knowledge and beliefs of certain sociocultural groups about the upbringing of children [19, 20, etc.]. The ethnic parenting theories reflect knowledge and representations on a range of positions – from the duration of breastfeeding and the degree of emotional support to developmental milestones and the value of educational activities in a child's life.

For example, it was repeatedly stated that children's education was far more important for Asian parents than for European and American parents which, for example, results in higher rates of educational activities in Chinese families [21, 22]. It is shown that representatives of a certain cultural community in terms of parental ethnotheories reflect the norms and expectations of the social environment not only in the upbringing of children but also in their perceptions [15].

* Corresponding author: tikho@mail.ru

Moreover, the dependence of the gender specificity of parental ethnotheories on the level of socio-economic development is shown (for example, [23]). Studies report culture-mediated maternal and paternal positions regarding "male" and "female" activities [24, 25].

In this study, we focused on the characteristics of parental perceptions of children of primary and secondary school age from Russia and Kyrgyzstan.

The samples of schoolchildren from these two countries are of particular importance for the purposes of this study. First, Russia and Kyrgyzstan represent European and Asian communities, respectively. Second, these countries have different levels of socio-economic development. Thus, according to the Human Development Report, the Russian Federation and Kyrgyzstan are in different groups of countries, according to the Human Development Index (United Nations Development Program, [26]). Russia occupies the 49th place in the rating and is included in the group of countries with a very high level of development, while Kyrgyzstan is on the 120th position and is included in the group with an average level. Third, the Kyrgyz education system is similar to the Russian education system including classes in Russian in a number of schools starting from first grade. Thus, these similarities and differences open the opportunity to analyze the specificity of the perception of the relationship of mothers and fathers in countries that tend to form European and Asian models of family relationships, using common methods of measuring parental attitudes.

2 Methods

2.1 Participants

The study involved 1962 children of primary and secondary school age from Russia and Kyrgyzstan. The schools in Russia and Kyrgyzstan were selected according to the level of socioeconomic status including characteristics of the teaching staff, education quality and the name of curricula for school disciplines.

The Russian sample included 501 primary school students aged 6.8 to 11.7 years (49.9% boys) and 438 adolescents aged 10.8 to 16.8 years (47.1% boys).

The Kyrgyz sample included 510 primary school students aged 6.6 to 11.8 years (48.5% boys) and 513 adolescents aged 10.3 to 16.8 years (46.3% boys).

All students filled out questionnaires aimed at assessing the factors of perception of maternal and paternal attitude. Written informed consent was obtained from all parents of the children participating in this study. The analysis of the results was carried out on un-identified data.

2.2 Measure

Maternal and paternal attitude was assessed with the Russian-language version of the Children's Report of Parental Behavior Inventory (CRPBI) [1, 27].

The Children's Report of Parental Behavior Inventory has a four-factor structure, in which the following scales are distinguished: 'Acceptance', 'Positive involvement', 'Rejection' and 'Hostile detachment' [1]. The scale 'Acceptance' consists of 8 statements (for example, 'Cheers me up when I'm sad'); 'Positive involvement' includes 7 statements (for example, 'Is very interested in what I am learning at school'); 'Rejection' consists of 7 items (for example, 'Almost always complains about what I do' and 'Gets cross and angry about little things I do'); 'Hostile detachment' includes 8 statements (for example, 'Wishes I were a different kind of person').

All participants fillled out the questionnaire for both parents.

3 Results

3.1 Descriptive statistics

Table 1 presents the descriptive statistics for maternal and paternal perception on the Russian and Kyrgyz samples of primary school children.

Table 1. Means and standard deviations (in brackets) for maternal and paternal attitude on the sample of primary school children.

	Russian	Kyrgyz
Acceptance	20.1 (2.7) 19.5 (3.9)	21.1 (2.9) 20.6 (3.7)
Positive Involvement	17.8 (2.4) 17.3 (3.0)	18.5 (2.5) 18.1 (3.3)
Rejection	10.1 (2.9) 10.0 (3.1)	9.7 (3.2) 9.6 (3.4)
Hostile Detachment	11.7 (3.5) 11.7 (3.6)	11.0 (3.8) 11.0 (4.0)

Note: top line – maternal attitude, bottom line – paternal attitude.

According to Table 1, higher average values for positive perceptual factors of both maternal and paternal attitudes (Acceptance and Positive Involvement) were obtained on the Kyrgyz sample of primary school students than on the Russian sample. On average, primary school age children report higher emotional acceptance and positive involvement of mothers than fathers.

For negative factors – Rejection and Hostile Detachment – the indicators of Russian schoolchildren are higher than of their Kyrgyz peers, both for mothers and fathers. Table 1 also shows that both Russian and Kyrgyz children perceive the negative attitude of both parents to the same extent.

Table 2 presents descriptive statistics for paternal and maternal attitude on Russian and Kyrgyz samples of adolescents.

In adolescence, unlike at primary school age, the mean values of both positive and negative factors of the parental attitude practically coincide for the Russian and Kyrgyz samples. For example, the average value of maternal Hostile Detachment for schoolchildren in both samples was 10.7, and Russian and Kyrgyz children estimate Positive Involvement at 17.8 and 17.9 points, respectively.

Table 2. Means and standard deviations for paternal and maternal attitude on adolescent sample.

	Russian	Kyrgyz
Acceptance	20.0 (3.2) 18.9 (4.2)	20.2 (3.1) 19.5 (3.8)
Positive Involvement	17.8 (2.5) 16.5 (3.4)	17.9 (2.6) 17.1 (3.1)
Rejection	9.6 (2.7) 9.5 (3.2)	9.7 (2.9) 9.0 (2.6)
Hostile Detachment	10.7 (2.9) 11.0 (3.7)	10.7 (3.8) 10.6 (3.2)

Note: top line – maternal attitude, bottom line – paternal attitude.

For positive aspects, maternal attitude for both age groups was rated slightly higher than paternal attitude. For negative aspects, there were multidirectional tendencies for mothers and fathers.

3.2 ANOVAs

To study the cross-cultural differences in the perception of a child by parents, a one-way ANOVA was applied. The analysis was carried out separately on two age-specific samples: primary school age children and adolescents. Being a resident of the Russian Federation or the Kyrgyz Republic was used as a categorical factor and the indicators of maternal and paternal attitude were consistently introduced as dependent variables.

Levene's test was used to test the hypothesis of the equality of variances of all distributions of the analyzed variables for the compared samples.

Table 3 summarizes the results of the variance analysis on the perception of parental attitude conducted on both samples. Maternal (top line) and paternal attitude (bottom line) were analyzed: Acceptance (A), Positive involvement (PI), Rejection (R) and Hostile Detachment (HD).

According to Table 3, there are small but statistically significant differences in the perception of parental attitudes among Russian and Kyrgyz schoolchildren. To the greatest extent these differences are manifested on the sample of primary school age. Thus, Kyrgyz children perceive the attitude of mothers and fathers as more emotionally accepting and less rejective than their Russian peers. In particular, among the aspects of children's perception of maternal attitude, significant effects of the country were found for such indicators of family microenvironment as Acceptance, Positive Involvement and Hostile Detachment. At the same time, Kyrgyz children's perceptions of maternal attitude are higher for positive scales (Acceptance and Positive Involvement) and less for Hostile Detachment compared to Russian children. Attention is drawn to the small effect size for these scales – from 1% to 3%. For the aspects of perception of paternal attitude, similar results were obtained: cross-cultural differences were obtained for all analyzed aspects with effect sizes of 1–2%.

Table 3. Estimation of the effect of the country on indicators of parental attitude.

Sample	Indicator	SS	F	p	η^2
Primary school age	A	275.5 282.9	35.1 19.6	0.00 0.00	0.03 0.02
	PI	107.2 129.9	17.5 13.0	0.00 0.00	0.02 0.01
	R	32.4 46.4	3.5 4.4	0.07 0.04	0.00 0.01
	HD	126.5 127.9	9.3 8.7	0.01 0.01	0,01 0,01
Adolescents	A	16.4 62.9	1.7 3.9	0.19 0.04	0.00 0.01
	PI	3.4 71.0	0.5 6.8	0.47 0.01	0.00 0.01
	R	0.5 41.1	0.1 5.0	0.80 0.03	0.00 0.01
	HD	0.1 39.8	0.01 3.4	0.92 0.07	0.00 0.00

Note: SS – sum of squares, F – F-statistic, p – significance level, η^2 – effect size

On the sample of adolescents, cross-cultural differences were only found in the perception of paternal attitude. In particular, Kyrgyz adolescents perceive paternal attitude as more emotionally supportive and less rejecting than Russian adolescents. It should be noted that the effect sizes are minimal – 1% of the variance of Acceptance, Positive Involvement and Rejection. Perceptions of maternal attitude did not differ on the samples of Russian and Kyrgyz adolescents.

3 Discussions

According to the results of this study, regardless of the conditions of the macroenvironment, primary school age children and adolescents perceive parental attitude more as emotionally accepting and less as rejecting.

At the same time, for the positive aspects of the parental attitude – Acceptance and Positive Involvement – differences in the perception of maternal and paternal attitude were revealed. The children assessed the maternal attitude as more emotionally accepting than the attitude of fathers. In addition, it was found that for children maternal attitude was related to positive involvement in their lives more than paternal attitude.

Similar results were obtained in a comparative study of the educational impact of fathers and mothers on a sample of older preschool children [1, 9]. In particular, according to parents' self-reports mothers encouraged the information flow for a child more than fathers meeting the needs of the child and participating in child's activities and games [9]. According to the literature, in most cultures the closest parent is a mother who spends more time with the child than their father [7]. In a number of studies this fact is used as an explanatory category in interpreting the exposure model of the family microenvironment influence on test indicators of abilities assuming that the effect size of parents' influence is directly proportional to the time of their communication with the child [10, 28].

The study also shows that the negative aspects of parental attitude – Rejection and Hostile Detachment – do not differ in terms of perceptions of both maternal and paternal attitudes.

According to the results of this study, features of the macroenvironment affect the perception of parental attitude. At the same time, the macroenvironmental effects are more pronounced in children's perception of paternal attitude.

Indeed, research on child-parent relationships reported stable cross-cultural differences in the degree of emotional acceptance and the nature of parental involvement in child's activities. These differences are associated with the existence of parental ethnotheories suggesting the knowledge and views of parents from a particular cultural group regarding the upbringing and child development [19, 20, 29, etc.]. It was shown, for example, that Chinese parents (both residing in the US and the People's Republic of China) were more involved in the process of educating their children than European parents [21, 22].

It is reported that during the school age child-parent relations and their perception by the growing child are undergoing multiple changes [1]. According to our results, cross-cultural differences in the perception of maternal and paternal attitude are subject to developmental patterns. In particular, cross-cultural differences in the perception of maternal attitude are only manifested at primary school age: Kyrgyz children assess the attitude of mothers as more hostile with positive involvement and less rejection. At the same time, similar cross-cultural differences in the perceptions of paternal attitudes are observed both at primary school age and in adolescence.

It turns out that in less favorable socio-economic conditions of the macroenvironment, the perception of parental attitude is more positive. At first glance, this might seem a paradoxical result. However, it may be explained from the position of a higher level of requirements for the knowledge and skills of the child when entering the school in more favorable conditions of the macroenvironment, in particular, the conditions of education. Thus, Russian children perceive the attitude of their mothers to a lesser extent as accepting and associated with positive involvement at primary school age. According to the data of the Russian longitudinal study, maternal attitude to the child is most influenced by the macroenvironment at older preschool and primary school age, when the child prepares for and / or starts going to school [30]. In particular, an increase in exigence, increased control over the actions of the child and more active participation in child's education were reported.

Thus, the more favorable is the macroenvironment (and, therefore, the higher is the quality of education), the more actively mothers are included in the learning process aimed at increasing the level of knowledge of a preschool child. Such activity of Russian mothers may result in a decrease in child's perception of maternal attitude on the positive aspects of the family microenvironment. On the contrary, in less favorable macro-environment conditions, which imply a lower level of education and lower requirements for children entering schools, maternal attitude is less subject to change. Thus, the features of the macro environment affect the perception of maternal attitude associated with emotional acceptance and positive involvement only at primary school age.

At the same time, this study shows that cross-cultural differences in perceptions of paternal attitudes are manifested at both primary and secondary school age: Kyrgyz children assess paternal attitude more positively than their Russian peers. In particular, Kyrgyz schoolchildren perceive the attitude of their fathers as more emotionally accepting with positive involvement and less emotionally rejecting compared to their Russian peers. This trend might be inversely related to the amount of time a child spent with the father. This fact confirms the analysis of the composition of the families participating in the study and the employment of mothers. In particular, the number of unemployed mothers (and, consequently, overworking fathers) in the sample of Kyrgyz schoolchildren was greater than in the sample of Russian schoolchildren.

Thus, the effects of the influence of the macro environment on the perception of parental attitude are subje to developmental patterns. Features of the macro environment determine the specificity of perception of mothers only at primary school age: Kyrgyz children perceive the attitude of mothers as more emotionally accepting and less rejective than Russian primary school children. Perception of fathers depends on the characteristics of the macro environment throughout the primary and secondary school years: Kyrgyz children assess paternal attitude as more accepting than their Russian peers.

This study was supported by the grant from the Russian Science Foundation [grant RSF №17-78-30028].

References

1. T.N. Tikhomirova, S.B. Malykh, *Cognitive bases of individual differences in academic achievement* (Nestor-History, Moscow, 2017)
2. E. Pougnet, L.A. Serbin, D.M. Stack, A.E. Schwartzman, Canadian Journal of Behavioural Science/Revue canadienne des sciences du comportement, **43**,173 (2011)
3. C.S.-S. Cheung, E.M. Pomerantz, Child Development, **82**, 932 (2011)
4. G.T. Harold, J.J. Aitken, K.H. Shelton, Journal of Child Psychology and Psychiatry, **48**, 1223 (2007)

5. T.N. Tikhomirova, Psychology. Journal of High School of Economic, **4**, 133 (2004)
6. C. Kagitcibasi, Journal of Cross-Cultural Psychology, **36**, 403 (2005)
7. O.A. Karabanova, *Psychology of family relations and the basics of family counseling* (Gardariki, Moscow, 2004).
8. R.P. Rohner, R.A. Veneziano, Review of General Psychology, **5**, 382 (2001)
9. T.N. Tikhomirova, Voprosy psihologii, **1**, 85 (2011)
10. T.N. Tikhomirova, S.B. Malykh, I.A. Lysenkova, A.P. Belova, O.N. Ovcharova, E.D. Gindina, D.A. Gaysina, Theoretical and experimental psychology, **6**, 33 (2013)
11. I. Tsaousis, K. Mascha, T. Giovazolias, Child Psychiatry & Human Development, **43**, 238 (2012)
12. J.C. Schwarz, M.L. Barton-Henry, T. Pruzinsky, Child Development, **56**, 462 (1985)
13. J. Roksa, D. Potter, Sociology of Education, **84**, 299 (2011)
14. A. Lareau, *Unequal childhoods: Race, class, and family life* (University of California Press, Berkeley, CA, 2003).
15. J.W. Berry, *Cross-cultural psychology: Research and applications* (Cambridge University Press, Cambridge, UK, 2002)
16. R.K. Chao, Journal of Applied Developmental Psychology, **21**, 233 (2000)
17. S.L. Pong, L. Hao, E. Gardner, Social Science Quarterly, **86**, 928 (2005)
18. D.Y.F. Ho, *The psychology of the Chinese people* (Oxford University Press, New York, 2008)
19. S. Harkness, P.O. Zylicz, C.M. Super, B. Welles-Nyström, M.R. Bermúdez, S. Bonichini, ... & C.J. Mavridis, Journal of Family Psychology, **25**, 799 (2011)
20. K.H. Rubin, O.B. Chung, *Parenting beliefs, behaviors, and parent-child relations: A cross-cultural perspective* (Psychology Press, New York, 2013)
21. M. Rodic, X. Zhou, T. Tikhomirova, W. Wei, S. Malykh, V. Ismatulina, E. Sabirova, Y. Davidova, M. Tosto, J-P. Lemelin, Y. Kovas, Developmental Science, **18**, 165 (2015)
22. X. Zhou, J. Huang, Z. Wang, Z. Zhao, L. Yang, Y. Zhengaheng, Early child development and care, **176**, 763 (2006)
23. C. Kagicibasi, *Family and human development across cultures: A view from the other side* (Erlbaum, Mahwah, 1996)
24. A.H. Eagly, W. Wood, Behavioral and Brain Sciences, **28**, 281 (2005)
25. C.L. Martin, O. Kornienko, D.R. Schaefer, L.D. Hanish, R.A. Fabes, P. Goble, Child Development, **84**, 921 (2014)
26. United Nations Development Programme, *http://hdr.undp.org/sites/default/files/2016_human_development_report.pdf* (2016)
27. S. Schludermann, E. Schludermann, *Notes of the CRPBI-30.* (University of Manitoba, Winnipeg, Manitoba, Canada, 1988)
28. T.N. Tikhomirova, S.B. Malykh, The European Proceedings of Social & Behavioural Sciences, **33**, 367 (2017)
29. H. Keller, B. Lamm, M. Abels, R. Yovsi, J. Borke, H. Jensen , ... & Y. Su, Journal of Cross-Cultural Psychology, **37**, 155 (2006)
30. I.A. Luzshetskaya, O.N. Pavlova, *Parents and children* (Kogito-centre, Moscow, 2003)

AUTHOR INDEX